Boilerplate:
Practical Clauses

Second Edition

Richard Christou
Solicitor

LAW & TAX

ISBN 0752 001884

Published by
FT Law & Tax
21–27 Lamb's Conduit Street
London WC1N 3NJ

A Division of Pearson Professional Limited

Associated offices
Australia, Belgium, Canada, Hong Kong, India, Japan,
Luxembourg, Singapore, Spain, USA

First published 1990
Second edition 1995

A CIP catalogue record for this book is available from the
British Library.

Printed by Bell and Bain Ltd., Glasgow

Contents

iii

Preface

The scope and purpose of this book remain unchanged since the first edition was published some five years ago. I have, however, taken advantage of the second edition to enlarge it somewhat by refining and updating the existing text and clauses, in the light of developments in the law, and adding new material where this seemed necessary or useful.

In particular, I have revised parts of Chapter 6 (Standard Warranties, Guarantees and Indemnities) to deal with the impact of the new law on acceptance and satisfactory quality brought in by the Sale and Supply of Goods Act 1994; and enlarged Chapter 7 (Exclusions of Liability) to cover consumer contracts, with a detailed commentary on, and explanation of the implications of, the Unfair Terms in Consumer Contracts Regulations 1994, which implement (with effect from 1 July 1995) the Council Directive on Unfair Terms in Consumer Contracts (93/13/EC).

R Christou
London
May 1995

Tables

TABLE OF CASES

TABLE OF STATUTES

TABLE OF STATUTORY INSTRUMENTS

EUROPEAN AND INTERNATIONAL LEGISLATION

Chapter 1

Introduction

The purpose of this book

Lawyers too often use the term boilerplate in a derogatory sense, and content themselves, after fierce negotiations on the substantive part of the contract, with attaching at the end of the contract, often at the last minute and late at night, a selection of standard clauses which they call boilerplate, and to which neither they nor the other side give a great deal of attention. Indeed those who insist on ploughing through the boilerplate in detail are often regarded as timewasters and pedants. However, when litigation on their contract has taken place, many draftsmen have found to their cost that it was a so called boilerplate clause (its significance overlooked by both sides at the time of drafting) which decided the issue.

The term 'boilerplate' is most properly used in its widest sense to describe the clauses, common to nearly all commercial contracts, which deal with the way in which the contract itself operates, as opposed to the rights of the parties under the particular transaction that they have agreed upon and embodied in the substantive clauses. Boilerplate clauses regulate, control, and in some cases modify, these substantive rights and their operation and enforcement. They are thus a vital part of every contract, without which the substantive rights of the parties embodied in the agreement would have little meaning.

If one can take an analogy from the field of computing, boilerplate is like the operating system of a computer, while the substantive content of the contract relating to the particular transaction could be likened to the application software. All commercial contracts have an underlying 'operating system' that is (at least in the

1

jurisdictions based on common law and even in some others) approximately the same.

In the absence of boilerplate the parties must rely on the general system of law applicable to the contract, and ask the court to apply this in settling disputes. In extreme cases, however, even the systems of law to be applied, and the question of which court has jurisdiction, would have to be decided by reference to some system of private international law. This approach defeats the whole aim of commercial contracts: to create certainty in dealings between the parties, and an easy method of enforcement of rights where necessary.

The purpose of this book is to give guidance on how to draft this basic framework for commercial contracts and to provide precedents for clauses in common usage by most draftsmen of commercial contracts.

Lawyers and law students who are drafting commercial contracts for the first time will find that the approach of this book gives them a useful introduction to the whole subject, together with precedents which, having already seen practical use, should enable them to draw up contracts which have, at least from their operative point of view, a fair degree of familiarity and acceptability to the parties and advisers on the other side of the transaction. The experienced draftsman may find the ideas and the precedents expressed here contain much that is familiar, but it is hoped that he too will find it convenient to have them all gathered in one place.

It should be stated that the precedents in this book, like all precedents, need to be applied with care, and only after due consideration of their suitability and necessity for particular circumstances. It is not the aim of this book to help draftsmen create longer and longer lists of boilerplate clauses which add nothing to the contract. It is intended instead to restore the reputation of 'boilerplate', and to enable the draftsman to use it more intelligently.

Drafting a commercial contract

Before considering the precedents in the following chapters, a few general comments on the drafting of commercial contracts may be useful.

(1) The process of drafting the contract is not the time to

negotiate matters of principle. This must be done before drafting commences.

(2) Always strive for clarity and certainty of expression. It is a common trap in negotiations for one party to try to rely on what he regards as an ambiguity in expression. Any ambiguity in a clause is often construed by a court against the person who is trying to rely on it, particularly if he is the person who has drafted the clause (*contra proferentem* rule). The end result is that neither party finds it has attained what it wants.

(3) Do not assume that you are achieving the best result for your client by drafting in every safeguard and exception, thus producing the longest possible contract, heavily weighted in favour of your client. In rare circumstances the client may give express instructions to this effect, but in the absence of such instructions you should aim to produce a reasonably balanced contract and persuade your client of the advantages of this. Negotiations on this basis will be speedier, and the end result is more likely to be a transaction with which both parties are happy.

(4) Do not be unnecessarily adversarial in your approach to drafting or contract negotiations. The best way to regard the process of entering into a contract is not as a contest but as an attempt by the two sides to find their way to a mutually beneficial bargain. The draftsman should try to aid this process by recording clearly what the parties have agreed and assisting them to clarify their thoughts so as to assess the consequences of their agreement. The draftsman should help the parties resolve inconsistencies by bringing them to their attention and working, where possible, for a fair and reasonable compromise.

(5) In both drafting and the negotiations, concentrate on dealing with the essential points first. Do not allow trivia to obscure these, and thus delay both the drafting of the contract and its finalisation.

(6) Say what you have to say in plain English and try to use short sentences and sensible punctuation. Do not rely on punctuation to correct defective sentence construction, but use it sparingly (particularly commas) to help to clarify the meaning. Another useful device, clearer than sets of commas, is to use brackets to separate parenthetical phrases.

(7) Do not be elegant or original at the expense of clarity. It

is better to repeat words and phrases to make a point rather than use pronouns or references to previous clauses. Never express the same idea in two different ways in different places in the agreement: it is better to repeat the same sentence. For instance, never use the phrase 'to the best of the Vendor's knowledge and belief' in one place, and the phrase 'to the best of the Vendor's knowledge' in another. If the agreement is ever interpreted by a court it will assume that different things are meant by different phrases, since the draftsman will be presumed to have used different wording after careful consideration.

(8) Use standard clauses wherever possible: there is no point in 'reinventing the wheel'. Such clauses not only save valuable time and are more likely to cover all the relevant points, but they will be familiar to the other side, which will help negotiations.

(9) Never draft in isolation. Always be aware of law which can affect the contract. The first area to consider is competition law both domestic and (in relevant cases) that of the EC. The next area is any regulatory provisions, particularly in the area of exchange control and export licensing, which may prevent the contract being put into effect or may even render it illegal. Finally, one should consider the relevancy of any legislation affecting exclusion clauses, such as the Unfair Contract Terms Act 1977 in the United Kingdom.

(10) Be vigilant for the impact of consumer protection legislation in relevant contracts. This can range from control of exclusion clauses, through strict liability for defective products, to the regulation of the way consumer credit is granted. The impact of both domestic and EC law in this area should be considered, particularly as it now relates to 'unfair terms' under the EC Directive on Unfair Terms in Consumer Contracts (EC Directive 13/1993).

(11) Be concerned with the effect on the agreement of taxation legislation. Obtain expert advice in this area where necessary.

(12) Ensure that you are fully aware of which system of law governs the agreement and, with the aid of local advice if necessary, be certain that you have taken into account the full impact of that system. It is not enough to specify a governing law in the agreement since, in some cases, the law of the place of performance may contain provisions which wholly or partially override such a clause.

The different parts of a commercial contract

(a) Designation of the parties

At the head of the contract it is usual to set out the names and identifying details of each of the parties. Although it is not uncommon to preface this section with a statement such as 'This Agreement is made the ....day of ....19........', this is not legally necessary. It is vital, however, that the agreement states from what date it is effective. The actual date upon which the agreement is signed (if this is different to the effective date) is therefore desirable but not essential.

(b) Recitals

After the details of the parties, a set of paragraphs called recitals will usually appear. These set out the background to the transaction and the purpose for which the parties are entering into the transaction. Without express words later on in the agreement, the legal status of these recitals is often ambiguous—they are not regarded as a part of the agreement which actually gives rise to legal obligations, and yet they will be taken into account by a court which has to interpret the substantive portion of the agreement. For this reason, recitals should be drafted as carefully as the substantive portions of the contract, and there is reason to include an express provision later in the agreement that the recitals are to be regarded for all purposes as an integral part of the parties' agreement.

(c) Definitions

Although it is possible to insert definitions in any of the foregoing or in substantive parts of the agreement, where there are a great many definitions it is usual to arrange them together in a separate section straight after the recitals. As a drafting tip, it can be easier to insert definitions throughout the agreement, as drafting the clauses throws up the need for them, and then to remove these definitions at the end, collect and edit them, and arrange them in suitable order (either alphabetical or logical) in the initial definition section.

The definitions form part of the substantive agreement because they prescribe that certain terms *shall* mean certain things. This prescriptive language can take various forms. The most unambiguous, and therefore the most desirable, is: 'In this Agreement A shall mean B'. A less desirable style, but still often used, is: 'Where the context so admits, in this Agreement A shall mean B'. The following example, which is undesirable, is a partial definition: 'In this Agreement [where the context so admits] A includes B'. An example of this is: 'In this Agreement taxation includes income tax, corporation tax and value added tax'. We do not have a complete definition of 'taxation', but do know some items which are included in the term. The parties are left free to argue, by reference to the ordinary dictionary meaning of taxation, whether other items such as stamp duty or inheritance tax fall within the definition or not.

Besides pure definitions, this section will also contain general interpretation clauses. The more important definitions and interpretation clauses are discussed and set out in Chapter 2.

(d) Substantive clauses

After the definitions follow the main clauses of the agreement—the substantive provisions. These clauses are sometimes introduced by: 'Now it is hereby agreed as follows . . .'. Although customary, this phrase does not appear to serve any legal purpose, since the substantive clauses will obviously be seen as matters upon which the parties are agreeing.

(e) Schedules

To ensure that the logical flow of the substantive clauses is not interrupted and obscured with a great deal of detail, it is useful to put many of the more detailed substantive provisions into schedules. A clause in the substantive part of the agreement could then read: 'All orders for the Products placed by the Buyer with the Seller shall be upon the terms and conditions set out in Schedule . . .'. The schedule concerned could then carry a detailed set of conditions of sale which, had they been left within the main clauses, would have completely disrupted the sequence.

Another use for schedules is to remove transaction-specific details so that the main document can be more easily used as a standard form. Standard form distributor or agency agreements, for example, usually place details of the products, territories covered and sales targets within the schedules.

Schedules are a substantive and integral part of the agreement, and there should always be a specific provision in the main clauses stating that this is so.

(*f*) *Appendices*

Where documents are referred to in an agreement they are often attached as appendices so that they can be easily referred to. Such appendices are usually signed by the parties by way of identification of the document concerned.

Such documents are not necessarily part of the agreement. For instance, a warranty can be given that a set of accounts, or a copy of a memorandum and articles attached as an appendix, is true and correct. The document is then attached for reference but its provisions are not incorporated in the agreement. Where a document is actually incorporated by reference (for example a set of standard conditions of sale or a technical specification) the document is sometimes also attached as an appendix. However, even in this case, the *provisions* of the document are incorporated by reference in the main clause, but the appended copy of the document only serves as a record of those terms and is not itself a part of the agreement.

(*g*) *Signature section*

This section should come after the schedules and before the appendices. It is often, but need not be, introduced with wording such as: 'The duly authorised representatives of the parties hereto have hereunto set their hands, the day and year first above written'. A shorter and equally acceptable method is 'Signed by X for and on behalf of ABC Ltd' followed by X's signature.

Commercial agreements do not normally need witnesses to the signatures; they are certainly not necessary under English law.

Most commercial agreements are just signed ('under hand') and not executed as deeds ('under seal'). Since commercial agreements will obviously contain the necessary consideration to make them enforceable, in jurisdictions where the concept of consideration exists, a deed is not necessary to obtain a legally enforceable document. One great advantage (or drawback depending upon which party is concerned) to the use of a deed under English law, is that the statute of limitations prescribes 12 years for an action on a deed, but only six years for a document under hand.

Deeds are also used by bodies such as local authorities in England and Wales whose processes for authorisation of signature of contracts are very complicated, while the use of documents under seal is a well-established part of their procedure.

(h) Counterparts and copies

Copies of commercial documents are usually supplied for each of the parties: these are signed by all the parties and include a special counterpart clause inserted to make each of them fully signed original copies for purposes of enforcement. As an alternative to counterparts, there is sometimes only one original, with the other parties being given certified copies which are regarded as equivalent to originals.

Conformed copies are sometimes produced. These are copies of documents which contain manuscript amendments made at the last minute, or illegible signatures. The manuscript (including the signatures) is reproduced in the documents in typed form. Such copies are obviously not originals and are often just used for ease of reference, but they may also, of course, be certified copies.

(i) Headings and contents pages

Headings to clauses, sections and schedules, and contents pages are often introduced into long documents for ease of reference. Such matters should not be part of the agreement or their drafting becomes too complicated and they no longer serve the purpose of providing easy reference guides. Usually a provision appears in the substantive clauses stating that this is the case.

(j) Contract numbering systems

Numbering systems can vary. Traditionally they consist of hierarchical mixtures of arabic and roman numerals and letters of the alphabet. In a long document one spends more time than it is worth working out and adjusting such hierarchies and keeping them consistent. The aim of all numbering systems is to provide a unique and easy way of referring to each part of each clause of the contract. This is best achieved by using a system of arabic numerals separated by decimal points. Thus the numbering goes: clause 1, sub-clause 1.1, paragraph 1.1.1, sub-paragraph 1.1.1.1, and so on through as many levels as necessary. Once this system has been set up there is actually no need to refer to clauses, sub-clauses, paragraphs, sub-paragraphs and so on. References to clause 1 or clause 1.1 or clause 1.1.1 are now perfectly clear. A similar kind of numbering can be used in schedules, starting a new hierarchy for each schedule, although here one traditionally refers to paragraphs rather than clauses.

One further advantage of this kind of numbering system is that it is well suited to the automatic numbering features which are available in many of the more advanced word-processing programs. Proper use of such features (which in effect assign a unique number to each clause or sub-clause of the agreement) enables one to delete or add clauses or sub-clauses, and to renumber the whole agreement automatically. However, such programs do not always provide an easy means of automatically updating cross-references between clauses, and care must be taken when using them to make sure that all cross-references have been picked up and amended, if necessary manually.

An extreme form of the decimalised numbering system is one which gives the first number in the series to the main sections of the agreement. In such systems, typically the parties are 1, the recitals 2, the definitions 3 and the substantive clauses 4. More conventional forms start with the main clauses, the first of which is the definition clause. The parties section has no number, and each paragraph of the recitals is designated by a letter of the alphabet.

Chapter 2

Definitions and Interpretation

Designation of the parties

The first task is to state the parties to the agreement in a clear and unambiguous way. Then one must decide how to refer to them throughout the body of the agreement. Identification of the parties is usually made by reference to the full name and an address at which they can normally be traced, principally for the purpose of service of notices or legal proceedings. In the case of legal entities, details about their incorporation and their registered office if they have one, or principal place of business if they do not, are usually also provided. Under EC law it is now necessary for each limited company incorporated in a member state of the EU to have a registered number of incorporation and it is useful to quote this as part of the description of such parties.

The parties can be referred to in the body of the agreement either by means of definitions or by the old system of referring to parties of the first part, second part and so on. This, however, is not only archaic but also confusing and seems to serve little useful purpose. It is better to define the parties at the beginning of the agreement when first stating their identity rather than waiting until the definition clauses appear. In this way a great deal of superfluous naming is avoided, particularly where there are extensive recitals, or the parties have long or similar names.

It is useful to choose definitions which relate to the parties rather than abbreviations. For instance in a purchase agreement between ABC Ltd and XYZ Ltd, it is better to define the two parties as the 'Vendor' and the 'Purchaser' rather than 'ABC' and 'XYZ'. The advantages of this are to make the agreement more comprehensible and also easier to adapt as a precedent for future use. The latter is particularly important where one is concerned

10

with a series of identical agreements, such as agency or distribution agreements.

The following examples show ways in which parties can be identified and defined at the beginning of an agreement. The first is a standard opening for an agreement between two limited companies incorporated in the United Kingdom, while the following two show the more extensive descriptions of the parties which are usual in international agreements.

2.1
This Agreement is made between the ACME MANUFACTURING COMPANY LIMITED whose registered office is at .... (the 'Vendor') of the one part and the EQUILATERAL TRADING CORPORATION LIMITED whose registered office is at .... (the 'Purchaser') of the other part.

2.2
This Agreement is made between (1) AMALGAMATED ENGINEERING CORPORATION INC, a company organised and existing under the laws of the state of Delaware, whose principal place of business is at .... Texas in the United States of America (the 'Principal') and (2) IMT LTD, a company organised and existing under the laws of England whose registered office is at .... (the 'Distributor').

2.3
Made in .... on ...., by and between
(1) MAT SpA, a company organised under Italian law, having its registered office at ...., a paid in capital of Lit ...., registered with the Court of .... under No .... of the Register of Companies, Chamber of Commerce of .... No ...., VAT and Tax Code No .... (hereinafter the 'Seller')
(2) ABC PLC, a public company incorporated in England under registration No .... having its registered office at .... (hereinafter the 'Buyer')
(3) Sr ...., an Italian citizen of .... Italy, (hereinafter the 'Guarantor').

It may still be necessary to use the words 'party' or 'parties' in the body of the agreement when referring to events which could affect any of the parties (for example 'if a party becomes unable to pay its debts in the ordinary course . . .'). It is therefore useful to include in the interpretation section a short clause such as:

2.4
Any reference in this Agreement to a party shall mean either the Vendor,

the Purchaser or the Guarantor, and any such reference to parties shall (as the case may be) mean all or any two of them.

For the sake of clarity it is desirable to avoid using the term 'third party' in an agreement.

Successors and assigns

Once the parties have been properly designated it is necessary to specify the extent to which the benefit and/or the burden of the agreement will be binding upon their successors in title either through assignment or by operation of law. It is also necessary to bear in mind that assignment may be prohibited elsewhere in the agreement unless the consent of the other parties is obtained (see Chapter 11) and that succession in title by devolution of law (for example in the case of insolvency) may be undesirable. In such circumstances the agreement will give the other parties the option of termination, if it is not terminated automatically (see Chapter 3).

Bearing these factors in mind a 'successors and assigns' clause must not contradict any such prohibitions or rights of termination further on in the agreement. Typical examples for such clauses are:

2.5
References in this Agreement to the parties shall include their respective heirs successors in title permitted assigns and personal representatives.

2.6
This Agreement shall be binding upon and inure to the benefit of the parties and their respective successors.

2.7
The expressions 'Seller' and 'Purchaser' shall include their respective successors and permitted assigns.

Extensions of the parties

Although a particular entity may sign as party to an agreement it may be intended that further entities connected with that party should also be joining in the agreement, taking the benefit and burden of it in conjunction with the signing party. This raises problems of the extent to which the signing party has power to sign on behalf of such entities: but this is usually dealt with elsewhere in the agreement (see Chapters 6 and 11). However, the definition and interpretation sections do need to extend the definition of a party to cover such entities. Very often employees, servants and agents of a party are required to be bound like the party whom they serve, but the extension of parties can be widened to cover other persons or entities linked by ownership influence or control to the signing party.

Commercial agreements with legal entities usually involve referring to groups of companies, holding and subsidiary companies and to directors. It is necessary first to define these terms before drafting the extension clause. When dealing with natural persons it is important to clarify other persons (natural or legal) connected with that person, such as close relatives or companies within their control so that a definition of the term 'connected person' is less ambiguous.

The definitions of groups of companies has become complicated in the United Kingdom because of the changes brought about by the Companies Act 1989. As well as introducing the concept of 'subsidiary undertaking' for the purpose of Group Accounts only (see the Companies Act 1989, ss 5, 21, 22 and Sched 9), in order to implement the EC Seventh Company Directive on Group Accounts, the Act also amended the definition of 'subsidiary' for non-accounting purposes by substituting s 736 in the Companies Act 1985 and adding ss 736A and 736B to that Act.

The definition of 'subsidiary' has been shifted from ownership to control and will therefore include legal entities which previously were not considered to be subsidiaries. For accounting purposes the definition of 'subsidiary undertaking' is even wider. Here there are three possible tests any one of which is by itself sufficient:

(a) ownership, or
(b) control, or
(c) the exercise of a 'dominant influence' or of the power to direct the policy of the undertaking.

A subsidiary undertaking, for the purposes of group accounts, need no longer be an incorporated entity but also includes unincorporated associations such as partnerships. Companies can be part of two different groups, one for accounting purposes and one for the general purposes of the Companies Act 1985 under s 736, the members of which could be different and, in the former case, include unincorporated associations.

It is possible to produce a compact series of definitions for use in an agreement by reference to the 1985 Act, s 736 (as amended by the 1989 Act), using the more conventional definition of subsidiary in the usual Companies Acts context.

2.8

'Holding Company' 'Subsidiary Company' and 'Wholly-Owned Subsidiary' shall be defined in accordance with the Companies Act 1985, Section 736 and Section 736A as substituted by the Companies Act 1989, Section 144.

'The Seller's Group' shall mean the group composed of the Seller, its Holding Company (if any), and all [Wholly-Owned] Subsidiary Companies of the Seller and of the Seller's Holding Company (if any).

The definitions can be compiled by reference to the 1985 Act, s 258 (as amended by the 1989 Act), using the accountancy definition of subsidiary undertaking. However, the accountancy definition is not normally to be recommended, except in warranties relating to the sale or purchase of a member of the group, where certain assurances about the relevant group and its consolidated accounts are required. The question of whether or not a dominant influence or policy direction is exercised must be to some extent a subjective matter determined by the auditors of the group in question or, in the last resort, by a decision of the court.

By the Companies Act 1985, s 229 (as amended by Companies Act 1989, s 5), it is possible to decide to exclude certain subsidiary undertakings from the group consolidated accounts on a voluntary basis; also one must exclude any subsidiary undertakings whose activities are so different from those of other undertakings within the group that their inclusion would distort the group's accounts.

A decision must be taken whether undertakings excluded for the purpose of group accounts should or should not be included within the definitions of 'undertaking' for the purposes of the agreement. Generally they should not be included for matters relating to group accounts (for example warranties) but should probably be included for other matters (for example confidentiality obligations and non-competition covenants). Precedent **2.9** shows one way of achieving the partial exclusion.

Considerable thought is, however, required to fit the circumstances of each case. For instance, a party to the agreement, particularly where it is not the parent company of the whole group, could be a subsidiary undertaking included for the purposes of accounting consolidation in one group, but could also be a subsidiary undertaking in another group but excluded from that group's accounting consolidation by virtue of s 229. In these circumstances it is important to clarify whether one or both of the groups concerned should be bound by or included in the effect of the agreement and for what purposes.

From many view points the accountancy definitions could be left to the accountants for their own purposes, with lawyers relying on the more conventional Companies Acts definitions other than in exceptional cases.

2.9
'Undertaking' 'Parent Undertaking' and 'Subsidiary Undertaking' shall be defined in accordance with the Companies Act 1985, Sections 258 and 259 as substituted by the Companies Act 1989, Section 5.

'The Seller's Group' shall subject as hereinafter provided mean the group composed of the Seller, its Parent Undertaking (if any), all Subsidiary Undertakings of which the Seller is the Parent Undertaking, and all Subsidiary Undertakings of which the Seller's Parent Undertaking is the Parent Undertaking [PROVIDED HOWEVER THAT [for the purposes of interpretation of Schedule .... only] such group shall not include Undertakings which have been excluded (pursuant to the Companies Act 1985, Section 229 as substituted by the Companies Act 1989, Section 5) from the group accounts into which the accounts of the Seller have been consolidated.]

Another alternative is to set out explicit definitions in the agreement. These could reproduce the provisions of s 736 in the agreement or make use of conventional definitions of subsidiary, holding and associate company based on a general concept of control or upon the ownership of voting stock. It is possible to define 'control' more closely, for instance by reference to the Companies Act 1985, s 258, but in this case unless special provision is made the full extent of the definition of 'subsidiary undertaking' will not be effective in that unincorporated associations will not be caught.

2.10
A 'Subsidiary' of a party hereto shall mean any corporation of which [more than fifty] [one hundred] per cent of the voting stock is directly or indirectly owned or controlled by that party.

The 'Holding Company' of a party hereto shall mean any corporation which directly or indirectly owns or controls [more than fifty] [one hundred] per cent of the voting stock of that party.

An 'Associated Company' of a party hereto shall mean any corporation which is a Subsidiary of that party's Holding Company.

The 'Group' of a party hereto shall mean the group composed of that party together with its Holding Company and all of its Subsidiaries and Associated Companies.

2.11

An 'Affiliate' of a party hereto shall mean any corporation controlling (directly or indirectly) or under common control with that party.

A 'Subsidiary' of a party hereto shall mean any corporation controlled (directly or indirectly) by such party.

The 'Group' of a party hereto shall mean the group composed of that party together with all of its Subsidiaries and Affiliates.

[For the purposes of this definition one corporation is controlled by another if the controlled corporation is a 'subsidiary undertaking' (in accordance with the definition contained in the Companies Act 1985, Section 258 as amended by the Companies Act 1989, Section 5) of the controlling corporation.]

The definitions of 'directors' and 'connected person' are best dealt with on the basis of the Companies Act 1985, ss 741 and 346 respectively.

2.12

'Director' shall mean in relation to a company a person duly appointed as director thereof, any person occupying the position of director, by whatever name called, and a person (other than a person advising in a professional capacity) in accordance with whose directions or instructions the directors of that company are accustomed to act.

2.13

'Connected Person' shall be defined in accordance with the Companies Act 1985, Section 346.

With all the above definitions the clauses extending the parties now become simple. The following are a number of possible alternatives.

2.14

This Agreement shall be binding upon and inure to the benefit of the Seller and all other members of the Seller's Group.

2.15

The expression the 'Seller' wherever used [in this Agreement] [in Schedule ....] includes every member of the Seller's Group to the intent and effect that each reference therein to the Seller shall be construed as a reference to the Seller and as a reference to each such member.

2.16

The expression the 'Seller' wherever used [in this Agreement] [in Schedule ....] includes every Subsidiary [and Affiliate] of the Seller to the intent and effect that each reference therein to the Seller shall be construed as a reference to the Seller and as a reference to each such Subsidiary [and Affiliate].

2.17
References in this Agreement to the parties shall include their respective directors, employees, servants and agents.

2.18
The expressions 'Seller' and 'Purchaser' shall include their respective Directors and all persons who are, in relation to the Seller and the Purchaser respectively, Connected Persons.

Territories (particularly the EU)

The definition of territory is an important part of agreements, particularly agency and distributorship. The two most important elements are certainty of definition at any one time and the method of dealing with fluctuations in the geographical extent of that territory brought about by political events. The following clauses address these points in a variety of ways.

2.19
'The Territory' shall mean the countries listed in Schedule ....

2.20
'The Territory' shall mean the state of .... as constituted on and with the geographical boundaries as defined on the date of signature of this Agreement.

2.21
'The Territory' shall mean the member states for the time being of the European Union. For the avoidance of doubt if a state shall cease to be a member state or shall become a member state of the European Union it shall thereupon cease to be or become, respectively, part of the Territory.

Following the advent of the Treaty of European Union of 1993 (the Maastricht Treaty) the old terminology of the European Economic Community has become obsolete, and a number of new terms have appeared.

The European Economic Community (EEC) was originally one of three separate European communities, the others being the European Coal and Steel Community (ECSC) and the European Atomic Energy Community (EURATOM). The members of these three communities are now to be regarded as members of the new European Union which came into force under the Maastricht Treaty. The legislative basis for this Union is the three original treaties, which have been somewhat modified by the Maastricht Treaty, and the Maastricht Treaty itself. The three former treaties deal with economic aspects of the Union. The EEC Treaty in particular was amended by the Maastricht Treaty to include a section on common economic and monetary policy, and its name was changed to the European Community (EC) Treaty. The Maastricht Treaty overlays common foreign and security policies for the Union and a regime for co-operation in justice and home affairs.

Opinion is divided as to whether one should now refer to the European Union (EU) or the European Community (EC). Most people suggest that the term 'EU' should be used when dealing with the member states' activities in the areas covered specifically by the Treaty of Maastricht (such as common foreign policy initiatives) while the term 'EC', or 'the Community', could be used when considering the economic activities of the member states derived from the provisions of the old EEC (now EC) treaty.

So far as the old references to EEC law were concerned (for instance EEC competition law) it is still correct to refer to EC law since the provisions regulating that law are contained not in the Maastricht Treaty but in the EC Treaty. Thus, as they are adopted under the EC Treaty, directives will continue to be called EC Directives, and the Commission in Brussels will continue to call itself the Commission of the European Communities (since it still deals with all three of the original communities, in so far as they now have a separate existence, and acts under the EC Treaty). However, the EC Council has renamed itself the Council of the European Union since it acts both under the EC Treaty and the Maastricht Treaty.

Finally, the European Economic Area extended the EC single market in goods and services, and thus provisions of the EC Treaty such as those relating to competition, public procurement and free movement of goods, to five of the member states of the European Free Trade Association (EFTA), namely Austria, Finland, Iceland, Norway and Sweden. As from 1 January 1995, Austria, Finland and Sweden have become full members of the EU which now comprises 15 member states: Austria, Belgium, Denmark, Finland, France, Germany, Greece, the Republic of Ireland, Italy, Luxembourg, the Netherlands, Portugal, Spain, Sweden and the United Kingdom. At the time of writing, however, the EEA still has relevance for dealings between the EU and Norway and Iceland.

Confusion is often encountered over the varying descriptions of the territories covered by the United Kingdom. The following sets out the correct terminology as provided by the Interpretation Act 1978, Sched 1.

2.22

'England' means, subject to any alteration of boundaries under Part IV of the Local Government Act 1972, the area consisting of the counties established by Section 1 of that Act, Greater London and the Isles of Scilly.

2.23

'Great Britain' means England, Scotland and Wales.

2.24

The 'United Kingdom' means Great Britain and Northern Ireland.

2.25

The 'British Islands' means the United Kingdom, the Channel Islands and the Isle of Man.

Periods of time

It is important to understand and use correctly the definitions of months, days, years and business days. Loose references to months and years in agreements are to be avoided.

In general commercial usage, and as a rule by statute (see the Interpretation Act 1978, Sched 1) reference to a month is taken as a calendar month. The Law of Property Act 1925, s 61 provides that in all deeds, contracts, wills, orders and other instruments executed, made or coming into operation after 1925, 'month' means calendar month unless the context otherwise requires. A calendar month is defined as a period of time consisting of 30 days if the period commences in April, June, September and November, and of 31 if it commences in the remainder of the months, except in February when it consists of 28 days, or 29 in leap years. A year is defined as 12 calendar months.

It is a common error to consider that a calendar month commences on the first day of a named month. In fact a calendar month can commence on any day of the named month and will simply run the requisite number of days into the next named month. When counting the number of days the day on which counting begins is included. For example, the calendar month starting on 1 February ends on 28 February (28 days inclusive), the calendar month starting on 15 November ends on 14 December (30 days inclusive) and the calendar month starting on 2 October ends on 1 November (31 days inclusive).

When dealing with the running of time periods, a common phrase is 'within .... days/months [after the happening of some event] [from a specified date]'. The common law considers that in such wording the day upon which the event in question occurs or from which the period is calculated is not to be included in the period. Thus the period 'within one month from 30 May' is one calendar month commencing on 31 May and terminating on 30 June. An illuminating discussion of these matters is to be found in *Radcliffe* v *Bartholomew* [1896] QBD 161 and the authorities cited in that case.

It is possible to use periods of months and years in commercial agreements with a high degree of certainty but many draftsmen prefer to use periods of days to avoid any ambiguity. Thus termination of an agreement is likely to be expressed as by 30 days' notice rather than one month's notice. When using days it is sometimes important to distinguish between days and business days and to define business hours. The criterion often used is whether or not banks are open for business. This is useful for business days but causes problems with business hours. Banks are usually open to the public for a shorter period of time than is usually regarded as full business hours. It is probably better in this instance to specify the actual hours in question.

The following clauses should be sufficient for dealing generally with periods of time.

2.26
'Day' shall mean a period of twenty-four hours ending at twelve midnight.
'Month' shall mean calendar month.
'Year' shall mean any period of twelve consecutive Months.
'Business Day' shall mean any Day on which [clearing banks generally are open for business in the City of London] [commercial [ordinary] banks in .... generally are open for business].
'Business Hours' shall mean [9 am to 5 pm inclusive on any Business Day] [those hours on the Business Day in question during which the relevant [clearing] [commercial] [ordinary] banks generally are open for business in ....].
References to dates which do not fall on a Business Day shall be construed as references to the immediately subsequent Business Day.
Wherever in this Agreement a period of time is referred to, the Day upon which that period commences shall be the Day after the Day from which the period is expressed to run, or the Day after the Day upon which the event occurs which causes the period to start running.

Scope of undertakings

It is useful to state clearly that when an undertaking not to do something is given the party giving the undertaking must not only observe it himself but must also seek to prevent a third party from committing acts which amount to a breach of the undertaking. It may be worded as follows:

2.27
Any undertaking by either party not to do any act or thing shall be deemed to include an undertaking not to permit or suffer the doing of that act or thing.

Agreed terms

It is convenient to refer to ancillary documentation such as side letters, appendices or specifications as being 'in agreed terms' or 'in agreed form'. The following clause gives a definition and its inclusion would prevent repetitive phrases occurring throughout the agreement.

2.28
References to any document being in agreed [terms] [form] are to that document in the [terms] [form] agreed between the parties and [signed by or on behalf of the parties for identification] [initialled (for the purposes of identification only) by the parties' respective solicitors].

'Knowledge' and 'awareness'

Warranties are often qualified as being to the giver's knowledge, or as true and correct so far as the giver is aware. While there is a certain amount of case law about the standard of knowledge or awareness required it is best to impose an express standard to avoid later controversy.

The first issue to note is that while the state of actual knowledge or awareness of a natural person is (at least in theory) a simple matter of fact, the actual knowledge or awareness of a legal person can only be that of its officers, servants or agents. Here the problem is whether actual knowledge or awareness of any of these people (whatever their status in the organisation) can always be imputed to the legal person in question. For instance, if a receptionist has received a writ against the company for which he or she works, read and understood what it is, but not yet passed it on to the company secretary, can the company be said to be aware of the litigation, and thus in breach of a warranty that, so far as the company is aware, no litigation has been instituted against it? Most people would argue that the company was in truth aware only once the company secretary had received the writ, but would the situation be different if the writ had been served upon the company's external legal adviser, and he had not yet told the company about it? All of these situations can only be properly resolved by express drafting.

The second issue, which clearly can apply to both natural and legal persons, is the extent to which constructive knowledge or awareness should be caught. Here the question to be answered is how stringent an obligation to make enquiries should be imposed. Where legal persons are concerned this question is also clearly tied up with the class of natural persons whose actual knowledge is to be regarded as the actual knowledge of the legal person involved. In this situation, the concept of constructive knowledge can only have meaning once this class has been defined and an obligation imposed upon its members to make further enquiries of a defined nature or to a further defined class of persons. This is one way of solving the problem of knowledge actually held by employees lower down in an organisation which is not actually known to the senior executives. The awareness of the senior executives could be stated to consist of what they actually know, and what they would have discovered if they had made proper enquiries of relevant subordinates.

The first clause (2.29) shows a number of alternatives for dealing with actual knowledge. So far as the references to legal persons are concerned the three choices in square brackets are in ascending order of severity, and there are of course many other possible combinations. The third choice is so far-reaching that it is unlikely to be commercially acceptable in most situations.

The second clause (2.30) deals with actual and constructive awareness. It is assumed that the vendor is a legal person. Part (i) of the clause could be replaced, with suitable adaptation, by any of the possibilities in part (ii) of Clause 2.29. Three examples are shown in part (ii) of Clause 2.30 of the standard of constructive awareness which might be imposed, but these can of course be greatly expanded if the bargaining power of the party seeking to impose the clause is sufficiently great to achieve this. In most cases, where one is dealing with warranties relating to the sale of a company the choice in the third set of square brackets is likely to be commercially the most acceptable.

In order to cope with actual and constructive knowledge or awareness of a natural person, part (i) of Clause 2.29 could be combined, with suitable adaptation, with the relevant concepts contained in part (ii) of Clause **2.30**.

2.29
As used in this Agreement, the term 'to the knowledge' of any Person shall mean (i) in the case of a natural Person, within the actual knowledge (as at the relevant date) of that Person [and of any [senior] employee [or agent] of that Person], (ii) in the case of a legal Person, within the actual knowledge (as at the relevant date) [of any director or the company secretary of that Person] [of any of its directors or of any of its senior executives who report directly to any of such directors] [of any of its directors, officers (including its auditors), employees, contractors, servants or agents].

2.30
Where any of the warranties is qualified by the expression 'so far as the Vendor is aware', or any similar expression, such awareness shall refer (i) to the actual awareness of the directors [and senior executives] of the Vendor, as at the relevant date, and (ii) to the awareness, as at the relevant date, that such persons would have had had they exercised [reasonable] due diligence in making enquiries in relation to the matter in question from [all sources of information [reasonably] likely to provide them with knowledge of the same] [the employees, servants, or agents of the Vendor] [the officers (including directors and auditors) and [senior] employees of each of the companies to be sold by the Vendor to the Purchaser].

Headings

It is usual to provide headings for the main sections of agreements whether these be clauses, paragraphs or schedules, for the purpose of easy reference, although they should not be included as part of the agreement. In this way headings provide an aid to reading the agreement, sometimes in conjunction with a table of contents. In the absence of such provisions headings would become unacceptably long to ensure that they did not limit the operation of the clause or have some other unintended effect upon the agreement. A variety of clauses for the purpose of excluding headings is set out below.

2.31
The headings in this Agreement shall not affect its interpretation.

2.32
The headings in this Agreement are for ease of reference only and shall not be taken into account in the construction or interpretation of any provision to which they refer.

2.33

The titles of clauses of this Agreement are for descriptive purposes only and shall not control or alter the meaning of this Agreement as set forth in the text thereof, and do not in any way limit or amplify the terms of this Agreement.

References to legislation

Agreements often make reference to various statutes or statutory instruments. The problem here is the extent to which later modifications of such legislation shall be deemed automatically to apply to the agreement. The Interpretation Act 1978, ss 17 and 23 states that if there is no express provision regulating the matter a reference to a statute is presumed to be a reference to it as repealed, re-enacted or amended. For instance, if there were not the provision to the contrary in the Companies Act 1989, s 144(6), an agreement having no express provision on the point, and which applied the Companies Act 1985 definitions for subsidiary and holding companies, would make the radical changes in the Companies Act 1989 apply automatically with, perhaps, consequences unintended by the parties. The way such legislative changes apply is best regulated by a special clause in the agreement rather than relying on transitional provisions in the amending legislation.

A useful provision is one which extends a reference to any statute to include a reference to any statutory instruments or subordinate legislation made under that statute. In many cases statutes are enabling acts and a great deal of the relevant substantive legislation is effected by statutory instrument.

The following clauses deal with these matters relatively simply.

2.34

References to any statute or statutory provision include a reference to that statute or statutory provision as from time to time amended extended or re-enacted.

2.35

Any reference to a statutory provision shall include any subordinate legislation made from time to time under that provision.

The following clause combines the two previous ones and extends the definition of subordinate legislation.

2.36

Any reference to any Act of Parliament shall be deemed to include any amendment, replacement or re-enactment thereof for the time being in force and to include any by-laws, statutory instruments, rules, regulations, orders, notices, directions, consents or permissions (together with any conditions attaching to any of the foregoing) made thereunder.

The following clauses deal with the problem of unintended changes to the agreement by reason of reference to legislation which is amended after the agreement is entered into. The first such clause excludes all amendments effected after the date of the agreement. The second excludes all subsequent modifications which have made a substantial change to the relevant legislation. Where statutory amendments after the date of the agreement are taken account of it is desirable to preserve references to old legislation which may be necessary if proceedings are taken in relation to a cause of action which has arisen under the old legislation in force prior to the amendment. This latter point is in fact provided for in Clauses **2.34**, **2.36** and **2.38** by using the word 'include'.

2.37
References to statutory provisions shall be construed as references to those provisions as respectively amended or re-enacted prior to but not after the date of this Agreement.

2.38
Any reference to a statutory provision shall include that provision as from time to time modified or re-enacted provided that in the case of modifications or re-enactments made after the date of this Agreement the same shall not have effected a substantive change to that provision.

Finally, it is often useful to have a clause which incorporates by reference statutory definitions such as those contained in the Companies Acts. In this case, it is usually wise to exclude subsequent legislative changes.

2.39
Words and phrases the definitions of which are contained or referred to in the Companies Act [1985] shall be construed as having the meaning thereby attributed to them but excluding any statutory modification thereof not in force on the date of this Agreement.

Persons

The expression 'person' is frequently used in commercial agreements and it is useful to define it at the beginning of the agreement in a way which enables it to be used as a shorthand reference to undertakings as well as to natural persons.

2.40
The expression 'person' where used in this Agreement shall mean any person firm or company or other legal entity.

2.41
References to persons include bodies corporate and unincorporated associations and partnerships.

2.42
'Person' shall mean an individual, corporation, government or governmental subdivision or agency, business trust, estate, trust, partnership, or association, two or more persons having a joint or common interest, or any other legal or commercial entity or undertaking.

2.43
'Person' shall mean any natural person, partnership, joint venture, corporation, limited liability company, trust, firm, association, government, governmental (or supra-governmental) agency or department, or any other entity, whether acting in an individual, fiduciary or other capacity.

Singular, plural and genders

It is usual for reasons of grammatical simplicity to include a clause which clarifies the references to the singular as including the plural and vice versa and references to one gender as including references to other genders. This avoids, for instance, unwieldy constructions such as using 'he she or it' every time one uses a pronoun in place of the term 'person'. Although not all clauses do this, they can be limited by reference to some phrase like 'whenever required by context'.

2.44
Words importing the singular number shall include the plural and vice versa and words importing the masculine shall include the feminine and neuter and vice versa.

2.45
The singular includes the plural and vice versa and any gender includes any other gender.

2.46
Throughout this Agreement [whenever required by context] the use of the singular number shall be construed to include the plural, and the use of the plural the singular, and the use of any gender shall include all genders.

References to recitals, clauses and schedules

Where it is desired to make recitals, schedules or other appendices part of the agreement this fact should be clearly spelt out.

2.47
The Recitals [A through C] constitute an integral part of this Agreement.

2.48
All of the Schedules to this Agreement constitute an integral part hereof.

2.49
The Schedules to this Agreement and the Appendices A to H referred to in such schedules and attached to this Agreement form part of and shall be deemed to be incorporated in this Agreement.

The following clause saves the continuous use of words such as 'hereof', 'hereto' or 'herein' when referring to various sections of the agreement.

2.50
References to Recitals Clauses and Schedules are to Recitals Clauses and Schedules of this Agreement, and the words 'hereunder', 'hereof', 'hereto', and words of similar meaning, shall be deemed to be references to this Agreement as a whole and not to any particular Recital, Clause or Schedule of this Agreement.

Where an agreement has a large number of sections such as schedules or appendices and where other documents are incorporated by reference, it is wise to include a clause regulating the order of precedence between them in case of conflict.

2.51
In the event of a conflict between any of the terms of this Agreement, including its schedules and appendices, the conflict will be resolved according to the following order of priority: the Clauses of the Agreement, [Schedule 1, Schedule 2, Schedule 3, Appendix 1, Appendix 2], the Recitals.

2.52
In the event of an inconsistency between the various provisions of this Agreement (including any documents incorporated herein by reference) the inconsistency shall be resolved by giving such provisions and documents the following order of precedence:
  (a) the Clauses of this Agreement;
  (b) the Schedules to this Agreement;
  (c) the Technical Specifications referred to in Clause ....;
  (d) the Acceptance Test Procedure referred to in Clause ....;
  (e) the Recitals to this Agreement.

2.53

The several constituent parts of this Agreement and the Attachments hereto shall be read and construed together in the following manner and order of precedence:

(a) the provisions of this present document ('the Agreement') shall prevail over all the Attachments hereto;

(b) attachments II (the Contractor's Exceptions and Qualifications to the Customer's Tender Specifications) and VIII (the Company's Pricing Proposal) shall prevail over all the remaining Attachments;

(c) attachments III to VII inclusive and IX to XII inclusive shall prevail over Attachment I.

It is intended that a reading and construction of the documents in the above order of precedence shall produce a clear, consistent and integral Agreement between the parties hereto. In the event of any remaining conflict or discrepancy between the various constituent documents or the Agreement, or any parts of any one of the same, the same shall be resolved by consultation and agreement between the respective Project Managers of the Customer and the Contractor with the intent that an interpretation should be agreed upon that will result in the most efficient, expeditious and economical performance of the various obligations assumed by each party under this Agreement. In the event of failure to reach such agreement the matter shall be determined by arbitration pursuant to Clause [.....].

A commonly used clause is one where a special agreement (often a purchase agreement) is expressed to prevail over the standard terms and conditions that are found on various forms (such as purchase order forms) that pass between the parties for the purpose of calling off orders under the agreement. In the absence of such a clause the standard terms and conditions may well come to apply to a particular order, in addition to, or instead of, the terms in the special agreement, through the operation of the common law rules on offer and acceptance which often result in what is known as the 'battle of the forms' (see *Butler Machine Tool Co Ltd v Ex-Cell-O Corporation (England) Ltd* [1979] 1 All ER 965; *Chichester Joinery Ltd v John Mowlem & Co plc* (1987) 42 Build LR 100; and *G Percy Trentham v Archital Luxfer* [1993] 1 Lloyd's Rep 25, CA).

2.54

Unless otherwise specifically agreed in writing the terms and conditions of this Agreement shall apply to any Order placed by the Purchaser. In the event of any inconsistency between these terms and conditions and any other terms and conditions printed or written upon any other document passing between the parties (including without limitation the

Customer's Purchase Order) the terms and conditions of this Agreement shall prevail. No variation of the terms and conditions of this Agreement shall be applicable to any such Order unless expressly accepted in writing by the Company.

References to amended agreements

One occasionally sees clauses which purport to clarify, just as in the case of legislation, the status of amendments to any agreement deed or instrument which is referred to in a primary agreement, and has been amended after the date that that primary agreement was signed. A similar issue arises in relation to a primary agreement which is itself later amended. Do the references to 'this Agreement' in the primary agreement refer to the agreement in its original form, or as amended?

Although common sense suggests that references to the primary agreement should be to that agreement as amended from time to time, this may not be the case with all or some of the ancillary agreements or documents. If the clause is drafted too widely it may catch documents which are intended to apply only upon the terms which were in force as at the date of signature of the primary agreement. For instance, a set of terms and conditions of sale appended to a purchase agreement should not suddenly be replaced (without the consent of the buyer) by a new edition which the seller has issued subsequent to the date of the purchase agreement.

This point is best tackled by providing that amendments to ancillary agreements and documents cannot take effect for the purposes of the primary agreement (although such amendments may in some cases be effective for other purposes in relation to the ancillary agreements or documents themselves) unless both parties have agreed to this. The worst that can be said about such a clause is that it imposes a certain discipline on the parties, when amending the ancillary documents or agreements, to decide whether or not to invoke it. Failure to do so will mean that, so far as the primary agreement is concerned, the ancillary documents or agreements will apply in their unamended form.

2.55
In this Agreement, (i) references to this Agreement (including the Schedules and Recitals hereto) mean this Agreement as amended or modified from time to time by the mutual consent of the parties in accordance with the procedure contained in Clause ..... and (ii) references to any other agreement, deed, instrument or document (collectively

a 'document') are to such document as in effect at the date of signature of this Agreement provided that where that document has been subsequently amended or modified, the parties hereto may from time to time mutually agree that such references shall for the purposes of this Agreement be deemed to be to that document as so amended or modified at the date of such agreement, such mutual agreement being implemented by a written agreement referring to this Clause and signed by the duly authorised representatives of the parties hereto.

'Including without limitation'

It is common practice in agreements to use general terms and then to add to them, by way of example, or for the avoidance of doubt, a list of specific terms which it is intended are to be included in the general definition. For instance, one could refer to a requirement that A procure the release of B from all liabilities and obligations to C 'including any guarantees given by B to C's bankers'; or one could provide for the sale by A to B of all of the assets owned by A and used in relation to a defined business 'including those set out in Schedule . . .'. The prudent draftsman will fear that the particular nature of his specific examples will somehow constrain and limit the generality of the initial description, so that his client will not obtain all of the intended benefit of the all-embracing general clause. This can be avoided by prefacing the specific list with a phrase like 'without prejudice to the generality of the foregoing' in each case, but a neater way to deal with the problem is to continue to use the natural English of 'include' or 'including', and to add the following clause to the interpretation section of the agreement.

2.56
In this Agreement the word 'including' shall mean 'including without limitation or prejudice to the generality of any description, definition, term or phrase preceding that word, and the word 'include' and its derivatives shall be construed accordingly.

Interpretation of ancillary agreements

It is essential in many cases where one is dealing with a set of agreements (often a master agreement of some kind, with a set of ancillary agreements) to ensure that consistent definitions and interpretation are used throughout the set. The easiest way to achieve this is to cross reference all of the ancillary agreements to the definitions and interpretation clauses contained in the primary agreement, and then add in each ancillary agreement only those definitions which are specific to that agreement. The following clause deals with the point. It should be noted that this not only achieves consistency, but also shortens the ancillary agreements considerably. The method can also be applied to other common clauses which it is desirable should be the same throughout the whole set of agreements, such as choice of law, arbitration, severability and so on. If so, one would insert into the clause the phrase 'and governed' as currently shown in square brackets after the word 'interpreted', and extend appropriately the list of numbered clauses to be referred to.

2.57
In this Agreement all capitalised terms not defined herein shall have the meanings ascribed thereto in the Master Agreement made between the parties on . . ., and this Agreement shall be interpreted [and governed] in accordance with Clauses .... of the said Master Agreement which shall be deemed to be incorporated by reference, *mutatis mutandis*, into this Agreement.

Chapter 3

Commencement and Termination

'Subject to contract'

The following clause deals with the situation of a heads of agreement or memorandum of understanding which is not intended to be legally binding; the true agreement only commences when the formal contract is agreed, drafted and executed. Care should be taken when such documents are made subject to the law of jurisdictions whose legal system is not based upon the common law. In many instances such jurisdictions may well regard the document as legally binding to some extent—often at least to the extent of imposing an obligation to negotiate in good faith and to compensate the other party for costs and expenses in the event of a refusal (other than in good faith and for reasonable cause) to enter into the final agreement upon the terms contemplated by the document.

3.1
These Heads of Agreement are subject to contract and are not intended to be legally binding nor do they represent a complete summary of the contractual or commercial aims of the parties, but express their desires and understandings subject to obtaining legal and other professional advice and executive approval. If executive approval is given, these Heads of Agreement will form the basis of negotiation of a detailed Agreement, but, save for the mutual obligation of confidentiality contained in Clause ..... hereof (which is, and is intended to be, legally binding), neither party is legally obligated to the other unless and until such an Agreement is signed by both parties and has become effective in accordance with its terms.

Date of commencement—effective date/date of signature

If there is no specific provision as to commencement an agreement will commence from the date upon which it is signed. It is, however, usual to include a provision which deals with this point, in order to avoid any misunderstanding. Where there is a starting date other than the date of signature there is no reason why this cannot be before the date of signature if the parties so wish.

3.2
This Agreement shall commence upon the date of signature hereof.

Where the date of commencement is other than the date of signature it is useful to define it as the effective date for reference in various clauses of the agreement, particularly the term.

3.3
This Agreement shall commence upon .... (the 'Effective Date').

Where the effective date is before the date of signature the following wording is more appropriate.

3.4
This Agreement shall be deemed to have commenced upon .... (the 'Effective Date').

Partial commencement subject to competition law notification

In order to avoid tainting all or part of an agreement with illegality it is usual to provide that any provisions of it which are notifiable or registrable under various competition law regimes shall not come into effect until duly registered or notified. The main competition law authority for United Kingdom agreements is the Office of Fair Trading.

Needless to say such clauses are not a complete answer to this problem in that the parties may actually have been operating the particular provisions even if they were not legally in force under the terms of the agreement. In these circumstances, since most competition laws can consider anti-competitive arrangements which are not legally binding, the clause will not safeguard the parties from sanctions.

3.5
No provision hereof by virtue of which this Agreement is subject to registration under the Restrictive Trade Practices Act 1976 shall take effect until the day after particulars of this Agreement have been

furnished to the Director General of Fair Trading pursuant to the terms
of Section 24 of the said Act.

Coming into force

Certain agreements, particularly those relating to exports and to
large capital goods, do not take effect immediately upon signature,
but are subject to various conditions precedent. The conditions
precedent fall into three main classes. Firstly, financial ones which
relate to the opening of letters of credit or the giving of bonds
so that one or sometimes both parties to the agreement will be
sure that the other can perform its obligations under the contract.
Secondly, regulatory ones which relate to the obtaining of
permissions from governmental or other authorities which are
necessary before one or both parties can perform. Typical examples
are export and import licences. Thirdly, there may be technical
or commercial matters to be agreed to enable the contract to be
fully efficacious. These matters usually relate to specifications or
acceptance tests for the products to be supplied under the contract.

Besides stating the relevant conditions precedent the clause must
legislate for the event of the conditions not being fulfilled. In most
cases the contract will lapse, but sometimes an extension of time
for their fulfilment is given instead. It is always necessary to consider
whether the parties will be under any liability to each other if the
contract is terminated for failure to fulfil a condition precedent.
Very often there is no liability but where one party is to blame
for the failure to fulfil a condition, it is not unusual to require
that he pay the reasonable costs of the party incurred to date in
preparing to perform the contract.

3.6

Notwithstanding the signature of this Contract by the Purchaser and
the Company, this contract shall become effective only when all the
following conditions shall have been complied with:

(i) receipt by the Company of a letter from the Purchaser confirming
that all relevant consents, import permits and licences necessary to
import and pay for the Goods in pounds sterling have been obtained;
and

(ii) confirmation by the Company that it has obtained any necessary
export licence for the Goods.

If all the above conditions are not satisfied within forty-five days of
the date of the Company's acceptance, the Company shall have the
right to amend the Contract Price and Delivery Dates by reasonable
amounts or alternatively terminate the order.

The following clause is more elaborate both in the nature of its conditions precedent and in the fact that it does not in all cases rely upon one party notifying the other that a particular condition has been fulfilled, but leaves the matter on an objective basis. It has been written from the viewpoint of the contractor rather than the customer.

3.7

Notwithstanding signature by the parties hereto, this Contract shall not come into force until all of the following conditions precedent have been fulfilled:

1 The Contractor shall have notified the Customer that the Contractor has obtained from the competent financial authorities in the United Kingdom confirmation of their approval of the financing conditions of the Contract.

2 The Letter of Credit in favour of the Contractor in respect of the advance payments referred to in Clause [........] shall have been received in London in a form satisfactory to the Contractor.

3 The Customer shall have notified the Contractor that the Customer has obtained from the competent authorities of [..............] all necessary approvals for performance of the Contract, and together with such notification delivered to the Contractor notarially certified copies of such approvals or other evidence of their grant satisfactory to the Contractor.

4 The Contractor has received a guarantee of all payments due under this Contract from the [..............] Bank or other bank acceptable to the Contractor.

5 The Contractor shall have confirmed to the Customer that it has received from the Customer all necessary documentation and information to enable the Contractor to proceed with the Contract, including but not limited to technical specifications.

6 The parties shall have agreed the detailed acceptance tests in accordance with the procedure set down in Clause [........].

The start date in the Contractor's implementation plan set out in Schedule [........] shall be the day the Contract comes into force as provided above.

In the event that the Contract does not come into force within six months of the date of signature of the Contract both parties shall be free to withdraw from this Agreement.

Upon such withdrawal by a party hereto this Contract shall thereupon terminate [and neither party shall be under any liability to the other by reason of such termination].

Fixed term

Some agreements are for a fixed term only in which case the

following clause is appropriate. In the interests of precision state the date of termination explicitly rather than the length of the term. Such clauses must of course allow for earlier termination by reason of breach, insolvency, and similar events.

3.8
This Agreement shall commence upon [.........................] [the Effective Date] [the date of signature hereof] and shall (subject to earlier termination pursuant to Clauses ....) terminate automatically without notice [upon ....] [three years from the date of its commencement] [upon the second anniversary of its commencement].

Renewable term

Other agreements, whether or not they have an initial fixed term, carry on for an indefinite period or are subject to periodic renewals. It is important to distinguish between an agreement which continues unless brought to an end by due notice and an agreement which will expire unless renewed. The administrative arrangements that the parties have to take to preserve the continuance of the agreement or to bring it to an end are very different. The following clauses are for an agreement with an indefinite term and for a renewable agreement.

3.9
This Agreement shall commence upon the [Effective Date] and (subject to earlier termination pursuant to Clauses ....) [shall continue in force for a period of .... and] thereafter shall continue unless and until terminated by one party giving to the other not less than [three months] notice to that effect [such notice not to be served prior to the expiry of the said period of ....].

3.10
This Agreement is effective as of the date first set forth above, and shall remain in effect up to and including [................] (the 'Initial Term'), unless earlier terminated pursuant to Clauses [................]. At the end of the Initial Term, or any subsequent term thereof pursuant to a renewal under this Clause (a 'Renewed Term'), this Agreement may be renewed for a period of one year by either party serving a notice offering such a renewal upon the other not later than forty-five days prior to the expiry of the Initial Term or the Renewed Term, as the case may be, and the other party serving upon the first party a counter-notice accepting such renewal, not later than thirty days prior to the expiry of the Initial Term or the Renewed Term, as the case may be.

Expiry by effluxion of time

There is a class of agreements which does not necessarily have a certain term (although it may have an end-date) which may terminate upon the happening of various events. The clauses which deal with these matters are the opposite of the coming into force clauses, in that they impose conditions whose subsequent fulfilment results in the termination of the agreement. These clauses are used in preliminary agreements which are likely to be replaced by a fuller agreement at a later stage. Memoranda of understanding often contain such clauses even if the memorandum in question is not legally binding. Another type of document which uses this clause is a consortium agreement to bid for a particular project. The following clauses have been taken from such agreements.

3.11
In the event that the Customer shall not have signed a Contract with the parties hereto resulting from their joint Offer to the Customer within one hundred and eighty days after [.......................], then this Agreement shall expire and cease to be binding upon the parties hereto, unless they shall mutually agree in writing to maintain it in force for a further period either subject to the same terms and conditions as are herein contained or subject to revised terms and conditions.

3.12
This Agreement shall terminate upon the first to occur of the following:
    (a) upon the signing of the supplementary Consortium Agreement referred to in Clause [.......] hereof;
    (b) upon the award of the Contract for the Works to a party other than both parties hereto acting jointly in Consortium or if it becomes apparent that the Purchaser has abandoned its intention to place a contract for the Works;
    (c) on [.......................] or such other date as the parties may agree;
    (d) upon the signature of any further Agreement between the parties which shall be expressed to supersede this Agreement.

Cancellation for convenience

There are circumstances in which one party wishes to cancel the contract he has entered into purely because it suits him to do so and irrespective of the fault of the other party. The following clauses set out various possibilities for this. These clauses are generally suitable for contracts which do not have express periods of duration but rather relate to the periodic supply of goods and service or to one-off transactions. Contracts with express terms are best terminated by using a clause permitting the service of notice of termination at the discretion of one party even when the other is not in default.

The following clause deals with the case where an important element of the parties' contract has to be agreed subsequent to the signing of the contract. This type of clause is useful where it is required that the majority of the provisions of the contract are to be binding and effective from the date of signature so that it is not appropriate to use a coming into force clause which would hold the contract in suspension until agreement was reached.

3.13
If the [User Specification] has not been agreed between the Seller and the Purchaser by .... the [Purchaser] [Seller] [either party] shall be entitled (but without prejudice to any other rights it may have) to rescind this Agreement and all other agreements made pursuant hereto or which otherwise relate to the subject-matter hereto without liability on its part.

The following clauses deal with various aspects of cancellation charges. (See Clauses **3.28** and **3.29** for an alternative approach.)

3.14
If the Purchaser cancels this Agreement or part thereof or any order placed hereunder after the same shall have become binding on the Purchaser it shall be liable by way of liquidated damages for the payment of charges in accordance with the following Schedule:
[sixty-one] or more days from the relevant date of delivery, [ten per cent] of the relevant purchase price.
[thirty-one]–[sixty] days from the relevant date of delivery, [twenty-five per cent] of the relevant purchase price.
[zero]–[thirty] days from the relevant date of delivery, [thirty-five per cent] of the relevant purchase price.

3.15
Before service is provided the customer may cancel an application by written notice to the supplier. Where such cancellation renders abortive preparatory work done, or expenditure incurred, by the supplier to meet the customer's requirements, a fair and reasonable cancellation charge shall be payable.

3.16
[Provided that there is a market for the Units subject to such cancellation] the Customer shall incur no liability whatsoever to the Supplier if the Customer cancels any one Consignment (whether wholly or in part)

save that if the Customer cancels all or substantially all of the Consignments the Customer shall be liable to pay the Supplier by way of agreed and liquidated damages the Supplier's reasonable costs and expenses of administration transport and storage relating thereto.

Termination by notice—without cause

Termination by notice is either for cause or for convenience. It can be distinguished in most cases from cancellation in that the contract is brought to an end in an orderly manner and not in *medias res*. These clauses are found in agreements such as rental, agency, distribution or licensing agreements which have either an indefinite term or are periodic (for example from year to year).

3.17
This Agreement may be terminated by the Customer as to any software on which thirty-six monthly payments have been made by giving the Supplier three months written notice to expire at the end of the relevant period of thirty-six months or at any time thereafter.

3.18
The Customer may elect, before the end of any term, to terminate the licence for the Software by returning the Software and all the associated materials to the Supplier together with a letter from a person authorised in that behalf by the Customer certifying that all copies of the Software have been destroyed and that the Customer has discontinued use of the Software. Once the Supplier has been so notified, the Customer shall not pay further for use of the Software, except for those amounts already due.

3.19
At any time after services have been provided the provision of any service under this contract may be terminated by either party by at least one month's written notice to the other whereupon the liability of the Customer to pay the relevant service charge and of the Supplier to provide the relevant service shall cease on the expiration of the notice, and if and when all the services to be provided under this Agreement have been so terminated then this Agreement shall thereupon terminate in its entirety.

3.20
The Licensee may terminate this Agreement by not less than thirty days prior written notice provided always that termination under this paragraph shall not entitle the Licensee to a refund of any part of the Total Licence Fee, or prevent the Company from recovering any balance outstanding thereof.

Termination by notice—with cause

The other circumstance in which a contract is terminated by notice relates to events which justify one party terminating it. These causes may be the breach of the other party or the occurrence of insolvency which make it impossible for the other party to perform his obligations. It is always a question as to whether these occurrences should automatically bring the contract to an end or whether they merely give the 'innocent' party the right to serve a notice of termination thereby giving him the option of leaving the contract in force. This is preferable since in the case of breach one often wants to give an opportunity to the party to remedy his default. In other cases of impossibility the time for performance may be extended to see if it can be achieved later. In insolvency cases the contract may be kept in existence so as to bargain on a stronger basis with the receiver or liquidator.

It is important to provide that the notice is summary (ie takes effect immediately upon service and not after the expiry of some period of time). Once a party has decided to terminate for cause it should not have to give a period of grace for doing so. The only exception to this is the so-called 'cure period' for deliberate breaches where it is usual to provide that summary notice can only be served if a party is in breach and has despite a request to remedy within a defined period failed to cure that breach. The following clauses deal with breach including failure to pay and the question of the cure period.

The first clause is a harsh one in that no cure period is permitted, so that even forgetting to make a payment through an oversight will trigger termination if the supplier so decides.

3.21

If the Customer:
    (a) fails to pay when due any sum payable under this Contract including any sum required by way of deposit; or
    (b) fails to observe or perform any of the provisions of this Contract;
the Supplier may (without prejudice to any other right or remedy) after notice summarily cancel the Contract and/or withhold delivery of services and/or stop any equipment in transit and the payment of the price of any equipment delivered shall become immediately due.

The next clause gives a general cure period for all breaches.

3.22

If the Licensee shall fail to observe or perform any of the conditions on its part to be observed and performed and fails to remedy any such breach within thirty days of notice thereof from the Company then the Company may serve a written notice on the licensee declaring that this Agreement is terminated at such future date as it may designate.

The following clause distinguishes between breaches relating to failure to pay sums due (which is treated more severely) and breaches where a longer cure period is permitted.

3.23
The Supplier may by giving written notice to the Customer terminate this Licence with immediate effect if:
(a) the Customer has failed to pay Licence Charges within fourteen days of despatch of a reminder that they are overdue for payment; or
(b) the Customer shall otherwise commit a [material] breach of its obligations hereunder and shall fail to rectify the same (and notify the Supplier of such rectification) within thirty days of being notified thereof by the Supplier.

The following clause treats the cure period flexibly. So far as the final category of breaches is concerned, if the second set of words in square brackets is used the period for remedy of the breach in the last resort would be determined by the court or an arbitrator.

3.24
Either party may terminate this Agreement at any time upon written notice to the other if the other party defaults by failing to perform any substantial obligation on its part. The termination will become effective thirty days after receipt of written notice unless during the relevant period of thirty days the defaulting party has remedied the default or (if the default is not capable of remedy within thirty days) is diligently proceeding to cure the default by taking active effective and continuing steps to do so and the default is in fact cured within [ninety days] [a reasonable period of time] after receipt of the relevant notice.

Other than in relation to breach, the reasons for termination with cause relate to insolvency, change of control, or disappearance or dissolution of a party.

The following clause deals with change of control in an agency, distribution or licensing agreement where the identity of the party matters. In supply agreements provided the party continues to be solvent it usually does not matter if there is a change of control. Although the clause gives the principal complete discretion as to whether or not to accept the new controller, it does provide for a period during which the principal must make up his mind.

3.25

This Agreement may be terminated by the Principal by summary notice given at any time to the Agent in the event that the person or persons now having control (within the meaning of Section 285 of the Companies Act 1985 as amended by Section 5 of the Companies Act 1989) of the Agent shall cease to have such control provided that any such notice shall be given within thirty days of the Principal having discovered that such change of control has occurred.

The following clause deals with the disappearance of a party through dissolution, death or insolvency. The exception relating to a solvent amalgamation or reconstruction should be noted since its absence would forbid perfectly harmless reorganisations, for instance of the structure of a group of companies.

3.26

The Contract may be terminated with immediate effect by either party giving notice of termination to the other party (the 'Defaulting Party'):
(i)   if the Defaulting Party (being a company) shall pass a resolution for winding up (otherwise than for the purposes of a solvent amalgamation or reconstruction where the resulting entity is at least as creditworthy as the Defaulting Party and assumes all of the obligations of the Defaulting Party under the Contract) or a court shall make an order to that effect, or
(ii)   if the Defaulting Party (being a natural person) shall die, or (being a partnership or other unincorporated association) shall be dissolved, or
(iii)   if the Defaulting Party shall cease to carry on its business or substantially the whole of its business, or
(iv)   if the Defaulting Party becomes or is declared insolvent, or convenes a meeting of or makes or proposes to make any arrangement or composition with its creditors, or
(v)   if a liquidator, receiver, administrator, administrative receiver, manager, trustee, or similar officer is appointed over any of the assets of the Defaulting Party.

Effects of termination—discharge or preservation of liabilities

Termination under the coming into force clauses and clauses relating to expiry of time or failure to reach agreement upon a significant term after the contract has been signed, may well be on the basis that both parties walk away from the transaction without further liability to each other to perform the contract. In such a case the following type of clause should be used.

3.27

Any termination under Clause [........] above shall discharge the parties from any liability for further performance of this Agreement.

An alternative is the type of clause that deals fairly with compensation for work in progress at the date of termination and the return of any advance payments made. The question arises in these circumstances whether the supplier should be entitled not only to compensation for work in progress but compensation for the opportunity cost of entering into a project which has not been completed so as to yield a full profit on the resources committed to it. The phrase in square brackets in the clause below goes some way towards this but much depends upon the precise circumstances of each contract negotiation, the circumstances in which termination takes place and the bargaining power of the two parties.

3.28

In the case of a termination by either party pursuant to Clause [........] the Supplier shall be entitled to be paid a reasonable sum for any work carried out by it prior to such termination [together with a reasonable profit thereon and on the uncompleted portion of the contract] and (subject to such payment) the Customer shall be entitled to be repaid forthwith any sums previously paid under this Agreement (whether by way of a deposit or advance payment or otherwise) provided that save as aforesaid neither party shall have any liability whatsoever to the other by reason of such termination.

Clauses for cancellation for convenience, particularly in large capital goods contracts, take into account not only these items but also third party cancellation charges and unrecovered overheads.

3.29

In the event of termination under Clause [........] by the Buyer the Seller shall be entitled to total termination charges (the 'Total Termination Charges') which shall be negotiated upon the basis of the direct and overhead costs (together with a reasonable profit thereon) incurred by the Seller, up to the date of such termination, in the performance of this Agreement, reasonable costs incurred by the Seller with respect to termination of this Agreement and with respect to settlement with vendors and sub-contractors as a result of such termination, and a reasonable amount by way of compensation for the recovery of the balance of overheads and profit which would have been achieved if the Buyer had completed the Contract.

[The Seller agrees to advise the Buyer of all proposed settlements with vendors and sub-contractors and the Seller further agrees not to enter into any binding settlement until the Buyer has approved the proposed settlement or until thirty days have elapsed from the date when such advice was furnished to the Buyer.]

The Total Termination Charges shall be determined in accordance with the Seller's standard accounting practice, supported by proper vouchers and records and verified by the Seller's auditors, who shall be an independent firm of chartered accountants. The Buyer shall pay the Seller the Total Termination Charges within sixty days of submission of the claim therefor verified to the Buyer by the Seller's auditors. Final payment shall be in the amount of the Total Termination Charges less the following:

(a) amounts, if any previously paid by the Buyer to the Seller pursuant to this Agreement;

(b) an amount equal to the direct and overhead costs (together with a reasonable profit thereon) incurred by the Seller in generating pursuant to this Agreement any items of inventory and work in progress which the Buyer does not wish to have delivered to it, and which the Seller agrees to retain for its own use.

In the event of such termination as aforesaid all inventory and work in progress generated under this Agreement except that which the Seller agrees to retain as specified in paragraph (b) above shall become the property of the Buyer.

[In no event shall the Total Termination Charges as aforesaid exceed the Contract Price.]

Irrespective of whether or not there is a release of the liabilities for future performance, termination for whatever reason is usually on the basis that accrued rights and liabilities are preserved. The following clauses provide a variety of provisions preserving such rights.

3.30

Any termination of this Agreement howsoever caused shall not affect any rights or liabilities which have accrued prior to the date of termination.

3.31

The termination of this Agreement for any reason shall be without prejudice to any rights or obligations which shall have accrued or become due between the Supplier and the Customer prior to the date of termination.

The clause can, however, be slanted towards one party. In this example the supplier preserves his rights which have accrued prior to his termination for the other party's breach.

3.32

The exercise by the Supplier of its right of termination under this Clause will be without prejudice to any right to damages or other remedy which the Supplier may have in respect thereof, whether under this Agreement or otherwise. The Supplier's foregoing right of termination shall not be affected by any previous waiver of its rights.

The type of wording can be applied on a basis of mutuality.

3.33
Exercise of the right of termination afforded to either party shall not prejudice legal rights or remedies either party may have against the other in respect of any breach of the terms of this Agreement.

Effects of termination—continuation in force

Certain provisions may be required to continue in force after the termination of the agreement. These are usually obligations of confidentiality and dispute resolution clauses. The intention to continue in force can be mentioned in each of the relevant clauses and the following sweep-up clauses can be used as part of the termination provisions.

3.34
The provisions of this Agreement expressed to have effect after termination shall do so no matter how this Agreement shall be terminated.

3.35
Any termination of this Agreement (howsoever occasioned) shall not affect the coming into force or the continuance in force of any provision hereof which is expressly [or by implication] intended to come into or continue in force on or after such termination.

An alternative is to provide for continuation only as part of the termination clause by stipulating that specific clauses will survive. The advantage of such a clause is that it is clear and gathers all the provisions for survival into one place where they cannot be overlooked. The draftsman should draft the whole agreement and then as a separate exercise decide which clauses should survive.

3.36
Termination or expiry of this Licence for whatever cause shall not put an end to the obligation of confidence imposed on the Customer under Clause ....

3.37
Notwithstanding anything contained elsewhere in this Agreement, the provisions of Clauses [........] shall survive the expiry or termination of this Agreement howsoever caused, and shall continue thereafter in full force and effect.

A special case of survival is that which relates to licences to use intellectual property rights of various kinds. There are circumstances in which a licence granted under an agreement survives termination. Care should always be taken to consider whether such a provision is appropriate. Where a party enjoys the benefit of such a provision it is usually because the termination took place without his default or the agreement has expired by effluxion of time.

3.38
If the Licensee should terminate this Agreement under the terms of Clause [........] above then the Licensee retains its right to use the Software.

Although such licence rights are granted irrevocably and free of charge care should be taken to make them non-exclusive and without any right to sub-license. Otherwise the owner of the rights will be hampered in his future use and exploitation of them.

3.39
Upon termination of this Agreement pursuant to Clause [........] the Licensee shall be granted an irrevocable non-exclusive royalty free fully paid up licence (but without power to sub-license) to use the Intellectual Property Rights throughout the world without limit of time.

Effects of termination—delivery up

The final point to consider regarding the effects of termination is the extent to which termination will enable one party to retrieve property which he has delivered to the other pursuant to the terms of the contract. The clauses in this section deal with the relatively simple issues but do not touch upon retention of title clauses which are dealt with in Chapter 8.

Delivery up clauses are widely used in confidentiality agreements and licences of software or knowhow. It is not sufficient for the recipient of the information or the software to promise not to use it any longer. The other party must ensure the return of all of the information or software delivered together with all copies of it which the recipient has made.

3.40
Each party shall:
    (a)   upon the termination of this Agreement, return to the other party all documents and materials (and all copies thereof) containing the other party's Confidential Information and certify

in writing to the other party that it has complied with the requirements of this sub-clause; and

(b) notwithstanding return of documents and materials as aforesaid, continue to be bound by the undertakings of confidentiality in relation thereto set out in Clause [........].

3.41
Upon termination of this Agreement the Licence shall be forthwith determined and within thirty days thereafter the Licensee shall cease to use the Software, shall erase the machine readable parts thereof from the memory of the Licensee's computer, and shall return all copies of the Software or any part thereof in the possession or control of the Licensee and not erased as aforesaid, together with all associated documentation, to the Supplier or dispose of it as the Supplier may require in writing.

3.42
Within seven days of termination (whether under this Licence or otherwise) the Programs (including all copies and all modifications) must be destroyed by the Customer and all Associated Documentation returned to the Supplier at the Customer's expense. Written confirmation of destruction must be given.

The other area relating to delivery up is the recovery of inventory or stocks that a party may have in his possession upon termination. This is of most concern in distribution agreements where the principal requires control over the distributor and the stock he holds.

3.43
Upon termination of this Agreement from any cause whatsoever (including but without limitation expiry by effluxion of time) the Distributor shall at the request of the Principal promptly return to the Principal all documentation of any nature whatsoever in his possession or control relating to the Products, to the Principal, or to the activities of the Distributor in relation to the Products or to the Principal (other than correspondence between the parties which does not relate to technical matters).

Upon such termination the Distributor if so required by the Principal shall sell back to the Principal at cost or market value, whichever is the lesser, all or any of the Products purchased by the Distributor from the Principal and in the possession or under the control of the Distributor at the date of such termination provided that Products which are unmerchantable, obsolete, illegal, damaged, deteriorated, defective or otherwise unfit for sale shall be destroyed forthwith in the presence of the Principal or his authorised representative at the expense of the Distributor, and without making any charge upon the Principal.

The various delivery up provisions may need an enforcement

clause to enable the owner to enter upon the premises of the other party and recover the items himself if they are not delivered. The enforceability of such clauses is questionable, but they are often effective *in terrorem*, and may be added in suitable cases. They are often effective when dealing with a receiver or liquidator and are useful adjuncts to retention of title clauses.

3.44
In the case of termination of this Agreement for whatsoever cause (including without limitation expiry by effluxion of time), the Supplier shall be entitled to enter any of the Customer's premises and recover any equipment, materials, software (in whatever form), documentation, and any other items whatsoever, which are the property of the Supplier, and the Customer hereby irrevocably licenses the Supplier, its employees and agents to enter any such premises for that purpose.

Chapter 4

Confidentiality and Disclosures

The first task is to define the information which is to be subject to the obligations of confidentiality. The party seeking protection requires as wide a definition as possible while the party who is to be fixed with the obligations requires the definition to be certain and circumscribed. Where the obligations are mutual the factor which often influences a party is whether he feels he is likely to give more information than the other party, in which case he will seek a wider definition, or less information, in which case he will seek a narrower definition.

One other factor to consider is the question of proof if ever there is litigation over breach of the confidentiality obligations. In litigation it is often difficult to prove that the information was ever in the possession of the party who is alleged to be in breach. If a wide definition of information is used, particularly one which includes oral information, proof may be more difficult.

Defining information

There are a number of parameters to the definition of information.

The first is the class of information to be protected. This may be a narrow definition (such as 'technical information relating to Product X', or 'commercial information relating to the business and affairs of ABC Limited' or even 'the items of information listed in the Schedule hereto') or it may be a wide one, covering all information passing between the parties generally.

The second relates to the method by which the recipient obtains the information. Is only information which is deliberately disclosed by one party to the other to be protected, or should a party also be bound if he obtains information through his association with the other party even if there is no formal disclosure?

49

The third relates to the medium of transmission of the information. Should only information transmitted in writing or other material form be covered or should, for instance, oral information and information transmitted electronically (such as by electronic mail or fax) also be covered?

The fourth relates to the question of whether only information which the common law would regard as confidential (basically that sort of information which amounts to proprietary information or a trade secret) should be covered, or whether all information falling within the other three parameters should be prima facie regarded as within the definition irrespective of whether the common law would regard it as confidential or not. In the latter case the problem or whether information (which is clearly not confidential) should be protected is taken care of by the exceptions (see below) to the obligations of confidentiality imposed in respect of the defined information.

Clause **4.1** adopts the approach of a wide class of information, but is otherwise very restrictive, since the definition only applies to information deliberately disclosed in writing or other material form, which is designated as confidential. However, if the phrase in the third set of square brackets is included, the clause does allow for human error if the information is not actually designated confidential with a formal stamp or legend.

4.1
'Confidential Information' shall mean all information disclosed by one party to the other in [writing] [material form (including without limitation in a written document)] PROVIDED THAT each such item of information [would appear to a reasonable person to be confidential or] either contains or bears thereon (in either case in a prominent position), or is accompanied by, a written statement that the same is confidential or proprietary.

Clause **4.2** adopts a much wider definition, applying to all information in whatever form that is disclosed to or obtained by the recipient. Its operation is somewhat restricted if the final sentence in square brackets is included, since in practice most oral information when first disclosed fails to receive the necessary confirmation in writing and is often never stated to be confidential. Unless a sophisticated information administration system is installed the clause is not operated and oral information is not protected.

4.2
'Confidential Information' shall mean all information (including all oral

and visual information, and all information recorded in writing or electronically, or in any other medium or by any other method) disclosed to, or obtained by one party from, the other party or a third party acting on that other party's behalf, and without prejudice to the generality of the foregoing definition shall include but not be limited to (i) any information ascertainable by the inspection or analysis of samples, (ii) the information detailed in the Schedule hereto, and (iii) any information relating to a party's operations, processes, plans, intentions, product information, knowhow, designs, trade secrets, software, market opportunities, customers and business affairs [PROVIDED THAT information disclosed orally shall not fall within this definition if it is not identified as confidential at the time of its disclosure and confirmed as such in writing by the disclosing party within thirty days of such disclosure].

Clause **4.3** is a further example of a clause relating to the exchange of technical information. This clause is restrictive as to the class of information covered (the first parameter above), but very wide as regards the other three parameters.

4.3
'Confidential Information' shall mean all that technical information relating to [the Product] which is disclosed to the Receiving Party by the Disclosing Party, or is otherwise obtained by the Receiving Party from the Disclosing Party [including without limitation the information contained in the documents listed in the Schedule hereto].

Obligations of confidentiality

Having defined the information to be protected the obligations of confidentiality must be imposed. The following clause is a short form for this purpose. The obligations imposed in relation to staff and the limitation to five years are quite standard. Most confidentiality obligations are unlikely to be imposed for less than three years, and it is not unknown for perpetual obligations, without any time limit at all, to be imposed.

4.4
Each party will take all proper steps to keep confidential all Confidential Information of the other which is disclosed to or obtained by it pursuant to or as a result of this Agreement, and will not divulge the same to any third party and will allow access to the same to its own staff only on a 'need to know' basis, except to the extent that any such Confidential Information becomes public through no fault of that party. Upon termination of this Agreement, each party will return to the other any equipment and written data (without retaining copies thereof) provided for the purposes of this Agreement. Notwithstanding the

termination or expiry of this Agreement for whatever reason the
obligations and restrictions in this clause shall be valid for a period
of [five] years from the date of signature hereof.

The following clause requires the recipient of the information
to impose obligations of confidentiality upon its other group
companies and upon employees and agents who have access to
the information.

4.5

The parties will not [and will procure that no Associated Company
will, in each case] without the prior written consent of the other party,
during the term of this Agreement and for a period of [two] years
after its termination or expiry for whatever reason divulge or
communicate to any person any of the Confidential Information which
any of them ('the recipient party') may have learned from the other
('the disclosing party') before or during the term of this Agreement.

The recipient party undertakes not to disclose any Confidential
Information to any third party other than Sub-Contractors and Sub-
Licensees appointed pursuant to the provisions of this Agreement and
the professional advisers and responsible officers and employees of the
recipient party who require such disclosure where bona fide necessary
for the proper performance of their duties and who will individually
comply with all obligations of confidentiality imposed upon the recipient
party by the provisions of this Clause.

The recipient party undertakes to take all reasonable steps to minimise
the risk of disclosure of Confidential Information by such advisers,
officers and employees, and shall take all reasonable steps to restrict
them from divulging or communicating any Confidential Information.

It is not enough merely to prevent a recipient from disclosing
confidential information. He must also be prevented from using
it for his own benefit and restricted to using it solely for the purpose
for which it has been disclosed to him. For instance, where a
manufacturer has received technical knowhow for the purposes of
evaluation he should not be permitted to make use of it for any
other purpose, such as for commercial gain by applying it to his
own production processes. The following clause is a more elaborate
confidentiality undertaking and also deals specifically with this
point. Note should be taken of paragraphs (c) and (d) which require
the recipient not only to impose obligations of confidentiality upon
employees and others having access to the information but also
require him to enforce those obligations and indemnify the
disclosing party if he fails to do so.

4.6

In consideration of the mutual exchange and disclosure of Confidential Information, each party undertakes in relation to the other party's Confidential Information:

(a) to maintain the same in confidence and to use it only for the purposes of this Agreement and for no other purpose and in particular, but without prejudice to the generality of the foregoing, not to make any commercial use thereof or use the same for the benefit of itself or of any third party other than pursuant to this Agreement or a further agreement with the other party;

(b) not to copy reproduce or reduce to writing any part thereof except as may be reasonably necessary for the aforesaid purposes and that any copies reproductions or reductions to writing so made shall be the property of the disclosing party;

(c) not to disclose the same whether to its employees or to third parties except in confidence to such of its employees or directors who need to know the same for the aforesaid purposes and provided that (i) such employees and directors are obliged by their contracts of employment or service not to disclose the same, and (ii) the receiving party shall enforce such obligations at its expense and at the request of the disclosing party in so far as breach thereof relates to the disclosing party's Confidential Information;

(d) to be responsible for the performance of sub-clauses (a), (b) and (c) above on the part of its employees or directors to whom the same is disclosed pursuant to sub-clause (c) above; and

(e) to apply thereto no lesser security measures and degree of care than those which the receiving party applies to its own confidential or proprietary information and which the receiving party warrants as providing adequate protection of such information from unauthorised disclosure, copying or use.

The following clause as it is presently drafted, without any further definition of confidential information, is one with wide application but it does rely on, in effect, protecting only what the common law would regard as confidential information. Such a clause is useful where the agreement is not primarily concerned with the disclosure of confidential information but where such information may be obtained by a party incidentally during the operation of the agreement.

4.7

In performance of this Agreement, each party and its employees and agents may have access to confidential information owned or controlled by the other party relating (*inter alia*) to equipment, apparatus, programs, software and specifications, drawings and other documents, and such information may contain proprietary details and disclosures.

All such information so acquired by the receiving party or its employees or agents under this Agreement or in contemplation thereof shall be and shall remain the disclosing party's exclusive property. The receiving party shall use a reasonable degree of care, which in any event shall not be less than the same degree of care which the receiving party uses to protect its own confidential information, to keep and have its employees and agents keep, any and all such information confidential. The receiving party shall not copy, publish or disclose such information to others, or authorise its employees, or agents, or anyone else to copy, publish or disclose it to others, without the disclosing party's prior written approval, and shall return such information to the disclosing party at its request.

With respect to all such information to be kept confidential pursuant to this Clause, each party agrees:

1 Not to provide or make available such information disclosed by or acquired from the other party ('disclosed information') in any form to any person other than those employees, agents or sub-contractors of the receiving party who have a need to know consistent with the receiving party's authorised use of disclosed information;

2 Not to use or reproduce disclosed information except for use reasonably necessary for the performance of this Agreement;

3 Not to publish or disclose disclosed information to third parties other than as expressly permitted herein, without the disclosing party's prior written consent; and

4 To return or destroy all disclosed information which is in written or graphic form at the conclusion of its authorised use.

Exceptions

There are certain exceptions to obligations of confidentiality, many of which are standard and well recognised, and which represent, in effect, an acknowledgment of the limitations on what the common law is prepared to regard as truly confidential information deserving of protection. However, the limits of the common law principles are not always clear particularly in the area of what constitutes information in the public domain) and, in any event, can to some extent be overridden by contract. The best solution is therefore (with one eye, as it were, on the common law position) to spell out a set of sensible express exceptions suited to the parties' requirements.

Such exceptions can either be added to the definition of confidential information (so that information falling within the exceptions is excluded from the definition and never receives even prima facie protection in the first place), or can be added as exceptions to the obligations of confidentiality themselves. These obligations can then prima facie apply to a very general definition of information, without the need to consider whether all of the defined information is truly confidential or not. The first clause deals with the related issues of public domain and public knowledge and the knowledge of the recipient party.

4.8
The obligations of confidentiality under this Clause shall not apply to any information or material which the recipient party can prove:
1   Was already known to it prior to its receipt thereof from the disclosing party;
2   Was subsequently disclosed to it lawfully by a third party who did not obtain the same (whether directly or indirectly) from the disclosing party;
3   Was in the public domain at the time of receipt by the recipient party or has subsequently entered into the public domain other than by reason of the breach of the provisions of this Clause or of any obligation of confidence owed by the recipient party or by any of its Sub-Contractors or Sub-Licensees to the disclosing party.

The following clause contains more elaborate exceptions. The requirement to prove prior knowledge of the recipient party in paragraph (ii) should be noted.

4.9
The obligations of confidentiality under this Clause shall not apply to any part of the Confidential Information which:
(i) is in or comes into the public domain in any way without breach of this Agreement by the receiving party; or
(ii) the receiving party can show was in its possession or known to it by being in its use or being recorded in its files or computers or other recording media prior to receipt from the disclosing party and was not previously acquired by the receiving party from the disclosing party under an obligation of confidence; or
(iii) the receiving party obtains or has available from a source other than the disclosing party without breach by the receiving party or such source of any obligation of confidentiality or non-use towards the disclosing party; or
(iv) is hereafter furnished by the disclosing party to a third party without restriction on disclosure or use; or
(v) is disclosed by the receiving party (a) with the prior written approval of the disclosing party or (b) without such approval, after a period of [........] years from the date of receipt thereof.
The foregoing exceptions shall not however apply to:
(a) specific information merely because it is embraced by more general information which falls within any one or more of such exceptions; and

(b) any combination of features merely because individual features (but not the combination itself) fall within any one or more of such exceptions.

The following clause is another variation on the exception but particular note should be taken of exceptions 3, 4, 5 and 7. Exception 3 is a subtle way of excluding oral information and one needs to watch for this when reviewing a draft document. Exception 4 deals with information which is not quite in the public domain but is nonetheless at the least publicly available. An example could be an article published in a relatively obscure technical journal. Exception 5 is one of the most important. Should a recipient be permitted to develop information identical to that disclosed to him and then use his developed information without restriction? The exception permits him to do this if he has developed the information independently. The phrase in square brackets does make the clause rather fairer on the discloser since it requires the recipient to adopt what is often called a 'clean room' approach and start afresh with employees who have no knowledge of the disclosing party's information. If the phrase is not used it would still be prudent to adopt a clean room approach otherwise the recipient would have little chance of proving independent development in any ensuing litigation. The exception is most commercially acceptable where the recipient is a large company or group of companies with different divisions and locations. It is quite possible that what has been disclosed to one division may be developed independently by another.

Exception 7 is an attempt to encapsulate the concept of general skill and expertise acquired by individual employees which cannot really be said to form an identifiable body of confidential information. The phrase in square brackets is by way of example only. This is the kind of information that can easily be exchanged when two employees of different organisations work side by side. A useful discussion of this type of information and its exclusion from the common law obligations of confidentiality in relation to employees who acquire it from their employer can be found in *Faccenda Chicken* v *Fowler* [1987] Ch 117.

4.10

Nothing in this definition of Confidential Information shall be construed to limit each party's use or dissemination of information that:

1   Was in the lawful possession of the receiving party at the time of disclosure by the disclosing party without an obligation to keep it confidential;

2 Was in the public domain at the time of receipt or disclosure or subsequently becomes so;

3 Is not identified in writing as being proprietary or confidential;

4 Was originally considered proprietary under this Clause but which subsequently becomes part of the public knowledge or literature through no fault of the receiving party;

5 Is developed by or for the receiving party at any time independently of the information disclosed to it by the disclosing party [by persons who have had no access to or knowledge of the said information];

6 Has been or hereafter may be rightfully acquired from third parties without obligation to keep confidential;

7 Consists solely of generalised ideas, concepts, knowhow or techniques relating to [data processing].

Further exceptions to the obligations of confidentiality can be found in the area of governmental or judicial authorities or regulatory bodies such as stock exchanges. Here the general law or practice may require a party to disclose confidential information whether he wishes to or not. Such an exception clause covering these matters should routinely be inserted.

4.11

Notwithstanding the foregoing, the receiving party shall be entitled to make any disclosure required by law or by any governmental or other regulatory authority (including without limitation the [London Stock Exchange]) of the other party's Confidential Information provided that it gives the other party not less than two business days' notice of such disclosure.

A standard disclaimer is that the disclosure of confidential information does not of itself give a licence or any other rights to use the information other than for the purposes, if any, specified at the time of disclosure. Such disclaimers should always be inserted.

4.12

Each party reserves all rights in its Confidential Information and no rights or obligations other than those expressly recited herein are granted by or to be implied from this Agreement. In particular, no licence is hereby granted directly or indirectly under any patent, invention, discovery, copyright or other intellectual property right now or in the future held, made, obtained or licensable by either party. Nothing in this Agreement or its operation shall preclude or in any way impair or restrict either party from continuing to engage in its business otherwise than in breach of the terms of this Agreement.

It is useful to combine the foregoing clause with one which clearly states that the agreement for disclosure of confidential information shall not be capable of enforcement by the other party so as to require the discloser to reveal matters which would put him in breach of confidentiality undertakings to third parties or of legislation preventing disclosure such as the UK Official Secrets Acts 1911–1989.

4.13
Nothing in this Agreement shall be construed as requiring a party to disclose Confidential Information or to grant rights under licences, or to render any technical assistance, which would violate any confidentiality undertakings or other obligations which such party has towards third persons or which would violate any present or future law or decree of any government or supra-governmental institution or of any officer or agency thereof, and nothing contained herein shall require the disclosure of Confidential Information which would increase or impose any obligations on a party with respect to third parties.

Warranties

The final clause is a warranty of right to disclose. This clause is often sought by recipients but avoided by disclosers. Given the amorphous nature of information it is a difficult warranty to give and should at least be qualified by the inclusion of one of the phrases in square brackets.

4.14
Each party warrants that [to the best of its knowledge and belief] [so far as it is aware] [to its knowledge] it has the right to disclose its Confidential Information to the other party, and the right to authorise the other party to use the same for the purposes of this Agreement, and that [to the best of its knowledge and belief] [so far as it is aware] [to its knowledge] there is no competing claim of title or intellectual property infringement relative to the use of its Confidential Information.

The following clause also excludes any other warranties relating to confidential information. If a right to disclose is warranted other warranties should probably be excluded using the wording of the remainder of this clause.

4.15
Neither party makes any representations in respect to, or warrants, any Confidential Information provided to the other party but shall furnish same in good faith to the best of its knowledge and ability. Without restricting the generality of the foregoing, neither party makes any representations or warranties as to suitability quality merchantability or fitness for a particular purpose, or as to whether or not the exploitation of any such Confidential Information will infringe any patent or other rights of any other person.

It is of course possible to include full warranties and indemnities in relation to confidential information. The warranties and indemnities relating to intellectual property in Chapter 5 (see Clauses 5.22 to 5.33) can be studied and adapted accordingly.

Publicity

Apart from confidential information the parties may well be concerned about publicity surrounding an agreement or a transaction. It may be that the agreement and its terms should be kept confidential. The following two clauses deal with this in a simple way. However, such clauses should not be inserted as a matter of routine. Consideration should always be given as to whether the party does or does not want to give the transaction publicity. Some of the parties may wish to do so, in which case such a clause would not find favour.

4.16
The parties agree to keep confidential the terms of this Agreement, and neither shall make any announcement in relation to or otherwise publicise [its existence or] its contents.

4.17
No announcement concerning the transactions contemplated by this Agreement or any matter ancillary thereto shall be made by any party without the prior approval of the others.

The following, wider, clause prevents one party from making publicity out of a connection with the other party. Such a clause is often used in standard purchase contracts where the purchaser does not wish his supplier to use his connection with the purchaser for the purposes of advertising or publicity.

4.18
Each party agrees to keep the existence and nature of this Agreement and the provisions terms and conditions thereof confidential and not to use the same or the name of the other party in any publicity, advertisement or other disclosure with regard to this Agreement without the prior written consent of the other party.

There are cases in which publicity is desired by both parties but in a co-ordinated way and it is wise here to prevent disclosure by either party unless the other agrees. Where one of the parties is a publicly quoted company stock exchange disclosure is often either necessary or desirable. Other possible circumstances where disclosure is mandatory are, for instance, in relation to competition law authorities. The clauses that follow deal with the points that arise here.

4.19

The parties agree that neither of them will make any official press release, announcement or other formal publicity relating to the transactions which are the subject of this Agreement without first obtaining in each case the prior written consent of the other party [which consent will not be unreasonably withheld].

4.20

No announcement, other than to the extent required by The Stock Exchange, the Government, or any statutory body of competent jurisdiction shall be made by any one of the parties hereto concerning the transactions referred to herein without the consent of the other of them.

4.21

Terms, conditions and general provisions of this Agreement, and any agreements or arrangements entered into pursuant to it, shall be held in confidence by both parties, and only disclosed as may be agreed to by both parties or as may be required to meet stock exchange disclosure or export permit requirements. Neither party shall make public statements or issue publicity or media releases with regard to this Agreement or the relationship between the parties thereunder without the prior written approval of the other party.

The final clause takes a middle path by imposing an obligation to consult prior to any such release. The difference with the previous two clauses is that (once consultation has occurred) one party may disclose without the consent of the other.

4.22

The Vendor and the Purchaser shall consult together as to the terms of, the timetable for and manner of publication of any announcement (unless specified by law or The Stock Exchange) to shareholders, employees, customers and suppliers or to The Stock Exchange or other authorities or to the media or otherwise which either may desire or be obliged to make regarding this Agreement.

Chapter 5

Intellectual Property Rights

Definition

It is necessary to define intellectual property rights for various purposes in commercial contracts. In licensing or technology transfer agreements the purpose is to define what is to be transferred. In development contracts or in supply contracts where development or adaptation of a product may be involved, it is necessary for the purposes of providing who owns the various rights which either exist prior to the contract or arise during its execution. Even in supply contracts it is necessary to define them for the purposes of the warranties and indemnities relating to third party infringement which most suppliers will want when they purchase goods.

We start by considering the definition of knowhow. To some extent there is an overlap with the definitions of confidential information discussed in Chapter 4. In its broadest sense knowhow is purely information. Some contracts talk of 'trade secrets' or 'proprietary information' but knowhow is not an intellectual property right since no one can own information. Where information is embodied in a material object such as a document or an engineering drawing this material embodiment can be owned. Some of the definitions of knowhow refer not only to information but also to material embodiments of it. Where such definitions are used it is correct to talk of ownership of knowhow and some of the clauses in this section reflect this. At the very least ownership of a material embodiment of information enables a party to possess it and have access to the information contained therein.

Intellectual property rights exist in relation to and depend upon there being underlying information. Copyright appears in the expression of a piece of information in a document or as a computer program. A registered or unregistered design right can exist in the visual appearance of certain products or equipment. While copyright cannot directly protect information, but only particular embodiments of it (hence the old maxim that copyright does not protect ideas but only their expression), some information can be directly protected by intellectual property rights. The information relating to an invention can be protected by a patent while a registered design can confer a monopoly to exploit a product with a particular visual appearance.

As will be seen later in this chapter, there is an interplay between the definitions of 'knowhow' and 'intellectual property rights', so that one often finds it useful in the agreement (for purposes of technology transfer, warranties or indemnities) to define the 'knowhow' and then to deal with the 'intellectual property rights' (as defined) subsisting in the 'knowhow'.

When deciding how to define knowhow, as with confidential information, there is the usual conflict between parties with different interests. Tighter definitions favour a party who is to transfer knowhow or to give warranties about it. The receiving party usually requires the widest possible definition to ensure that he has all the knowhow to achieve his purposes in entering into the agreement and to give him the widest possible protection in relation to warranties.

In addition to deciding on the width of a particular definition, care should be taken to consider exactly what categories of knowhow should be comprised within a particular definition. Should commercial knowhow, for instance, be included as well as technical knowhow? One typical problem is whether to include software within the definition. Recipients will probably desire this but a great deal of thought should be given as to the way the definition will be applied. Matters that are appropriate for general information need special attention for software. This is particularly true where one is giving extended warranties and indemnities in relation to knowhow. What might be acceptable in relation to a technical specification in a written document could be far too onerous for a computer program.

The definition below, despite its apparently wide wording, is completely restrictive since it applies only to the defined items listed in a schedule. The removal of the reference would of course give a very wide definition.

5.1

The 'Knowhow' shall mean all those patentable and non-patentable inventions discoveries improvements and processes and copyright works [(including without limitation computer programs)] [excluding computer programs] and designs (whether or not registered or registrable) listed in Schedule [.........].

Knowhow is not of course restricted purely to technical matters. It can cover commercial, marketing and sales information and general business practices. The definition above, whether or not one chooses to restrict it by reference to items listed in a schedule, is slanted towards technical information. The following definition is a wide one with no listings in a schedule and it also refers not only to technical knowhow, but to the other categories as mentioned above.

5.2

'Knowhow' means all industrial marketing and commercial information and techniques including (without prejudice to the generality of the foregoing) drawings, formulae, test reports, operating and testing procedures, shop practices, instruction manuals, tables of operating conditions, administrative procedures, lists and particulars of customers, marketing methods and procedures, advertising copy, [and] [but excluding] computer programs.

It is possible to limit definitions of knowhow by reference to the purpose for which it is required and the amount of information needed to achieve that purpose. Clause **5.3** below shows various ways of doing this.

The knowhow is directed towards a particular product which will have been defined elsewhere in the agreement, probably by reference to a technical specification. The definition is aimed at capturing the knowhow needed to make and sell that product but goes further by giving a sort of warranty to the recipient. The bare wording 'necessary to manufacture the product' and the similar phrases in the definition give the recipient the assurance that he will get all of the knowhow needed to achieve his purpose and that the transferor of the knowhow has assumed an obligation to achieve this.

This obligation can be broadened in two ways. Firstly, the insertion of the word 'reasonably' broadens the class of knowhow beyond knowhow without which it is impossible to achieve the purpose for which it is being transferred. The grey area covers such things as engineering drawings, tooling specifications or some production processes. It may be desirable and reasonable for the recipient not to develop these things himself but, if he only gets what is necessary, items which he could develop himself (at whatever cost in time and money) are unlikely to be considered 'necessary'. The insertion of the word 'reasonable' broadens the categories of cases in which the knowhow will be regarded as necessary. The best solution for a recipient who wants a broader definition is to specify such items as a listed part of the knowhow and then insert the words 'reasonably' as an additional catch-all.

The second method of broadening is to define necessity in relation to the recipient. If the recipient is technically unsophisticated, he will need more training, for instance, in order to achieve the purpose for which the knowhow is transferred. He may need additional detail on manufacturing or testing processes in order to achieve proper manufacture. Transferors prefer to avoid such concepts and define the knowhow objectively. Particularly where training is concerned this is usually limited by reference to a schedule or else a charge is made per man day supplied. One of the frequent traps a transferor can fall into is to agree a lump sum and a reasonable royalty for a transfer of knowhow and then find that his return is eaten up by the expenses of fulfilling an open-ended obligation for training and technical assistance, where the transferee is not in fact technically competent to manufacture the product.

5.3

The 'Knowhow' shall mean:

A complete file containing (a) details of all manufacturing processes and formulae [reasonably] necessary [to enable the Licensee] to manufacture the Product and (b) a list and specifications of all plant and machinery and all quality control and other facilities [reasonably] necessary [to enable the Licensee] to manufacture pack store transport market and sell the Product; and

technical assistance and training [reasonably] necessary to transfer [to the Licensee] the Licensor's experience and methods in the field of manufacturing quality control and development of the Product; and commercial assistance and training [reasonably] necessary to transfer [to the Licensee] the Licensor's experience and methods in the field of marketing and selling of the Product.

It is now possible to define intellectual property either in isolation or in relation to knowhow. In this book the term 'intellectual property rights' or 'intellectual property' is used although some draftsmen use the term 'industrial property'. It is suggested that industrial property means all intellectual property rights other than copyright. However, in most modern commercial contracts, particularly those where software is involved, it does not make sense to exclude copyright from the provisions on intellectual property. If this is desired it is better to achieve the purpose in an unambiguous way by restricting the definition of intellectual property accordingly.

The following definition of intellectual property set out below would be linked to a specific definition of knowhow such as that contained in Clause **5.3**. Consideration should always be given as to whether trade marks and trading names should be included within the definition.

The definition deals with both United Kingdom and foreign intellectual property rights. Since there are certain rights equivalent to patents in foreign jurisdictions (such as *brevets d'invention* in France) and many varying design rights, it is important to widen the definition with the 'all other rights' wording towards the end.

When dealing with warranties and indemnities decide whether their operation will apply to intellectual property rights throughout the world or only to a particular jurisdiction. Careless use of a world-wide definition and no jurisdictional limitation can result in a warranty or indemnity that is wider than intended.

5.4
'Intellectual Property' means all rights which may subsist in any part of the world in the Knowhow including United Kingdom and foreign patents, registered and unregistered designs and copyright [and trade marks and trading names (whether or not registered)] [but excluding trade marks and trading names].

The following example excludes trade marks and is a general definition which does not depend upon a prior definition of knowhow.

5.5
'Intellectual Property Rights' means patents, registered and unregistered designs, copyright and all other intellectual property protection [(other than trade marks)] wherever in the world enforceable.

It is often convenient to have two stages of definitions in an agreement particularly with a technology transfer or licence agreement. Begin with two general definitions of knowhow and intellectual property (those in Clauses **5.2** and **5.5** would be appropriate) and then set up two further definitions which relate to the product or technology which is the subject of the agreement. A wide definition then exists which can be used generally in warranties and indemnities relating, for instance, to third parties' intellectual property and the possibility of its infringement, and a specific definition which can be used for the provisions relating to the knowhow to be transferred and the intellectual property in respect of which a licence is to be granted.

The two definitions below show how the specific knowhow and intellectual property definitions should be drafted. The phrase in the first set of square brackets is important in both clauses. If it is not present and a party undertakes an obligation to transfer in relation to the defined term he will have to procure the transfer of, for instance, intellectual property or information which is owned or controlled by third parties and this may not be possible. The problem is particularly acute in the area of third party software where the transferor will only be a licensee, and may not have the power to sub-license. The phrases in the remaining sets of square brackets can be used to widen or narrow the relevant definition.

5.6
'Relevant Intellectual Property' means all Intellectual Property [owned or controlled by the Licensor] relating to [and/or used in connection with] the Products [or their manufacture, marketing or sale], [including without limitation the Intellectual Property specified in Schedule ....];

5.7
'Relevant Knowhow' means all Knowhow [which the Licensor has unrestricted right to disclose] relating to [and/or used in connection with] the Products [or their manufacture, marketing or sale], [including without limitation the Knowhow specified in Schedule ....];

It is useful where the phrase 'ownership or control . . .' is used to insert a further paragraph at the end of the definition defining what is meant by control. The following is an example of what could be used.

5.8
For the purposes of this definition intellectual property shall be deemed to be within the control of a party if, as licensee thereof, he enjoys under the relevant licence, an unrestricted power to sub-license the relevant intellectual property [throughout the world] [in the Territory] to all persons.

The question of control in relation to third party rights existing in intellectual property rights is particularly important to computer programs which are only licensed and not sold. The following clause deals with the obligation on a transferor to procure the consent of relevant third parties for the use of such programs by the transferee. The phrases in square brackets obviously limit the extent of the obligation.

5.9
To the extent that the copyright in computer programs comprising part of the Knowhow is owned or controlled by third parties the Vendor will [use all reasonable endeavours to] obtain permission for the Purchaser to use such programs[, but shall have no obligation to make any payment in order to obtain such permission].

Ownership

In contracts which either require the use of intellectual property or are likely to generate new intellectual property as a result of their performance, it is important to establish between the parties the ownership of the various classes of intellectual property rights.

Pre-existing rights which each party already has but either contributes to or uses in the course of the performance of a contract are usually owned by the originating party. This class of rights is called 'background intellectual property rights'. Intellectual property rights generated or arising during the course of a contract are called 'foreground intellectual property rights'. The following clause deals with ownership of both classes of rights on the basis that they belong to the party performing the contract. This is most appropriate for a supply contract. The phrase in square brackets at the end of the first clause has to be used with caution in situations where EC law applies. Such 'no contest' clauses, certainly where they are included in licence agreements, contravene Art 85 of the Treaty of Rome and are very rarely granted an exemption by the European Commission under Art 85(3). They may have a chance of exemption in a supply agreement.

5.10
The Customer acknowledges that any and all of the Intellectual Property Rights used or embodied in or in connection with the System including the Supplier Products and any parts thereof are and shall remain the sole property of the Supplier or of such other party as may be identified therein or thereon (the 'Owner') [and the Customer shall not during or at any time after the completion, expiry or termination of this Agreement in any way question or dispute the ownership by the Supplier or the Owner of any such Intellectual Property Rights].
In the event that new Knowhow evolves or is generated or arises in the performance of or as a result of this Agreement, the Customer acknowledges that the same and all Intellectual Property Rights therein

shall belong to the Supplier unless otherwise agreed in writing by the Supplier.

Conversely, in a licence agreement it is most usual for improvements or other inventions generated by the licensee in the course of his activities to belong to the licensee.

5.11
The ownership of any and all Intellectual Property which exists in any Knowhow furnished to the Licensee under this Agreement shall remain with the licensor or third parties as appropriate and shall not vest in the Licensee.
The ownership of any and all Intellectual Property which exists in any changes, modifications, adaptations or improvements made to the Product or the Knowhow by the Licensee shall remain with the Licensee.

The following clause provides an example of a grant-back clause. Foreground rights generated by a licensee are usually the subject of a licence back to the licensor of the background technology to which the foreground technology is related. Such clauses are permitted under EC law, but only if they grant non-exclusive licence. The clause itself does not provide the detailed terms of the licence back which may, in appropriate cases, need to be the subject of a special and detailed licence agreement. It is very important to exclude the power to sub-license (see discussion below relating to joint ownership). The various alternatives in square brackets relating to the licence back will widen or narrow the scope of the grant-back licence as desired. In most cases the terms of the grant-back are as wide as possible and free of payment.

5.12
Any and all Intellectual Property Rights throughout the world resulting from any work carried out by the Licensee in order to adapt the Products to its customers' requirements [or relating to an improvement to the Products generated by the licensee] shall vest exclusively in the Licensee. The Licensee undertakes that it will grant an irrevocable [worldwide] non-exclusive licence [free of royalty or any other payment] [upon fair and reasonable terms] without limit of time and for all purposes [but excluding the power to grant sub-licences] of such Intellectual Property Rights to the Licensor.

Various issues arise as to the ownership of background and foreground rights in joint development situations. It is usually provided that each party owns the background that it contributes and the foreground that it generates on its own. Where foreground is developed jointly with a substantial contribution from both parties problems as to ownership arise.

In cases of joint development it is possible to provide that the two parties become joint owners. This, however, often gives rise to complications particularly in the area of patents. Under the Patents Act 1977, s 36(1) each co-owner of the patent is entitled (in the absence of express agreement to the contrary) to use the invention for his own profit without the permission of the other co-owners or the obligation to account to them for any profit he makes. However, under s 36(3) no one co-owner can license the patent without the consent of all the others unless the Comptroller of Patents makes a direction approving the relevant licence. It is also necessary to make provisions to cover decisions as to which jurisdictions to file the patents in when they are generated. Similar problems arise with copyright and registered design rights.

Wherever possible joint ownership of intellectual property rights should be avoided with one party taking the benefit and burden of ownership and the other being granted a licence. Provided the licence is properly worded it can confer all of the benefits of ownership without causing the complications of joint ownership.

Where this course is adopted Clause **5.13** could be used with some adaptation as follows. If the phrase in square brackets in the second line of the second paragraph is included the licence to the customer would include background as well as foreground rights; if it is excluded, only foreground will be licensed. It is not usual to grant a free licence for background rights. Usually background is licensed subject to payment, and only if the contractor is willing to grant a licence, while foreground is often licensed automatically and free of charge.

5.13
All Knowhow and all Intellectual Property Rights used in or generated from or arising as a result of the work undertaken by the Contractor for the purpose of the Contract shall (to the extent that they are not already vested in the Contractor prior to their use as aforesaid) vest in and be the absolute property of the Contractor.
The Contractor shall grant to the Customer a licence for the use of any Knowhow and Intellectual Property Rights [used in or] generated from or arising as a result of the work undertaken by the Contractor for the purpose of the Contract, such licence to be an irrevocable [worldwide] non-exclusive licence [free of royalty or any other payment] [upon fair and reasonable terms] without limit of time and for all purposes [but excluding the power to grant sub-licences].

The following clause (taken from an agreement on collaborative development) shows an alternative method of dealing with the issue, and provides clearer definitions of foreground and background intellectual property rights. Again it avoids the problems of joint ownership of intellectual property rights, but shows how each party's contribution to the development can be taken into account in deciding how to exploit the results of the collaborative development.

5.14

'Background Information' means Technical Information, excluding Foreground Information, owned or controlled by any party in the same or related fields to the research conducted under a Development Project; 'Background IPR' means all Intellectual Property Rights, excluding Foreground IPR, owned or controlled by any party in the same or related fields to the research conducted under a Development Project; 'Deliverables' means all Technical Information, and all tangible and intangible goods and services, delivered or otherwise provided, as the case may be, by one party for or to any other party pursuant to a Development Project;

'Development Project' means a program of research and development, approved by the parties in accordance with Clause ....;

'Foreground Information' means Technical Information, generated by any party in connection with a Development Project;

'Foreground IPR' means all Intellectual Property Rights of any kind generated by a party in connection with a Development Project;

'Intellectual Property Rights' means all intellectual property rights, including all letters patent, patent rights, utility models, registered designs, design rights and copyright, and other similar proprietary rights, all rights of whatsoever nature in computer programs, firmware, microcode and other computer software and data, and all intangible rights and privileges of a nature similar to any of the foregoing, and whether or not registered and including all granted registrations and all applications for registration in respect of any of the same;

'Technical Information' includes inventions, confidential information, knowhow, trade secrets and, in particular, all information concerning equipment and software (including firmware) pertaining to design, manufacture, maintenance, installation, operation and use, in whatever form including drawings, charts, manuals, schematic representations, software listings in source and object code, and on or in whatever medium, including paper, diskette, microfiche and tape.

1   Nothing in this Agreement shall affect the parties' ownership rights to Background Information and Background IPR.

2   Except as provided in Clause 3, Foreground Information and Foreground IPR shall be owned by the party generating the same and such party shall (subject to Clause 7) grant to the other parties a non-exclusive, non-assignable, non-transferable, personal, perpetual,

irrevocable, world-wide, free, unrestricted right and licence to use such Foreground Information and Foreground IPR for any purpose.

3 Jointly developed Foreground Information and Foreground IPR shall be owned by the Lead Developer and such party shall (subject to Clause 7) grant to the other parties a non-exclusive, non-assignable, non-transferable, personal, perpetual, irrevocable, world-wide, free, unrestricted right and licence to use such Foreground Information and Foreground IPR for any purpose.

4 Any party delivering Background Information to any other party for use in a Development Project thereby grants each of the other parties a free non-exclusive personal licence to use the Background Information and any of its Background IPR relating thereto in so far as necessary for the purpose of the Development Project.

5 To the extent that a Deliverable generated under a Development Project incorporates or is wholly or partially based on any Background Information of a party, that party grants each of the other parties (subject to Clause 7) a non-exclusive, non-assignable, non-transferable, personal, perpetual, irrevocable, world-wide, free, unrestricted right and licence to use the Background Information and any of its Background IPR relating thereto in so far as necessary to permit the other to use and exploit the Deliverable.

6 To the extent that a Deliverable is usable only in association with another product of any of the parties, being a product in which any Background IPR subsists, or cannot be used or exploited by one party without infringing a Background IPR of another party (not being a Background IPR referred to in Clause 5 above), the party owning the Background IPR grants to each of the other parties (subject to Clause 7) a non-exclusive, non-assignable, non-transferable, personal, perpetual, irrevocable, world-wide, free, unrestricted right and licence under such Background IPR in so far as necessary to permit the other to use and exploit the Deliverable.

7 Each party may grant any third person a licence or sub-licence under any Foreground IPR or Foreground Information or license or otherwise exploit any Deliverables (generated in connection with a Development Project) by way of licensing or sub-licensing (including sub-licences to end users in the ordinary course of business) PROVIDED THAT (i) it shall have no right to grant a sub-licence of any relevant Background Information or Background IPR owned or controlled by another party without having first obtained the consent of that party, and (ii) it shall previously have agreed with the other parties a fair and reasonable allocation of the proceeds of such sub-licence, taking into account particularly each party's contributions to the Development Project in respect of funding, Technical Information, and Intellectual Property Rights (including, where the relevant consent has been granted pursuant to (i) above, in respect of Background Information and Background IPR).

The clause below provides for joint ownership and exploitation, and a number of procedural matters which have to be dealt with. It should be noted that the suggestions in this clause for the resolution of disputes are relatively draconian on the basis that in most business relationships deadlock or a relatively undesirable outcome to a dispute often forces agreement or at least a commercial solution, perhaps on the basis that one party buys out the other.

Care should be taken with the phrases in square brackets in the first paragraph. These are mutually exclusive. The first phrase provides for the solution of a grant, in advance and for all cases, of the permission by each party to the other of the right to license. This provides for a situation of free exploitation by each joint owner except the right to grant a power to a licensee to sub-license. Granting a licence with power to sub-license means that (to the extent of the power to sub-license) the original licensor has lost control of the intellectual property right. It is an undesirable situation for joint owners to permit one of their number to open up the exploitation of their intellectual property rights to an indeterminate number of people by way of a sub-licence. The second phrase in square brackets restricts the right to grant licences quite considerably particularly in the area of granting sub-licences.

Where it is envisaged that a large amount of important intellectual property rights will be jointly owned detailed procedural arrangements should be dealt with in a separate agreement. This requires a specialist in intellectual property matters and is beyond the scope of this book.

5.15

Intellectual Property Rights and Knowhow jointly developed or funded for the purposes of the Contract shall be owned jointly by the parties as co-owners of equal undivided shares, and each party shall be entitled to exploit [including by way of licence other than a licence with power to grant sub-licences] any such Intellectual Property Right or item of such Knowhow without reference to the other party and without any obligation to account to that other party for any of the profits of such exploitation [PROVIDED THAT neither party shall grant a licence of any Intellectual Property Right or item of Knowhow without the consent of the other party (such consent not to be withheld without reasonable cause, except in relation to a term in a licence granting the licensee the power—whether or not on a restricted basis or subject to any consents terms or conditions—to grant sub-licences, when such consent may be withheld entirely at the discretion of the party whose consent is sought) unless, in relation to a United Kingdom patent only, the Comptroller of Patents shall direct otherwise under his powers contained in the Patents Act 1977, Section 37].

The parties hereby appoint [........................] of [........................]
as their firm of Chartered Patent Agents who shall act for the parties
in respect of all matters relating to the application for registration in
any jurisdiction of any Intellectual Property Right capable of
registration, and shall generally advise the parties as to the conduct
and administration of the matters provided for in this Clause.

The parties hereby set up a committee (consisting of one representative
from each party) which shall meet not less than four times a year which
shall decide (after consultation with the said firm of Chartered Patent
Agents appointed pursuant to the preceding paragraph above) on a
unanimous basis upon (a) the jurisdictions in which any jointly owned
Intellectual Property Right capable of registration shall be applied for
and registered, (b) whether or not to renew, surrender, or allow to
lapse, any such jointly owned Intellectual Property Right, and (c) the
institution and conduct of legal proceedings relating to the infringement
by a third person of any jointly owned Intellectual Property Right or
Knowhow.

In the event that the parties fail to agree unanimously in committee
as aforesaid upon any matter they shall use their best endeavours to
resolve the deadlock by consultation, failing which the matter in dispute
shall not go ahead and the status quo shall be preserved [except in
the case of failure to agree upon the institution of infringement
proceedings when one party may institute such proceedings without
the consent of the other on the basis that all costs, and any damages
or other compensation recovered, shall be for his account, and that
the other party shall, at his request and expense, render to him all
reasonable assistance, including joining in as a party to such
proceedings].

The fees of the said firm of Chartered Patent Agents and the costs
of the administration of the said committee and of the implementation
of all its decisions, including without limitation all fees costs charges
and expenses incurred in order to obtain maintain and protect any
jointly owned Intellectual Property Right capable of registration, and
in connection with infringement proceedings in respect of any jointly
owned Intellectual Property Right or Knowhow shall [subject to the
exception in the preceding paragraph] be borne by the parties in equal
shares.

Neither party shall assign or charge or otherwise dispose of or encumber
its interest in any jointly owned Intellectual Property Right or Knowhow
without the consent of the other, provided that if such consent is refused
then, at the option of the party seeking the same, the party refusing
such consent shall take an assignment of the other party's right title
and interest in the relevant Intellectual Property Right or Knowhow
at a fair and reasonable price to be fixed by agreement or (failing
agreement) by the said firm of Chartered Patent Agents acting as expert
and not as arbitrator.

A further problem related to joint ventures arises where employees seconded to the venture generate intellectual property or knowhow. The following clause provides for ownership to vest in the joint venture, although it is more usual for ownership to vest in the party from whom the relevant employee was seconded.

5.16
All Intellectual Property Rights arising from work done by an employee of one of the parties who is seconded to the Joint Venture shall belong to the Joint Venture and the relevant party shall execute or cause to be executed all deeds documents and acts as reasonably required to vest such Intellectual Property Rights in the Joint Venture.

The clause below makes a distinction between intellectual property and knowhow which is the subject of the contract and that which is the supplier's accumulated skill and expertise which is part of his general business assets. This is rather similar to the distinction between knowhow and expertise discussed in *Faccenda Chicken* v *Fowler* [1987] Ch 117.

5.17
Nothing in this Agreement shall be so construed as to require the Supplier to assign to the Buyer any rights whatsoever in relation to such ideas, knowhow, methodologies and techniques developed by the Supplier whether prior to or in the course of performance of this Agreement as together constitute the expertise which the Supplier brings to bear on the performance of its obligations hereunder.

Warranties and exclusion clauses

The question of whether or not warranties are provided depends not only on the respective bargaining powers of the parties but the type of agreement. In a contract where knowhow is being transferred together with a licence of the associated intellectual property rights, warranties in relation to the accuracy and efficacy of the knowhow are often sought together with warranties as to the licensor's right to transfer and license. Supply contracts deal with goods supplied which infringe the intellectual property rights of third parties. Agreements wholly relating to patents and trade marks are less likely to have warranties relating to security from infringement by third parties. Agreements dealing only with the disclosure of information for evaluation purposes are likely to have no warranties at all. Software licences are a special category of agreements, but warranties relating to right to license and infringements of third party rights are increasing.

The clause below deals with the warranty by exclusion of liability for infringement of third parties' intellectual property. This is suitable for a disclosure agreement but may well be imposed in technology transfer agreements or other licences if the transferor has enough bargaining power.

5.18
It is understood and agreed that there is no warranty either express or implied on the part of the Licensor that the Licensee can make use or sell the products free from any infringement of the intellectual property rights of third parties.

The following clause contains standard exclusions which most licensors would want included in their agreements and is certainly inserted in those relating purely to the disclosure of information. Paragraph (a) of the clause is particularly important. The licensor does not want the obligation of maintaining all relevant patents in force if he wishes to drop them, nor does he wish to be held liable in the event of failure to renew because of an error. The remaining paragraphs are there to exclude expressly and beyond doubt matters which might otherwise possibly be implied into the agreement.

5.19
Nothing contained in this Agreement shall (or shall be so construed as to):
  (a) require a party to file any patent application, to secure any patent or to maintain any patent in force, or constitute a warranty or representation as to the validity or scope of any patent or other intellectual property right;
  (b) constitute an agreement to bring or prosecute actions or suits against third parties for infringements of any Intellectual Property Rights;
  (c) confer any right to use, in advertising, publicity or otherwise, any name, trade name or trade mark, or any contraction, abbreviation or simulation thereof;
  (d) confer by implication, estoppel or otherwise upon a party any licence or other right (including a right of access) in or to any information or Knowhow or under any Intellectual Property Rights, except the licences and rights expressly granted to such party pursuant to this Agreement;
  (e) limit, in any manner, either party's right to discontinue or change the design or characteristics of any of its products or services at any time without notice and without liability.

Where warranties are being given, the first concern will be whether the transferor owns or controls the items being licensed or transferred. The following clause relates to a situation where the transferor (in this case the vendor of a business) owns the intellectual property rights to be transferred and warrants this fact. The first phrase in square brackets gives the main qualification used in most warranties where a party's bargaining power is great enough to impose it. The effect of the qualification is to remove liability for inadvertent errors made in good faith. Clauses can go on to qualify the phrase by specifying what enquiries the party will have to have made if the warranty is to be regarded as made to best knowledge and belief (see Clauses **2.29** and **2.30**).

The remaining set of square brackets contains an exception to warranties where, in a formal disclosure letter made before the agreement concerned is entered into, one party discloses to the other situations which are breaches of certain warranties but which nonetheless the disclosing party requires the other to accept and make no objection to, if he wishes to enter into the agreement.

5.20
All the Vendor's Intellectual Property is [to the best of its knowledge and belief] in the legal and beneficial ownership of the Vendor, and, where registrable, is registered in the name of the Vendor, or in that of its wholly owned subsidiary and there are no adverse liens, charges or encumbrances over it and it is not subject to any licence or authority or other permission in favour of another [(save only for such of the foregoing as have been disclosed)].

The other frequently required warranty relates to the right to license or disclose knowhow or intellectual property. If this is given it is usually in absolute form with no reference to best knowledge and belief. This warranty is mostly given in software licences or licences of unregistered intellectual property rights. Where a patent, registered design or registered trade mark is being dealt with the entries in the register are sufficient evidence of title for a licensee.

5.21
The Company warrants that it has the power right and authority to [license the use of the Software System to the Licensee] [disclose the Knowhow to the licensee and license the licensee to use the same].

Closely connected with warranties of title are warranties against infringement of third party rights. It should be noted, however, that because a party is willing to assume the obligation of warranting that it is the owner of a particular intellectual property right, and has the right to license it, does not mean that party will easily grant a warranty that no third party rights are infringed. In the case of registered rights such as patents it is possible for patents with potentially conflicting claims to be registered. It is then only as a result of legal proceedings that the claims can be properly interpreted and conflicts finally resolved. In the case of unregistered rights the party concerned may not know whether or not there has been an infringement. For instance, one of his employees may have copied some third party's copyright work and embodied it in his employer's documents.

This type of warranty is often combined with an indemnity relating to any third party claims of infringement. Further examples can be found in Chapter 6 relating to indemnities. The stand-alone warranty is usual when dealing with the sale of a business and there are a number of warranties governed by one overall set of indemnity provisions.

The clause below deals with the warranty. The phrases in square brackets cut down the liability. Instead of the first phrase it is possible to use 'To the best of the Vendor's knowledge and belief . . .'.

5.22
[So far as the Vendor is aware] the processes employed and products and services dealt in the Business [in the manner in which they are so employed and dealt by the Vendor in the Business] do not infringe any United Kingdom [or foreign] Intellectual Property Rights or Knowhow of third parties and [so far as the Vendor is aware] no claims of such infringement have been made or are the subject of litigation actual or threatened.

Other than infringement the main concern of a recipient of knowhow or the licensee of intellectual property rights is whether or not they are capable of being applied to achieve his particular purpose. Will the computer program work properly? Will he be able to manufacture the product concerned by using the knowhow? Transferors are normally very reluctant to warrant such matters. The following clause is a compromise in that at least some obligation is undertaken by the licensor.

5.23
The Licensor will make reasonable efforts to confirm the accuracy and efficiency of the Knowhow but it makes no representation or warranty that the Licensee can successfully manufacture the Products through use of the Knowhow.

An alternative clause is one which sets an objective standard. The transferor may be prepared to warrant either that he can make proper and effective use of the relevant knowhow or intellectual property or that anyone who is skilled in the relevant branch of industry can do so. The following would serve this purpose. The implication is that the knowhow and intellectual property is of itself complete and accurate and therefore sufficient to achieve the stated purpose if the licensee is competent to use it. Such warranties impose quite onerous obligations and are not to be undertaken lightly.

5.24
The Licensor hereby warrants that the Knowhow and Intellectual Property furnished to the Licensee hereunder will enable a Person skilled in the manufacture of [RF and digital telecommunications equipment] to manufacture use and sell [the Product] [products which conform to the specifications set out in Schedule ....].

5.25
The Licensor hereby warrants that by utilising the Knowhow and Intellectual Property furnished to the Licensee hereunder, the Licensor is able to manufacture the Products in the Licensor's own factory at [....................], but the Licensor makes no representation or warranty that the Licensee can successfully manufacture the Products.

Indemnities in general

Indemnities in relation to knowhow or intellectual property cover two main situations. The first occurs in a licence or other technology transfer agreement where the recipient of the technology attempts to exploit it and is then faced with a claim from a third party that intellectual property is being infringed. The second is in a supply contract where a third party claims that the supply or use of the goods or services infringe his intellectual property rights.

In either case the innocent party under the contract will seek an indemnity from the other for any loss or damage he suffers as a result of the proceedings taken against him by the third party. The innocent party is usually the recipient of the technology or the purchaser of the goods or services, but this is not always the case, as will be seen in some of the clauses discussed below. Such indemnities are usually given in supply contracts and software licences. In these cases they establish the right to good title or quiet possession of the items that the purchaser or licensee is contracting to be supplied to him. Other licences of knowhow or intellectual property may or may not contain indemnities (of varying scope and efficacy) depending upon the bargaining power of the parties.

Before commencing, one important distinction must be made between such indemnities (and, indeed, warranties) relating to the licensing of technology and those relating to the supply of goods. Warranties as to good title or freedom from infringement are not implied by law into licences of intellectual property or knowhow, nor is there any statutory provision requiring the licensor to give such warranties. The licensor is thus free to exclude all such warranties, or to give certain defined warranties and/or indemnities under which he undertakes precise and limited liabilities and to exclude any other liability.

This is not always the case with the supply of goods. Where the relevant contract is one to which the Unfair Contract Terms Act 1977 applies, the supplier cannot exclude liability for infringement of third party intellectual property by the goods he has supplied, since such infringement is regarded as a defect in the title to the goods (see *Microbeads* v *Vinhurst Road Markings Ltd* [1976] RPC 19, CA and *Niblett* v *Confectioners Materials* [1921] 3 KB 387), and he is prohibited from excluding liability in relation to the supply of goods with a defective title by ss 6 and 7 of the Act. This issue is considered in more detail in the precedents which follow.

Firstly we shall deal with indemnities relating to the supply of goods.

Indemnities and supply of goods

The first two clauses show simple, all-encompassing indemnities. The first is the usual indemnity that a supplier gives a purchaser.

In all of the precedents which follow reference is made to defined terms for intellectual property rights and knowhow. One limit on the operation of these indemnities is the way in which these terms are defined elsewhere in the agreement. For instance, whether the indemnity covers infringement claims throughout the world, or only in one jurisdiction, will depend upon the definitions adopted. Strictly speaking these indemnities should only cover infringements of intellectual property rights since there is no ownership in pure information. However, it is usual to insert references to knowhow as well given the points made about the material embodiment of knowhow on p 61.

5.26

The Supplier shall indemnify and keep the Customer fully indemnified against all losses, liabilities, costs and expenses in respect of claims on the grounds that the System or any part thereof or anything done by the Supplier hereunder infringes any Intellectual Property Right or Knowhow of any third party.

The second clause requires the purchaser to indemnify the supplier. This is not an unusual situation where the contract is for the supply of customised goods or services and the customer has had a part in their specification. It may be that the infringement is caused by the adaptation to the customer's specification, and that the supplier's standard, unadapted products or services would not (without such adaptation) have infringed the intellectual property in question.

5.27

The Customer shall indemnify the Supplier fully against all losses, liabilities, costs and expenses which the Supplier may incur as a result of work done in accordance with the Customer's specifications which involves or results in the infringement of any Intellectual Property Right or Knowhow.

The majority of indemnities are not as short as the two above. The indemnifying party normally requires considerable control over the claims against which he is indemnifying. The following clause sets out minimum conditions for such control the fulfilment of which is a prerequisite for the operation of the indemnity. If the party seeking indemnification fails to observe them he cannot rely on the indemnity. This point is important in two ways. Firstly, if the contract is one to which the Unfair Contract Terms Act 1977, ss 6 or 7 applies, then the customer will have an implied (or, perhaps, express) warranty as to good title, and he can fall back on a complaint that this has been breached. However, here he cannot use the wording of the indemnity simply to recover all of the loss he has suffered, in accordance with the terms of the indemnity, but is reduced to proving his damages for breach of warranty in accordance with common law principles on the recovery of damages for breach of contract, which will certainly be a more onerous task, and may not in the end enable him to recover to the extent he could have under the indemnity. Secondly, if the Act does not apply and any warranties as to title or liability for infringement (other than the express indemnity) have been excluded, he will be left with no remedy at all.

5.28

The Supplier will indemnify the Customer against liability under any injunction or final judgment or any settlement made by the Supplier under (iii) below for infringement of third party patents copyrights and/or registered designs by the Client's use of the Software subject to the following conditions:

(i) the Customer must promptly notify the Supplier in writing of any allegation of infringement;

(ii) the Customer must make no admissions without the consent in writing of the Supplier; and

(iii) the Customer must at the request of the Supplier permit the Supplier or its authorised representative at the Supplier's cost and expense to conduct and/or settle all negotiations and litigation and must give the Supplier all reasonable assistance in relation thereto.

The following example shows how the short wording of Clause **5.24** can be built upon to produce a longer version incorporating further control provisions. Paragraph (b) has wording in square brackets which if incorporated gives the customer some control over how the supplier settles a dispute. Such wording is not unusual. Paragraph (e) gives the supplier the option to modify the system to avoid any threatened or pending claim of infringement. The phrases in the square brackets at the end of paragraph (e) provide the customer with varying degrees of protection against receiving something other than what he contracted for. It should be noted that 'materially' and 'in any way' are mutually exclusive alternatives, the first providing less protection for the customer against unwanted alterations to the system.

The end of the clause contains a standard exclusion against any liability for claims of infringement which arise because the customer has combined the supplied equipment with other items which are not supplied by the supplier or specified for use by him. Since the supplier has no control over such actions by the customer he can be under no liability in respect of such claims for infringement, and should not accept it.

5.29

The Supplier shall indemnify and keep the Customer fully indemnified against all losses and liabilities costs and expenses in respect of claims on the grounds that the System or any part thereof or anything done by the Supplier hereunder infringes the Intellectual Property Rights or Knowhow of any third party provided that:

(a) the Customer shall promptly notify the Supplier in writing of any alleged infringement of which it has notice and shall make no [voluntary] admissions without the Supplier's consent; and

(b) the Customer shall allow the Supplier at the Supplier's request to conduct and settle [(on such terms as the Customer may approve, such approval not to be unreasonably withheld or delayed, and provided that any such settlement does not in any event include terms which might in any way restrict the Customer's use of the System)] all negotiations and litigation, all costs incurred or recovered in such negotiations and litigation being for the Supplier's account; and

(c) the Customer shall give the Supplier all reasonable assistance for the purpose set out in paragraph (b) above; and

(d) the Customer shall not incur any cost or expense for the Supplier's account without the Supplier's prior written consent; and

(e) if at any time any allegation of infringement is made or in the Supplier's opinion is likely to be made the Supplier may at its own expense procure for the Customer the right to continue using the infringing items on terms not restricting the Customer's use of the same as contemplated by this Agreement or modify or replace the infringing items so that the same cease to be infringing [provided that such modification or replacement does not [materially] detract [in any way] from the performance or quality of the System].

PROVIDED HOWEVER THAT the Supplier shall have no liability to the Customer hereunder for infringement as aforesaid which is based on the use of the System or of any of the Supplier's Products in combination with the Customer's equipment or other items not supplied by the Supplier other than in a combination and with equipment and items as specified or licensed by the Supplier.

The following clause is an example of an indemnity coupled with a limitation of liability. As such it will not be effective, as previously stated, in supply contracts where the Unfair Contract Terms Act 1977, ss 6 or 7 have application. The seller is only agreeing to pay any third party claimant a reasonable royalty so that the buyer can continue to use or sell the goods. Most cases relating to intellectual property infringement are settled by the payment of a reasonable royalty so this is not perhaps so unreasonable as it at first seems. Part of the first paragraph lists extensively the types of causes for infringement which are the responsibility of the buyer rather than the seller. Since this clause operates more as a limitation of liability than an extensive indemnity the second paragraph relating to the conduct of claims imposes obligations on the buyer but does not make their fulfilment a precondition to the operation of the first paragraph. Otherwise, the first paragraph could fail in its operation, if the buyer did not notify, and the limitation of liability would be lost. The third paragraph is the converse imposing obligations on the buyer. It is a warranty rather than an indemnity but is not subject to limitations and is potentially more far-reaching than the express indemnity given in the first clause.

5.30

The Seller shall indemnify the Purchaser against any claim for infringement of Intellectual Property Rights arising directly from the use or sale by the Purchaser of the goods, provided that any damages payable by the Seller shall exclude damages for loss of profit or business or of a consequential or indirect or special nature, and the liability of the Seller shall be limited to payment of a reasonable royalty to the owner of such Intellectual Property Rights. This indemnity shall not apply to any infringement caused by the Seller having followed a design or instruction furnished or given by the Purchaser nor to any use of the goods in a manner or for a purpose or in a country which shall have been specifically prohibited in writing by the Seller, nor to any infringement which is due to the use of such goods in association or combination with any other equipment not supplied by the Seller.
The Purchaser shall give the Seller the earliest possible notice in writing of any such claim being made or action threatened or brought against him and will permit the Seller at its own expense to conduct any ensuing litigation and all negotiations for a settlement of the claim.
Any design or instruction furnished or given by the Purchaser shall not be such as will cause the Seller to infringe any Intellectual Property Rights in the execution of the contract.

The following indemnity also contains elements limiting liability and, again, is therefore effective only in cases where the Unfair Contract Terms Act 1977, ss 6 or 7 have no application. It is not as far reaching as the previous clause in limiting direct compensation but excludes liability for indirect and consequential loss. However, the preconditions (in paragraph two) to accepting liability under paragraph one can be expressed as genuine preconditions to the indemnity, since the last paragraph has the effect that if the indemnity in paragraph one is lost the supplier is under no liability at all.

5.31

In the event that any third party claims that the System or any part thereof infringes such third party's Intellectual Property Rights then: (a) the Supplier shall have the right to conduct all negotiations with such third party, (b) the Supplier shall have the right to conduct the defence of any suit brought against the Customer by such third party, and (c) the Supplier shall (subject as provided below) pay all damages and costs awarded against the Customer in such suit.
The Supplier may at its option refuse to accept liability under the indemnity contained in the first paragraph above, in relation to any claim or suit, if the customer at any time: (a) fails to notify such claim

to the Supplier within fourteen days, (b) fails promptly to give the Supplier all necessary information and assistance to rebut such claim or defend such suit, and (c) makes any admission to such third party which might prejudice the Supplier's conduct of such suit or the negotiations relating to such claim.

The Supplier shall in no circumstances be liable for or grant any indemnity in relation to any infringement due to modification of the System by the Customer or any third party or arising from the use of the System with any adjunct or devices unless such modification or use is approved in writing by the Supplier specifically for the purposes of this Clause.

Other than as and to the extent herein provided the Supplier shall be under no liability for, and the remedies herein contained constitute the Customer's sole and exclusive remedies for, infringement of Intellectual Property Rights in relation to the System and in particular, but without prejudice to the generality of the foregoing, the Supplier shall not be liable for any indirect, special or consequential damages, or loss of profits, business, revenues or contracts, suffered by the Customer as a result of such claim.

As stated above, the law does not imply warranties as to good title or freedom from infringement into licences of knowhow or intellectual property, nor are such licences (if one leaves aside the thorny question of whether software is to be regarded as goods —which is certainly still not a settled question, though most commentators incline not so to regard it) subject to the Unfair Contract Terms Act 1977, ss 6 and 7. Thus the concept of restricting or excluding relevant warranties, and coupling them with a limited indemnity (which is expressed to be the licensee's sole remedy) is common in such agreements. Clauses **5.30** and **5.31** could be used in such agreements. In addition, set out below, is an example of a rather longer clause which could also be used in such a licence. Here the relationship between warranties, indemnities and limitations of liability is more clearly set out.

5.32

1   The Licensor represents and warrants to the Licensee that:

1.1   The Licensor has registered the Trade Mark in each of the countries listed on Schedule A;

1.2   The Trade Mark may be used by the Licensee in any country listed on Schedule A;

1.3   The Software, as used in the Licensor's business as of the date of this Agreement, does not require the use of any software owned or controlled by a third party.

2   The Licensor agrees to indemnify and hold harmless the Licensee against any and all Losses arising out of or related to (i) any breach

of the Licensor's warranty in Clause 1.3, or (ii) any claim that the Licensee's use of any of the Software infringes or violates the Intellectual Property Rights of any third party, or that the Licensor is not the owner thereof, or that the Licensee is not authorised to utilise the same, and the Licensor shall defend and settle at its sole cost, expense and control all suits or proceedings arising out of the foregoing. The foregoing indemnity is the Licensee's sole remedy for any such infringement or violation.

3 The Licensor agrees to indemnify and hold harmless the Licensee against any and all Losses arising out of or related to any breach of the Licensor's warranty in Clauses 1.1 and 1.2, and the Licensor shall defend and settle at its sole cost, expense and control all suits or proceedings arising out of any such breach; PROVIDED HOWEVER THAT the Licensor's obligations under this Clause 3 shall (i) only apply with respect to any claim for breach of such warranty for which notice thereof has been provided to the Licensor on or prior to [the first anniversary of the date of this Agreement], and (ii) be limited to £......... in the aggregate (including the Licensor's costs incurred in conducting such litigation, if any, arising out of such breach). The foregoing indemnity is the Licensee's sole remedy for any such breach.

4 The Licensor shall have no obligations under Clauses 2 or 3 to the extent that such Losses arise as a direct result of the Licensee's negligence or wilful misconduct or its material breach of the terms of this Agreement. The Licensee shall, with respect to any claim which is indemnifiable under Clauses 2 or 3, provide the Licensor with:

    (i) prompt notice of any such claim of which it learns;

    (ii) assistance in the defence of the action as the Licensor reasonably requires (at the Licensor's sole cost and expense); and

    (iii) control over the defence of such action.

[The failure to give any such notice referred to in this Clause 4 shall not affect the Licensor's obligations hereunder except to the extent the Licensor is actually prejudiced therefrom, and then only to the extent of such prejudice.]

5 In any infringement action provided for in Clauses 2 or 3, the non-prosecuting party, at its own expense, shall be entitled to non-controlling participation in such action through counsel of its own selection.

6 Except as provided in Clause 1, the Software is offered by the Licensor and accepted by the Licensee 'as is' and the Licensor makes no other representation or warranty, express or implied, regarding the Software, including but not limited to any implied warranty of suitability quality merchantability or fitness for a particular purpose.

7 Under no circumstances (including, for the avoidance of doubt, under Clauses 2 and 3) shall a party hereto be liable for any loss of business profits, contracts or revenues, or for any special, incidental or consequential damages suffered by the other party hereto (other than any such damages suffered by any third party for which the Licensor may be liable under Clauses 2 or 3 as the case may be), even if it has been or is hereafter advised of the possibility of such damages.

8   Except: (i) in the case of the Licensor's obligations under Clause 2 and (ii) in the case of the Licensee's failure to make any royalty payments due hereunder, the entire liability of each party and the exclusive remedy of the other party against it for damages from any cause whatsoever arising under this Agreement other than as a result of a wilful breach of, or wilful failure to perform, this Agreement, and regardless of the form of action, shall be limited to £...........; PROVIDED HOWEVER THAT the Licensee shall be entitled to a credit in an amount equal to the Annual Royalty (or a pro rata portion thereof) for any period during which the Licensee does not receive fundamentally all of the benefits of this Agreement.

Pursuing third parties for infringement

Finally, the question occasionally arises in licences of intellectual property as to how to deal with third parties who are themselves infringing the intellectual property rights which have been licensed under the agreement. Should the licensor or the licensee pursue them? Who should take the decision, and who should bear the costs involved? The following clauses show a common way of dealing with such issues.

5.33

1   In the event that the Licensee becomes aware of any actual or suspected unauthorised use or infringement of any Software (including any Intellectual Property Rights or Confidential Information relating thereto) or any infringement of the Trade Mark by any third party in the Licensed Area, the Licensee shall promptly notify the Licensor. The Licensee shall, at its sole cost and expense, have first option to take such action (including without limitation, bringing a suit against such third party) as may be reasonably required in order to protect fully the Software (including any related Intellectual Property Rights) and/or the Trade Mark. In such event, the Licensor (at the Licensee's sole cost and expense) shall provide any assistance in the prosecution of such action reasonably requested by the Licensee, including (if necessary) assigning to the Licensee the Licensor's right to prevent and protect against the unauthorised use or infringement of the rights referred to in this Clause 1.

2   In the event that the Licensee determines not to act pursuant to the provisions of Clause 1 above, it shall promptly so notify the Licensor. Upon receipt of such notice, the Licensor shall have the right, but shall not be obligated, to take such action, at the Licensor's sole cost and expense, to protect fully the Software (including any Intellectual Property Rights or Confidential Information relating thereto) or the Trade Mark. In such event the Licensee shall provide, at the Licensor's

sole cost and expense, any assistance reasonably requested by the Licensor in the prosecution of such action.

3   Any recoveries, damages or settlement amounts received by the prosecuting party as a result of any action taken hereunder shall, unless otherwise agreed by the parties hereto, be retained by the prosecuting party [PROVIDED THAT, if such amounts represent in part any Losses that the non-prosecuting party suffered as a result of the matter which is the subject of the action, such non-prosecuting party shall receive its proportional share of such recoveries, damages or settlement amounts (by reference to the relevant harm suffered by the Licensor, on the one hand, and the Licensee, on the other hand), after deducting the prosecuting party's reasonable legal fees and other costs incurred in conducting such litigation].

Chapter 6

Standard Warranties, Guarantees and Indemnities

There are a number of standard warranties and guarantees which are required in most types of commercial contracts. These divide roughly into the two areas of legal compliance and of the quality and conformance to contract of products or services. The first is of less importance in ordinary supply contracts but will be more significant in contracts relating to the transfer of capital assets, intellectual property rights, or business or share sales. In addition, there are certain standard indemnities which are often to be found in commercial contracts relating to compensation either for breach of contract or for injury and damage caused by defective goods which are dealt with in this chapter.

The clauses in this chapter do not address the problem of the extent to which various legal systems permit the restriction or exclusion of liability in contract law. These matters are dealt with in Chapter 7.

Warranty of authority

The warranty made by an individual that he has authority to sign the agreement on behalf of the party that he represents is normally implied under most systems of law, as it is under English law by the mere fact of his signing the document. It is useful to include such a warranty in any cases of doubt to ensure that the person signing obtains the necessary authority. The individual concerned will be personally liable for any breach of either the implied or the express warranty.

6.1
Each individual executing this Agreement on behalf of a party hereto represents and warrants that he has been fully empowered by such

party to execute this Agreement and that all necessary action to authorise execution of this Agreement by him has been taken by such party.

The other type of warranty of authority is given by the party itself that it has the necessary authority and capacity to enter into the transaction. Warranties of this type and those under the following section (good standing) are in a sense irrelevant. If the party signing either does not have the power to bind itself or does not properly exist as a corporation it may not be possible for any other aggrieved party to pursue the defaulting party for a breach of the warranty; however, there may be some remedy against the signatory or the persons controlling the defaulting party.

This problem is tied up with the concept of *ultra vires* when the party concerned is a corporation. The principle has now been abolished in certain parts of the United States and significant changes were made in English law by the Companies Act 1989.

Under the Companies Act 1989, s 108 the Companies Act 1985 contains three relevant sections—s 35 (which abolishes the *ultra vires* rule as regards third parties), s 35A (which provides that in favour of a person dealing with a company in good faith the power of the board of directors to bind the company shall be deemed to be free of any limitations under the company's constitution including its memorandum and articles, shareholders' resolutions and shareholders' agreements) and s 35B (which provides that a party to a transaction is not bound to enquire whether it is permitted by the company's memorandum or as to any limitations on the powers of the board of directors to bind the company or authorise others to do so). None of these provisions prevent shareholders from restraining such *ultra vires* or unauthorised acts nor from proceeding against directors who exceed their authority.

Because of doubts as to the enforceability of such warranties in any significant transactions it is considered normal and prudent procedure either to obtain independent verification of good standing, authority and capacity by checking public registers or obtaining certified copies of the relevant board or shareholders' resolutions or powers of attorney or, alternatively, and often in addition (particularly in the United States), to obtain warranties to be given by a third party, very often the party's external counsel, who has the means and opportunity of checking the status of these matters.

Where the warranties are put in the agreement they are often there to concentrate the mind of the party concerned. Where there is a gap between signature of the agreement and closing of the transactions detailed in it, their presence can be used to enable the other parties to the agreement to refuse to close if the warranties as to authority, capacity and good standing are breached between signature and closing.

The following clause shows a short form warranty relating to the obtaining of authority.

6.2

The execution and the delivery of this Agreement has been and the discharge of the covenants herein contained will have been on the Closing Date duly authorised by the Board of Directors of the Buyer without any further proceedings or action being required.

The clause below deals with a short form warranty not only for authority but also for capacity to enter into the transaction.

6.3

Each party hereto warrants and represents to each of the others that it has full authority, power and capacity to enter into this Agreement, and that all necessary actions have been taken to enable it lawfully to enter into this Agreement.

The following longer form concentrates firstly on the need to obtain requisite internal consents, but it is sufficiently wide to cover external consents (for example regulatory consents or export control licences). Secondly, it deals with the question of capacity by warranting the validity and enforceability of the agreement entered into.

6.4

Each party has full power capacity and authority, and has taken all necessary and proper action, (i) to execute and deliver this Agreement and the other agreements and instruments executed or to be executed in connection with this Agreement to which it is or is contemplated to be a party (collectively the 'Agreements'), (ii) to carry out its obligations under the Agreements, and (iii) to consummate the transactions contemplated by the Agreements.

In particular, but without limiting the generality of the foregoing, the execution and delivery by each party of the Agreements has been fully authorised by the Board of Directors and the shareholders of that party, and no other corporate or other proceedings on the part of that party are necessary to authorise the Agreements and the transactions contemplated thereby.

The Agreements constitute valid and binding obligations enforceable against each of the parties thereto, in accordance with their respective terms.

The following two clauses are longer and put emphasis on the area of external consents. The question of external consents is totally unaffected by such legislation as the Companies Act 1989, s 108 and even if advantage is taken of this legislation a warranty relating to external consents and permissions is still necessary and an action for its breach would properly and easily lie against the party giving it.

6.5
The Seller has and will on the Closing Date have the power and authority to own assets and property, exercise rights, carry on business, assume and discharge obligations and enter into and perform this Agreement and the covenants herein contained.
The Seller is not in any state of incapacity or restricted capacity, and no authorisation consent or approval of any Court authority or other person is or will on the Closing Date be required to authorise validate or ratify any of the actions of the Seller hereunder.

6.6
The Vendor has full power and authority to enter into and perform this Agreement, and this Agreement when executed will constitute a binding obligation on the Vendor in accordance with its terms.
The execution and delivery of, and the performance by the Vendor of its obligations under, this Agreement will not:
(i) result in a breach of any provision of the memorandum or articles of association of the Vendor; or
(ii) result in a breach of any order, judgment or decree of any court or governmental agency to which the Vendor is a party or by which the Vendor is bound.

Warranty of good standing

An alternative way of looking at capacity in the case of a party that is a corporation is to question whether it is in fact in good standing. Was it properly incorporated and does it at the time of the transaction exist as a properly functioning corporation under the law of the place of its incorporation? It is of no use entering into a transaction with a party which has been struck off its local companies' register! The Companies Act 1989 does nothing to remedy this problem although there are some limited provisions under most legal systems for restoring companies struck off the register.
The two clauses below are a long and a short form respectively of such a warranty.

6.7

The Buyer is and will on the Closing Date be a company duly incorporated existing and in good standing under the laws of its jurisdiction of incorporation.

6.8

Each of the parties is a corporation which is duly organised, validly existing and in good standing under the laws of [......................] and has the corporate power and authority to own, lease and operate its properties and to carry on its business as now being conducted.

The copies (attached hereto as Appendix A) of the Certificate of Incorporation, and all amendments thereto, of each of the parties as certified by [the Registrar of Companies], and of the Memorandum and Articles of Association of each such party, as amended to date, as certified respectively by each party's Company Secretary, are true, complete and correct copies of such Certificate of Incorporation and Memorandum and Articles of Association as amended and presently in effect.

Warranty of compliance with laws

Warranties of compliance with law are generally useful in most commercial agreements. Besides encouraging both parties to act in a lawful manner and providing the innocent party with a remedy, and an excuse that he did not condone the offence in the case of a breach, they also serve the useful purpose of imposing an obligation upon each party to obtain all necessary consents and permissions required by law to enable him to carry out his part of the bargain and, by implication, to obtain them at his own expense. Export licences and regulatory consents would also be covered here.

The first clause is a general short form imposing upon each of the parties the obligation to act in the performance of the agreement in accordance with law.

6.9

Each party warrants and undertakes to the other that in the performance of this Agreement it will comply with all laws, rules, regulations, decrees and other ordinances issued by any supra-governmental, governmental, state or other authority relating to the subject matter of this Agreement and to the performance by the parties hereto of their obligations hereunder.

The second clause is a warranty relating to the past and is appropriate in the sale of a business or other assets to which the warranty can be made to relate. The sweeping nature of such a warranty is qualified by the wording in square brackets at the beginning of the clause.

6.10
[To the best of the Seller's knowledge and belief] the Seller's business has at all times been conducted in accordance with applicable laws, regulations and by-laws in the United Kingdom and in any relevant foreign country and there is no investigation or enquiry, order, decree or judgment of any court or any governmental agency or regulatory body outstanding or anticipated against the Seller which may have a material adverse effect upon the Seller's business.

The following warranty is more detailed and concentrates upon the concept that the transactions contemplated by the agreement should not violate any relevant laws or breach or otherwise affect any obligations to third parties.

6.11
The Company warrants that [to the best of its knowledge and belief] neither the execution or delivery of this Agreement or any of the other agreements and instruments executed in connection with this Agreement to which it is a party, nor the consummation of the transactions contemplated hereby or thereby,

(i) requires any filing or registration with, or material permit, authorisation, consent or approval of, any supra-governmental, governmental or regulatory authority;

(ii) violates any law, rule, regulation, ordinance, order, writ, injunction, judgment, decree or award of any court or supra-governmental, governmental or regulatory authority;

(iii) violates or conflicts with any provision of, or constitutes a default (or an event which, with notice or lapse of time or both, would constitute a default) under, the Certificate of Incorporation or Memorandum and Articles of Association, as amended, of the Company;

(iv) violates or breaches any material provision of, or constitutes a default (or an event which, with notice or lapse of time or both, would constitute a default) under, any of the material terms of any deed of trust, franchise, licence, lease, agreement or other instrument, arrangement, commitment, obligation, understanding or restriction of any kind to which the Company is a party, or by which the Company or its property may be bound, except for those as to which requisite consents either have been obtained (and copies of which have been provided to the Purchaser) or the obtaining of which has been waived, in writing, by the Purchaser; or

(v) will cause, or give any Person grounds to cause, to be accelerated (with or without notice or lapse of time or both) the maturity, or to increase the amount, of any material liability or obligation of the Company.

Warranty of title and quiet possession

In many jurisdictions a warranty of good title and/or quiet possession is implied into contracts for the sale or hire of goods and the supply of work and materials (see the Sale of Goods Act 1979, s 12 and the Supply of Goods and Services Act 1982, ss 2 and 7). In many jurisdictions these warranties cannot be excluded by express provisions in the contract. Certain sections of the Unfair Contract Terms Act 1977 provide as follows:

(a) s 6(1)—no exclusion at all in the case of sale or hire-purchase goods;

(b) s 7(3A) (introduced by s 17(3) of the 1982 Act)—no exclusion in the case of other contracts under which the title to goods (ie supply of work and materials) passes; and

(c) s 7(4)—no exclusion in the case of contracts for the supply of goods other than those to which ss 6(1) and 7(3A) apply (ie in practice those where possession of goods but not title passes, such as contracts of hire, rental, lease or bailment),

unless the exclusion satisfies the Act's requirement of reasonableness.

Given this insistence on such warranties it is useful to set them out expressly. This also serves the purpose of ensuring that any general clause excluding all warranties 'other than those expressly set out in the agreement' will not be struck out as a whole and any protection granted by it negated, because of legislation such as the Unfair Contract Terms Act 1977, which condemns the clause for being so broad that it excludes warranties (such as that of title) which by law cannot be excluded (see also Chapter 7).

The clause below warrants the title of the vendor, and would also be suitable in the event that the goods are being hired to the other party.

6.12

The goods are the absolute property of the Vendor and none are the subject of any option, right to acquire, assignment, mortgage, charge, lien or hypothecation or other encumbrance whatsoever (excepting only liens arising by operation of law in the normal course of trading) or the subject of any factoring arrangement, hire-purchase, conditional sale or credit sale agreement.

The following clause warrants the vendor's good title and promises to pass it to the buyer.

6.13

The Seller, (i) holds full clear and unencumbered title in and to all of the goods, (ii) will on the date of delivery of the goods hold full clear and unencumbered title in and to all of the goods, and (iii) will on the date of delivery have the full and unrestricted right power and authority to sell transfer and deliver all of the goods to the Buyer hereunder whereupon the Buyer will acquire valid and unencumbered title thereto.

The following clause is a suitable warranty of quiet possession in a hiring agreement where title to the goods does not pass but only possession. By the Supply of Goods and Services Act 1982, s 7(2) a warranty may be made subject to any disturbance to quiet possession by the owner or other person entitled to the benefit of any charge or encumbrance over the goods disclosed or known to the bailee before the contract is made. Furthermore, s 7(3) states that such a warranty does not limit the hirer's powers to repossess the goods under an express or implied term of the contract.

6.14

The Hirer warrants to the Customer that the Hirer has the right to give the Customer possession of the goods, and that the Customer will have quiet possession of the goods in pursuance of, and for the period set out in, this Agreement, and subject to the Hirer's rights to repossess the goods as provided in Clause .... hereof. [This warranty does not apply to any disturbance of such quiet possession by the owner or other person entitled to the benefit of any charge or encumbrance over the goods disclosed or known to the Customer before concluding this hire agreement.]

Warranties relating to the quality of goods

The final class of warranties is that relating to the quality of goods supplied whether under a contract of sale, supply of work and materials or of hire. Most jurisdictions imply such warranties into these contracts and there are various restrictions as to the extent to which parties to a contract can exclude such warranties, particularly in the case of consumer transactions.

Under English law the relevant statutes are the Sale of Goods Act 1979 and the Supply of Goods and Services Act 1982. The basis of any contract for the supply or hire of goods is that the goods will conform to the description contained in the contract. Such warranties are implied by the Sale of Goods Act 1979, s 13 and the Supply of Goods and Services Act 1982, ss 3 and 8 respectively. In all contracts for supply or hire of goods the Unfair Contract Terms Act 1977, ss 6(2) and 7(2) prohibit exclusion of this warranty against persons dealing as consumers, and ss 6(3) and 7(3) prohibit such exclusions against all other persons except to the extent that they satisfy the Act's requirement of reasonableness (see s 11).

Under the Sale of Goods Act 1979, s 14 there were implied warranties of merchantable quality except for defects drawn to the attention of the buyer or defects which ought to have been discovered by an examination before the sale (if such an examination was actually made) and reasonable fitness for purpose where the buyer expressly or by implication made that purpose known to the seller (unless the buyer did not in fact rely, or it was unreasonable for him to rely, on the skill or judgment of the seller). Similar warranties were implied by the Supply of Goods and Services Act 1982, ss 4 and 9 in the case of contracts for work and materials and those for the hire of goods respectively.

Although the warranty of fitness for a particular purpose still continues in force under the Sale of Goods Act 1979, s 14, sub-section (2) of that section has been amended, with effect from 3 January 1995, so as to replace the implied warranty of merchantable quality by one of satisfactory quality. By the Sale and Supply of Goods Act 1994, s 1 the 1979 Act, s 14(2) now reads 'where the seller sells goods in the course of a business, there is an implied term that the goods supplied under the contract are of satisfactory quality'. The new s 14(2A) defines 'satisfactory quality' as 'the standard that a reasonable person would regard as satisfactory, taking account of any description of the goods, the price (if relevant) and all other relevant circumstances'. Section 14(2B) goes on to provide that 'fitness for all the purposes for which goods of the kind in question are commonly supplied, appearance and finish, freedom from minor defects, safety and durability' are all 'in appropriate cases aspects of the quality of goods'.

Section 14(2C) provides that the implied term does not extend to 'any matter making the quality of goods unsatisfactory' if it is 'specifically drawn to the buyer's attention before the contract is made', if it is one which 'where the buyer examines the goods before the contract is made . . . that examination ought to reveal' or, where the contract is one of sale by sample, 'which would have been apparent on a reasonable examination of the sample'.

Purely as a consequential amendment, the 1994 Act, s 1(2) amends the 1979 Act, s 15 (sales by sample) so that references in that section to defects which render the goods 'unmerchantable' are replaced by references to making the quality of the goods 'unsatisfactory'.

The new standard of satisfactory quality does not differ to a great extent from that of the old one of merchantable quality, but it has taken account of some of the case law built up around the concept of merchantable quality to provide a standard which is better defined, and should give contracting parties greater certainty. Section 14(2B) is, however, of particular interest in that it now expressly includes a fitness for general purposes test (as opposed to the fitness for specific purpose still contained in s 14(3)) and a consideration of durability. As to this last point, the Law Commission have stated that in their view durability requires that goods supplied under the contract should have 'those qualities which will enable them to last in reasonable condition for a reasonable time'. Many commentators have already argued that this standard is no more than that which was, in any event, implied by the concept of merchantable quality, or even fitness for a specified purpose under s 14(3), but it is certainly helpful to have an express statutory provision as a new basis for the concept.

Finally, it should be noted that equivalent changes have been made by the 1994 Act to the Trading Stamps Act 1964, the Uniform Laws on International Sales Act 1967, the Supply of Goods (Implied Terms Act 1973 (which governs hire-purchase sales) and the Supply of Goods and Services Act 1982. The treatment accorded to all of the relevant sections under the Unfair Contract Act 1977 remains unchanged, so that the new standard of satisfactory quality is dealt with in exactly the same way (so far as relates to its possibilities of exclusion) as was the old standard of merchantable quality.

The new law does not expressly supersede any other warranty as to quality or, indeed, merchantability, that might apply as a result of the common law. In the absence of any judicial precedent, where one is drafting clauses which exclude implied warranties it is still sensible to exclude any implied warranties not only as to 'quality' or 'satisfactory quality', but also to 'merchantability, just to be on the safe side. This practice has been followed in the precedents in Chapter 7 on exclusion clauses.

Since such implied warranties of quality are available to the customer under general law in most jurisdictions, at least in the absence of an express exclusion clause, and since there are considerable restrictions upon such exclusion, it must be asked why there is any need to include express warranties upon these subjects at all.

The first advantage for the customer is that of certainty: he can point the court to an express contractual warranty set out in the contract. In addition, such an express warranty can be more favourable than that implied by law. As an example, the implied warranty of fitness for a particular purpose in the Sale of Goods Act 1979, s 14(3) is subject to certain conditions and is not available in any contract where those conditions are not satisfied. It is a mistake often made by purchasers that this Act implies, in all cases, a general warranty of fitness for the specific purpose for which the purchaser intended to use the goods; only an express warranty of fitness for a specified purpose can achieve this.

However, by itself, an express warranty will not usually satisfy the customer. His legal remedy for breach of warranty is to sue for damages but what he actually wants (although he may want general damages as well—to compensate for economic loss, for example) is that either the goods supplied should be repaired or modified to remedy the defect or, if this is not possible, that they should either be replaced or his money should be refunded.

In most jurisdictions the general law only gives the customer the opportunity to invoke all of these remedies by rejecting the goods when they are delivered to him. This enables him to start afresh with the supplier or to go elsewhere if he is not satisfied. Once he has accepted them, however, he has to keep them and his only remedy is to claim damages for breach of warranty.

The Sale and Supply of Goods Act 1994 has made some changes to the law relating to acceptance as contained in the Sale of Goods Act 1979, ss 11, 33, 34 and 35. The 1994 Act, s 2 amends the 1979 Act, s 35 so that acceptance now takes place either when the buyer intimates to the seller that he has accepted the goods, or when (after delivery of the goods to him) 'the buyer does any act in relation to them which is inconsistent with the ownership of the seller'. All this is old law. However, the amendments to s 35 now provide that the buyer who has taken delivery of the goods without previously having examined them, is not deemed to have taken delivery until he has had a reasonable opportunity to examine them to ascertain if they are in conformity with the contract or (if under a sale by sample) in conformity with the sample.

It is true that the buyer is still deemed to have accepted the goods if he has not (within a reasonable time after delivery) told the seller that he rejects them, but the question of whether a reasonable time has elapsed depends (*inter alia*) upon whether the buyer has had a reasonable opportunity of examining the goods. Finally, an important provision, s 35 now provides that the buyer is not deemed to have accepted the goods merely because he asks or agrees for the seller to repair or arrange for their repair, nor because he has delivered them to a third party under a sub-sale or other disposition.

A new s 35A has also been inserted which provides for a right of partial rejection, either of the goods delivered under the contract as a whole or in respect of one instalment delivery under a contract for delivery by instalments.

Section 35 is of mandatory application in the case of a sale to a person dealing as a consumer (the same definition as the Unfair Contract Terms Act 1977 applies), but can be excluded by contract in the case of any other sale. Section 35A, however, only applies in the case of all contracts of sale, 'unless a contrary attention appears in, or is to be implied from, the contract'.

Section 4 of the 1994 Act has made some changes to the classification of the warranties to be implied into a sale of goods contract under the 1979 Act, ss 13, 14 and 15 which affect the right of rejection in sales where the buyer does not deal as a consumer. A new s 15A(1) is inserted into the 1979 Act which provides that where the breach of the warranty is so slight that it would be unreasonable for the buyer to reject the goods, the breach is to be treated not as a breach of condition (giving a right of rejection) but as a breach of warranty (imposing an obligation to accept the goods, subject only to a claim for damages for any diminution in value caused by the breach).

Similarly, s 15A(2) modifies the 1979 Act, s 30 by providing that, where a buyer does not deal as a consumer, he cannot reject the whole of a delivery by reason of a shortfall or an excess, where the shortfall or excess 'is so slight that it would be unreasonable for him to do so'.

In both cases the burden of proof is on the seller to show that the breach, shortfall or excess is so slight as to fall within the provisions of the section. However, while s 15A(1) only applies if it is not displaced by a contrary intention which appears in, or is to be implied from, the contract, s 15A(2) does not contain this wording, and therefore appears to be mandatory.

The 1994 Act also makes amendments, analogous to those contained in the new s 15A, to the Supply of Goods (Implied Terms) Act 1973 and the Supply of Goods and Services Act 1982.

Finally, it should be noted that, since the question of the extent to which the above provisions are to be mandatory has been covered in the provisions themselves, the 1994 Act has had no need to make, and has not made, any consequential amendments in this respect to the Unfair Contract Terms Act 1977.

Nevertheless, despite the changes made by the 1994 Act, once the goods have been accepted, the right to reject is lost, and damages remain the usual remedy. Any assertion (after acceptance) of breach of any warranty relating to satisfactory quality or failure to conform to description then raises the question of how long the product should continue to perform satisfactorily, and hence whether should be any guarantee as to the useful life of the product.

The warranty of conformance to description (as was also the case with the old warranty of merchantable quality) applied only at the time of delivery. However, the new warranty of satisfactory quality does provide some assistance on the question of product lifetimes. As discussed above, the Sale of Goods Act 1979, s 14(2B)(e) now makes durability one of the aspects of the quality of goods which is 'in appropriate cases' to be taken into account in determining if the goods are of 'satisfactory quality'. Presumably, the wording 'in appropriate cases' is there to deal with goods (such as fresh food or other perishables) where durability is not something the parties can reasonably be concerned with, unlike the case of, for instance, consumer durables like washing machines or motor vehicles, or capital goods like computers or plant and machinery.

In any event, clearly the standard of durability to be met must vary with 'the description of the goods, the price (if relevant), and all other relevant circumstances' (see the 1979 Act, s 14(2A)). For instance, a low priced felt tip pen with no facility for a refill can be expected to write for a reasonable but short period of time after purchase, while an expensive fountain pen can be expected to continue to be serviceable for a much longer period. Similarly, second hand goods, sold as seen, should not have to meet the same standard of durability as the equivalent goods when purchased new.

Nevertheless, in the absence of any specific legislative provisions laying down specific lifetimes for specific products, the definition of the period must be vague, and the relevant standard of durability will obviously be a question of fact to be determined (perhaps with the assistance of trade custom or usage) variously according to the different types, prices and qualities of the products in question.

In order to overcome all of these problems the customer will thus require in addition to express warranties, specific obligations as to the way in which the supplier must remedy any breaches of those warranties which occur within a specified period after the delivery or acceptance of the goods. These express remedies solve the problems of giving the customer the kind of redress that he really wants, even after acceptance and use, and of providing in effect a specific warranty as to the life of the goods.

In certain jurisdictions these express remedies are sometimes called guarantees. The term is often used under English law particularly in the area of consumer transactions (see the Unfair Contract Terms Act 1977, s 5). It is also common practice to call them 'warranties' and to refer to the specified period for remedying breaches as a 'warranty period'.

Such express remedies are often drafted as an obligation to rectify defects in design, material or workmanship. The warranties implied by English law relating to quality, conformance to description and fitness for purpose could all be breached by any of these defects, although design defects are more closely related to warranties of fitness for purpose and defects in workmanship and materials to warranties of satisfactory quality.

From the point of view of the supplier, express warranties coupled with express remedies as described above serve the purpose of marketing tools, if the remedies are sufficiently attractive to customers, and also give some degree of certainty to the transaction.

It is questionable whether the inclusion of an express warranty or guarantee by implication excludes any terms upon the same subject otherwise implied by law. Despite certain rules of construction at least in English law that support this contention, sometimes referred to as *inclusio unius exclusio alterius*, the matter is far from certain. Certainty can only be safely achieved if the express warranties or guarantees in the contract are expressly stated to be the only ones given and all others which would otherwise be implied under the law of jurisdiction are expressly stated to be excluded (see for instance the Sale of Goods Act 1979, s 55 and the Supply of Goods and Services Act 1982, ss 11(1) and (2) which permit express exclusions in a contract of warranties otherwise implied by the Acts, subject to the Unfair Contract Terms Act 1977, but do not regard an express condition or warranty as negating one implied by the Acts unless the express one is inconsistent with the implied one).

However, the party for whose benefit an express warranty or guarantee has been inserted will want to insure that he also has the benefits of his rights under the general law, making the express provisions 'cumulative'. To achieve this beyond doubt he should insert a provision to this effect. This can either be a general clause at the end of the agreement (see for example Clause **12.21** and the relevant commentary) or a phrase in the warranty indemnity or remedy itself. In consumer transactions in the United Kingdom such an insertion is required by law in all such clauses plainly stating that they are in addition to and do not affect the consumer's statutory rights.

The supplier is mainly concerned with coupling express warranties and guarantees with provisions excluding all other rights in order not only to clarify but also to restrict his liability to the customer. This is discussed in Chapter 7. The following precedents are drafted from the point of view of the customer on a cumulative basis and not as exclusion clauses.

In the precedent below the first paragraph restates the warranties that would be implied in most jurisdictions in a supply of goods. The last sentence of the first paragraph disposes of any arguments which could be raised under the Sale of Goods Act 1979, s 14(3) to show that the buyer took upon himself approval of a product and could no longer rely on the seller's skill or judgment in order to raise a claim that the product was not fit for its intended purpose.

The remaining paragraphs state the buyer's remedies and the period of time in which those remedies will be available.

The bold sentence in the final paragraph provides a 'revolving warranty'; that is, the repaired or replaced goods, since they are stated to be subject to the provisions of the agreement, are also themselves subject to the warranty. The result in extreme cases is that the warranty continues indefinitely until one of the repaired or replaced items can survive for the duration of the warranty period. Revolving warranties are not usually given in capital goods contracts but are quite common in consumer contracts, particularly in the area of mass-produced goods where it is cheaper for the supplier to continue providing a replacement rather than incur the problems and expense of repair.

6.15

The Seller warrants that all items delivered under this Agreement will be free from defects in material and workmanship, conform to applicable specifications and drawings and, to the extent that detailed designs have not been furnished by the Buyer, will be free from design defects and suitable for the purposes intended by the Buyer. The Buyer's approval of designs furnished by the Seller shall not relieve the Seller of its obligations under any provisions of this Agreement including the warranty contained in this Clause.

The Seller's warranties hereunder shall extend to any defect or non-conformity arising or manifesting itself within [two years] after delivery. With respect to items not in accordance with any such warranties, the Buyer, without waiving any rights or remedies provided by law and/or elsewhere under this Agreement, may require the Seller (1) to correct or replace such items at the Seller's risk and expense or (2) to refund such portion of the price as is equitable under the circumstances. **Items corrected or replaced shall be subject to the provisions of this Agreement in the same manner as those originally delivered hereunder.** If the Seller refuses or fails promptly to correct or replace such items when requested by the Buyer, the Buyer may itself, or through any agent or sub-contractor, or otherwise, correct or replace such items and the Seller agrees to reimburse the Buyer for the costs incurred thereby. All warranties shall survive acceptance and payment.

The following two clauses are express remedies. These can, on their wording, stand alone as 'guarantees' but could be coupled with express warranties if desired. In these clauses the purchaser is trying to limit his liability not by excluding the remaining rights at law of the customer but by hedging the express remedy with certain restrictions. If these restrictions disqualify the buyer from relying upon the express remedy for redress, he will have to go to court and claim general damages for breach of warranty— a much harder task and with the burden of proof upon the buyer. The clauses are therefore less favourable for the buyer because of the procedural steps that must be taken by him, before the seller will implement the remedies that he has offered.

In the following clause if the phrase in square brackets in paragraph (ii) is included the guarantee will become even less favourable. Since the question of the seller's responsibility for defects would then be judged solely by the seller, the guarantee would become optional for the seller. If the buyer were dissatisfied at the seller's failure to implement the remedy he would have to claim for general damages for breach of warranty. The clause does, however, contain a revolving warranty in the third paragraph.

6.16

The Seller shall free of charge either repair or, at its option, replace defective goods where the defects appear under proper use within [.........] months from the date of delivery, PROVIDED THAT

(i) notice in writing of the defects complained of shall be given to the Seller upon their appearance; and

(ii) such defects shall [be found to the Seller's satisfaction to] have arisen solely from faulty design, workmanship or materials; and

(iii) the defective goods shall be returned to the Seller's works at the Purchaser's expense if so requested by the Seller.

Any repaired or replaced goods shall be redelivered by the Seller free of charge to the original point of delivery but otherwise in accordance with and subject to these Conditions of Sale.

Alternatively the Seller shall be entitled at its absolute discretion to refund the price of the defective portion of the goods in the event that such price shall already have been paid by the Purchaser to the Seller.

The remedies contained in this Clause are without prejudice to and in addition to any warranties indemnities remedies or other rights provided by law and/or statute and/or under any other provision of this Agreement for the benefit of the Purchaser.

In the clause below, note the disclaimer by the seller of responsibility for the buyer's designs which reverses the point made in Clause **6.15** as to who is responsible in this area for fitness for purpose.

The last paragraph of the clause also provides for the possibility of varying warranty periods for different parts of a system. In a computer, for example, fuses or indicator lights would have much shorter warranty periods than disk drives. The provision is also one way of dealing with items incorporated in a system or assembly which are supplied by third parties under warranty periods of differing lengths. The seller includes them in his warranty but he can specify the relevant warranty period for each item and have full back to back cover through reliance on the warranty of corresponding length given to him by the third party.

The warranty is not a revolving one on its own terms since it relates only to an obligation to remedy faults or defects in the system as a whole for a fixed period.

6.17

The Seller will make good, by rectification, repair or replacement or at its option by the supply of replacement parts, faults or defects which, under proper use, appear in the System within the period of [........] months after the System has been accepted or has been deemed to have been accepted and arise solely from faulty material or workmanship or faulty design (other than a design made, furnished or specified by the Customer for which the Seller has disclaimed responsibility in writing); PROVIDED THAT in respect of the items specifically listed in the quotation (if any) there will be substituted for the period of [........] months the periods set against such items respectively, and PROVIDED FURTHER THAT (in the case of goods) the defective parts have been returned to the Seller if the Seller shall so require. The Seller shall refund the cost of carriage on such returned parts and the repaired or new parts will be delivered and installed at the Buyer's premises free of charge.

The remedies contained in this Clause are without prejudice to and in addition to any warranties indemnities remedies or other rights provided by law and/or statute and/or under any other provision of this Agreement for the benefit of the Buyer.

The following clause is a further example of the limited type of guarantee. Note should be taken of the penultimate paragraph which shows how to prevent a revolving warranty arising by an express provision.

6.18

Products delivered by the Seller are subject to inspection and test by the Buyer and, in the event that during a period of one year from date of installation at the Buyer's premises any product is found to be defective in material or workmanship, or not in conformance with the relevant specifications, the Buyer shall have the right to reject the same.

The Buyer shall notify the Seller and return such product with an attached failure report to the Seller, at the Seller's expense.

The Seller shall then use its best efforts to repair or replace, at the Seller's option, and at the Seller's sole expense, such product within fourteen days of receipt of such product, and to return the same, at the Seller's expense, to the Buyer.

If the Seller is unable to repair or replace such product in accordance with the requirements of the relevant specifications, the Seller shall, upon the Buyer's request, accept the return of such product, and refund in full any amounts paid by the Buyer therefor.

A replacement of such product, or replacement parts supplied for such product, or repairs made to such product, during the original warranty period for such product, shall be warranted for an additional period of three months after the Buyer's receipt of such replacement or replacement parts or repaired product, or until the expiry of the original warranty period, whichever is the longer period.

This warranty does not cover defects in or damage to the products which are due to improper installation or maintenance, misuse, neglect or any cause other than ordinary commercial or industrial application.

The remedies contained in this Clause are without prejudice to and in addition to any warranties indemnities remedies or other rights provided by law and/or statute and/or under any other provision of this Agreement for the benefit of the Buyer.

Remedies relating to goods damaged in transit

Express undertakings are often given for repairing or replacing goods damaged or lost in transit. Under general law in most contracts for the supply of goods risk in the goods passes to the buyer on delivery and, in many contracts for the sale of goods, delivery is deemed to take place when the goods are given to the carrier to transport to the buyer. Given the foregoing, in many cases the seller will be under no responsibility for damage in transit. Goods in transit insurance policies are widely available, often on a blanket basis, to protect the buyer.

It is not uncommon for suppliers to offer an express remedy for goods lost or damaged in transit. Given the difficulty of proof of whether such damage or loss occurred in transit or through handling on the customer's premises, such remedies are usually hedged with a number of conditions, for example the giving of timely notice, and are often expressed as optional remedies requiring proof to the seller's satisfaction. In the absence of such a provision or if the seller refuses to implement the remedy where it is optional for him to do so or because the buyer has failed to comply with any relevant condition, the buyer would be put to proving that risk had not passed to him before he was able to claim for breach of contract on the part of the seller.

The following clause concentrates upon damage and requires a short notice period.

6.19
The Seller will replace free of charge any goods [proved to the Seller's satisfaction to have been] damaged in transit provided that within three days after delivery both the Seller and the relevant carriers have received from the Purchaser notification in writing of the occurrence of the damage, and also, if and so far as practicable, of its nature and extent.

The clause below deals with both loss and damage and is slightly more flexible as to notice periods.

6.20
The Seller shall only accept responsibility for:
(i) damage to the Products caused in transit if the same is externally visible, and is notified to the Seller and the carrier (if not delivered by the Seller) within seven days of receipt of the Products by the Customer;
(ii) an actual or apparent discrepancy between any delivery note and items delivered, if the same is notified to the Seller and the carrier (if not delivered by the Seller) within seven days of receipt of the Products by the Customer;
(iii) non-arrival, if the same is notified to the Seller within a reasonable period from the date that the Seller informed the Customer that the Products or the relevant consignment thereof were due to arrive.

Where the Seller accepts responsibility under this Clause, it shall, at its sole option, repair or replace (as the case may be) the items concerned which are proved to the Seller's satisfaction to have been lost or damaged prior to delivery to the Customer.

General indemnities

The customer is not only concerned with having an express remedy to correct defects in goods supplied. He also needs to ensure that he is compensated for any other loss or damage caused either as a result of the defect or as a result of the failure of the other party to perform the contract properly or at all. A contract for services also benefits from having an express provision for indemnification for loss or damage caused by its negligent performance.

Such remedies are usually given by way of an indemnity rather than a warranty. As it is understood under English law and most common law jurisdictions an indemnity is an express obligation to compensate for defined loss or damage, as opposed to a warranty which is only a contractual promise whose breach gives rise to an action for damages for breach of contract. Proceedings under an indemnity are easier to enforce at law and an indemnity avoids certain problems as to the common law rules on remoteness of damage if it is drafted widely enough. It is different to the express remedies for the supply of defective goods discussed above, since the only remedy here is to pay money. An indemnity therefore falls between a warranty and a guarantee.

As discussed in the case of warranties and guarantees relating to the quality of goods supplied, these indemnities may or may not be cumulative or by implication take away rights otherwise implied at law. Since indemnities only give express remedies for payment of money in defined circumstances it is harder to construe them as implicitly excluding other rights and remedies, still less other warranties, but the problem still remains and the situation can best be resolved by an express provision either way.

In any event, even if the indemnity is cumulative the party who gives the indemnity may hedge it with conditions on the basis that if these are not complied with the indemnity falls away and the easy method of obtaining a remedy is lost. The party suffering loss will then have to prove breach of contract and the extent of his damages by reference to the general law.

The clause below provides for failure to perform contractual obligations in general. It can be used in any contract for the supply of goods or services. Its width and generality are such that it does not need any provision making it cumulative.

6.21

The Supplier undertakes that it will indemnify the Customer against all proceedings costs expenses liabilities injury death loss or damage arising out of the breach or negligent performance or failure in performance by the Supplier of the terms of this Agreement.

The following clause is an indemnity limited to death, personal injury and damage to tangible property only. Subject to this its terms are wide. If the phrase in square brackets is excluded the supplier becomes strictly liable for all acts or omissions even if they were not wilful or negligent. The addition of the last paragraph makes clear that it is cumulative and without prejudice to other rights, for instance to recover damages for economic loss.

6.22

The Supplier shall indemnify and keep the Customer fully indemnified against all liabilities costs and expenses in relation to death or injury to persons or loss of or damage to tangible property to the extent that such death injury loss or damage is attributable to the [wilful or negligent] acts or omissions of the Supplier its officers employees agents or sub-contractors.

The remedies contained in this Clause are without prejudice to and in addition to any warranties indemnities remedies or other rights provided by law and/or statute and/or under any other provision of this Agreement for the benefit of the Buyer.

The following clause accepts wide liability for third party claims for loss or damage but imposes conditions on acceptance which enable the indemnifier to have the conduct of the claims against which he is to indemnify the other party. Again, the last paragraph preserves the cumulative nature of the remedy.

6.23

The Contractor shall indemnify and keep the Customer fully indemnified against all liabilities costs and expenses in respect of claims brought against the Customer by third parties in relation to death or injury to persons or loss of or damage to property where and to the extent that such death injury loss or damage is attributable to the [wilful or negligent] act or omission of the Contractor its employees agents or sub-contractors.
PROVIDED HOWEVER that the Customer:
(i) promptly notifies the Contractor of such claims;

(ii) allows the Contractor if the Contractor so requests to conduct and control (at the Contractor's sole cost and expense) the defence of such claims and any related settlement negotiations; and

(iii) affords all reasonable assistance to the Contractor (at the Contractor's sole cost and expense) and makes no admission prejudicial to the defence of such claims.

The remedies contained in this Clause are without prejudice to and in addition to any warranties indemnities remedies or other rights provided by law and/or statute and/or under any other provision of this Agreement for the benefit of the Buyer.

The following clause gives a general mutual indemnity for third party claims where services are provided by one party to the other. Again, because of its width and generality a specific cumulative provision is not necessary.

6.24

A party receiving any [technical assistance] pursuant to this Agreement from another party thereto shall indemnify and hold harmless that party from any and all claims (made by third parties against that party) for damages, losses, expenses or costs (including counsel's fees and expenses) arising out of the furnishing of such [technical assistance] and the party receiving such [technical assistance] hereby waives any claims that it might have or might pretend to have against that party or its employees and agents, for or arising from the provision of such [technical assistance].

The final indemnity relates to the situation where the customer has rendered himself liable to third parties or has suffered loss himself because of his own mishandling of products supplied by the supplier. In these circumstances, the supplier does not want to get drawn into the controversy, even though in the last analysis he is unlikely to have any liability.

6.25

The Customer will indemnify the Supplier against all claims in respect of any loss or damage of whatsoever nature suffered by the Supplier or its subsidiary or associated companies or by any employee, former employee, beneficiary or contingent beneficiary of the Supplier or of any other person or institution arising from the use of the Software (except in any circumstances where Clause .... (*force majeure*) of this Agreement applies) by or for the Customer, where and to the extent that:

(a) the Customer supplies or uses incomplete or incorrect information or fails to verify any data input on its behalf by the Supplier; or

(b) the results of program or calculation routines have been corrupted by malfunction of telecommunication or computer or terminal equipment or programs not supplied by the Supplier; or

(c) the Customer uses material supplied hereunder otherwise than strictly in accordance with the specifications and instructions of the Supplier [and the equipment manufacturer]; or

(d) the Customer allows any person who has not been trained in working with the System to operate the System or any part thereof; or

(e) the Customer permits any person other than authorised representatives of the Supplier to effect any modifications or changes to the Software unless expressly authorised by the Supplier.

Consumer guarantees

Finally, although many of the guarantees and indemnities set out above are in theory suitable for use with consumers, the practice is now (particularly with the advent of the Unfair Terms in Consumer Contracts Regulations 1994 (SI No 3159) which are discussed in detail in Chapter 7) to use shorter and more 'user-friendly' guarantees for consumer transactions. Set out below are a short form and long form example of such clauses. It should be noted that both clauses contain the notice relating to the consumer's statutory rights, which is required by the Consumer Transactions (Restrictions on Statements) Order 1976 (SI No 1813), and the omission of which amounts under the Order to a criminal offence.

6.26

We guarantee that if [the goods] fail to satisfy you in any way, and you return them by post (together with proof of purchase), within [one month] of purchase, to the address stated below, we will refund you their purchase price, and the cost of postage, by return. This guarantee is in addition to and does not affect your statutory rights.

6.27

All our goods are guaranteed for a period of [twelve months] against defective workmanship and materials. In the event of any such defect please return the goods to us [in their original packaging] together with proof of date of purchase, and we will refund you your postage (if any) and, at our choice, refund you their purchase price, or repair and return them to you, or send you new goods as a replacement. Goods which have become defective for any other reason, such as accidental damage or failure to use in accordance with the operating manual, are not covered by this guarantee. If you return such goods to us, we will notify you of this, and we will, according to your choice, either repair the goods or return them to you, in each case to the extent possible and at your expense. This guarantee is in addition to, and does not affect your statutory rights.

Chapter 7

Exclusions of Liability

Preliminary

The drafting of clauses which exclude or restrict liability is a complex task. In most jurisdictions courts are reluctant to accept that a party can ostensibly undertake contractual obligations and then insert a clause which enables him to escape the liability normally imposed by law upon him in the event of his default. This has led courts to evolve various devices to defeat such exclusion clauses. The most widely used is that of strict construction of the clause. Where a party relies on such a clause the court will only permit him to do so if the wording clearly covers the event of default for which he is seeking to avoid liability.

The party relying on the clause has to convince the court that the clause is drafted in such a way that it covers the breach in question. (The discussions in the Court of Appeal in *Flying Colours Film Co Limited* v *Assicurazioni Generali SpA* [1993] 2 Lloyd's Rep 184, and in *Summers* v *Congreve Horner & Co* [1992] 40 EG 144, are instructive in their emphasis on the need to establish that the facts of the situation fall properly within the relevant exclusion clause.) Any ambiguity is always construed against the party attempting to rely on the clause.

Under English law, this principle has long been applied to defeat the operation of general exclusions of liability. For instance, in the *Suisse Atlantique* case [1967] 1 AC 61, the court held that exemption clauses cannot be construed to apply to fundamental breach unless clearly stated to do so. However, in *Photo Production Limited* v *Securicor Transport Limited* [1980] AC 827, an exclusion clause was found to be drafted so widely as to exclude liability for a wilful default which was also a fundamental breach of the contract.

Nevertheless, the courts are particularly hostile to this type of exclusion, and require the plainest and clearest drafting before they are prepared to hold that such an exclusion clause can cover the defendant's negligence or wilful default (see *EE Caledonia Ltd* v *Orbit Value Co Europe* [1993] 4 All ER 165, *Glebe Island Terminals Pty Ltd* v *Continental Pty Ltd and Another* (the 'Antwerpen') [1994] 1 Lloyd's Rep 213, Supreme Court of New South Wales, CA, and also *Morley* v *United Friendly Insurance plc* [1993] 3 All ER 47, for a discussion of what amounts to 'wilful').

In modern times, more and more jurisdictions impose by law restrictions on the ability of the parties to contract out of certain liabilities by way of express clauses in contracts. Such legislation often prescribes that basic warranties in certain contracts (sale of goods is the most frequent instance) will be implied into the contract if the parties have not expressly included them and that, in defined types of contracts, or in particular circumstances, any attempt by a party expressly to exclude such warranties will be ineffective. In addition, exclusions of liability for certain kinds of loss or damage (usually death or personal injury), or for failure to perform generally, are often prohibited or controlled by some requirement as to reasonableness. Such legislation is frequently but not exclusively directed at consumer protection and needs to be looked at together with more general measures for consumer protection (such as the EC directive on strict liability for consumer products) which in many cases accompany it.

For ease of reference in this chapter where mention is made of exclusion of liability it should be taken to include partial restriction or limitation of liability as well as total exclusion.

Where the draftsman is dealing with exclusion clauses the following rules will assist:

(1) Before deciding to use exclusion clauses consider drafting the positive obligations under the contract in a narrower way. In many jurisdictions this will avoid legislation relating to exclusion clauses entirely. For instance, instead of stating a firm delivery date and using an exclusion clause to escape liability for failure to keep to it, use a clause which states clearly that there is no firm delivery date, but that reasonable endeavours will be made to deliver by the date specified. (Plainly stating what contractual obligations are undertaken, and showing clearly that others are not, is to be recommended particularly as a style for drafting consumer contracts.)

(2) Decide which warranties, guarantees and indemnities must

be included in the contract under its governing law, depending upon the type and subject matter of the contract, the parties to the transaction and the negotiations between them. Include all of these expressly.

(3) Draft clauses or include phrases in the relevant express provisions which clearly exclude all other warranties, guarantees, indemnities, remedies and liabilities which would otherwise be implied by law or prior negotiations between the parties in relation to the matters covered under (2) above.

(4) Decide using the criteria in (2) above the extent to which further limitations on liability are desirable and possible, and include these in a series of separate exclusion clauses. These would typically relate to *force majeure*, economic loss, liquidated damages and perhaps an overall limitation of liability by reference to a sum of money.

(5) Avoid general exclusion clauses which have too wide a cover. If these are declared illegal all protection is lost. Always make use of the principles of severability (see Chapter 11), by drafting a series of exclusion clauses. If one or more is then struck out by a court, others may survive and to some extent be effective in reducing liability.

(6) Do not be too greedy. It is better to settle for a lesser amount of protection which is legally effective, than to go too far and lose the right to rely on the clause altogether.

(7) Always draft with the utmost clarity and remember that the clause will only ever be invoked in court in the context of a dispute with the other party.

So far as the United Kingdom is concerned there are two legislatory regimes which control exclusion clauses. The first is the Unfair Contract Terms Act 1977, which regulates both business to business and consumer transactions. The second is the Unfair Terms in Consumer Contracts Regulations 1994 (SI No 3159), which implements the Council Directive on Unfair Terms in Consumer Contracts (93/13/EC), which applies only to consumer transactions and comes into force on 1 July 1995.

It should be noted that the Directive provided for a coming into force on 1 January 1995, so the UK government appears to be in default of the Directive by reason of a late implementation date. Neither the 1994 Regulations nor the Directive contains any provision as to the effect on contracts concluded before the implementation date (whatever the correct date may be) but still in existence on the effective date. The principles of EC and UK law conform to the concept that legislation should not have a retrospective effect, unless clearly stated to do so. (Contrast, for instance, the wording in the Commercial Agents (Council Directive) Regulations 1993 (SI No 3053) which expressly states that existing agency agreements were caught by the 1993 Regulations.) Thus, although the wording of the 1994 Regulations is, on the face of it, broad enough to affect any contract in force on the implementation date, the better view would be that contracts entered into before that date are probably not caught.

The only note of caution is that if the UK government is in default of its obligations in respect of the implementation of the Directive by delaying it beyond 1 January 1995, all contracts entered into after that date may in fact be caught (see the two European Court cases, *Francovich* v *Italy* [1991] ECR I-5357 and *Faccini Dori* v *Recreb Srl* (Case C-91/92, Judgment of 14 July 1994).

Despite some bodies of opinion which suggested that the 1977 Act should be amended to bring it into line with the Directive, so as to provide one comprehensive piece of legislation regulating consumer contracts, the UK government has decided not to take this option. Thus, so far as contracting with consumers is concerned, there are now two regulatory regimes, one under the 1977 Act and one under the 1994 Regulations which, while overlapping to some extent, are not by any means identical. This causes obvious difficulties for businesses dealing with consumers, but provides consumers the best of both worlds. They can take advantage of areas in either regime which are not overlapping, and also plead their case in the alternative to the extent that there is an overlap.

So far as business to business transactions are concerned, these are still regulated under the 1977 Act as before and, by definition, the 1994 Regulations can have no effect on them.

The Unfair Contract Terms Act 1977

This Act applies not only to consumer transactions but also to certain business to business transactions. It is, however, limited, so far as ss 2–7 are concerned to transactions carried out in the course of a business, so that these sections do not apply to contracts between private individuals (s 1(3)). Whether one is drafting business contracts or consumer contracts, a thorough knowledge of this Act is vital if one is to deal effectively with warranties, indemnities or exclusion clauses.

The basis of the 1977 Act is to prohibit certain exclusion clauses altogether, and to permit the existence of others only if they satisfy the criterion that they are fair and reasonable (usually referred to as the 'reasonableness test'). The test is defined in s 11 of the 1977 Act. The burden of proof that an exclusion clause is reasonable lies upon the party seeking its protection.

The Unfair Contract Terms Act 1977 prohibits any attempt to exclude a warranty of good title and quiet possession on sale of goods (s 6(1)) and on the supply of goods under contracts for work and materials (s 7(3A)), whether in consumer or business sales. The corresponding warranty of quiet possession, under contracts where possession of, but not title to, goods passes (such as a hire contract), can only be excluded whether in consumer or business sales if the excluding term satisfies the requirement of reasonableness (s 7(4)). The implied warranties as to satisfactory quality, fitness for purpose, conformance with description or sample, whether for sale of goods, supply of work and materials or hire of goods (the Sale of Goods Act 1979, ss 13–15 and the Supply of Goods and Services Act 1982, ss 3–5, 8–10 respectively (as amended by the Sale and Supply of Goods Act 1994)) cannot be excluded at all in consumer transactions (the Unfair Contract Terms Act 1977, ss 6(2) and 7(2)) and may only be excluded in business transactions if they satisfy the requirement of reasonableness (ss 6(3) and 7(3)).

Under the Unfair Contract Terms Act 1977, s 2(1) the exclusion of liability in business to business and consumer contracts for death or personal injury caused by negligence is prohibited. In the case of any other loss or damage caused by negligence, liability can only be excluded to the extent it is reasonable (s 2(2)). Therefore, under the 1977 Act to the extent that defects in products or defaults in the performance of the contract are caused by negligence and may cause death, personal injury, loss or damage, s 2 would regulate attempts to exclude liability, whether by way of restricted warranties and indemnities or by general exclusion clauses.

Under s 3 it is not possible, for a party who is dealing on his written standard terms or conditions in a business transaction, or at all in a consumer transaction, to exclude liability in respect of a breach of contract, or claim to render a performance substantially different to what was reasonably expected of him, or, in respect of the whole or part of his contractual obligations, not to perform at all, except if the relevant contract term satisfies the 1977 Act's test of reasonableness. This section does not limit the terms of express warranties or indemnities, nor does it prevent the narrow drafting of contractual obligations as described above. To some extent this overlaps with s 8 of the 1977 Act.

Under s 8, the 1977 Act also prevents any attempt to exclude liability under the Misrepresentation Act 1967, for pre-contract misrepresentations, unless this exclusion satisfies the reasonableness test. This section is of the very widest application. It is not limited, as are ss 2–7 of the Act, either by s 1 to business to business and consumer transactions, or by the exception of the operation of those sections from the classes of contracts set out in Sched 1 to the Act. The ambit of s 8 is thus defined purely by the 1967 Act, and this applies to all contracts of any nature, whether or not business to business, entered into with a consumer, or non-business transactions between private individuals.

The 1977 Act has most impact in dealing with consumer transactions. Its effect, together with more general consumer legislation, is to make it hardly worthwhile to exclude liability in consumer transactions. The more fruitful course is not to promise to undertake liability (to the extent that the law permits) rather than to make promises and exclude liability for their subsequent breach. For the remainder, the only refuge is in insurance.

In commercial transactions the 1977 Act has most impact in the area of standard form contracts with its control of exclusion clauses under s 3 and very little in arm's length one-off negotiated contracts where the parties are presumed to have access to proper advice. The only mandatory provisions relating to negotiated contracts are s 6(1) (warranty of title in sale of goods) and s 2(1) (liability for death or personal injury).

All other applicable sections of the 1977 Act (s 2(2), the remainder of s 6 and ss 7 and 8) are subject to the reasonableness test which is usually easier to satisfy under the circumstances of a negotiated contract.

The 1977 Act does not apply to international supply contracts (s 26) nor to contracts the governing law of which would not (in the absence of any express proper law clause) be the law of some part of the United Kingdom (s 27).

The Unfair Terms in Consumer Contracts Regulations 1994 (SI No 3159)

The Directive implemented by the Unfair Terms in Consumer Contracts Regulations 1994 is a harmonisation measure requiring member states to equalise the level of protection granted to consumers when they enter into contracts with traders, businessmen or professionals, whether such contracts are oral or written. The Directive applies to trades, businesses and professions of both a public and a private nature, so that state-owned enterprises are included within its ambit. The Directive is not aimed at controlling merely exclusion clauses, although it clearly affects them. It is concerned with regulating contract terms which are in general 'unfair'. This goes far beyond the purpose and scope of the Unfair Contract Terms Act 1977.

The 1994 Regulations implement the text of the Directive quite literally, and the scheme is a very simple one.

Regulation 2 contains a number of necessary definitions. 'Consumer' is defined as any natural person who is contracting for purposes which are outside his business. 'Seller' and 'supplier' are defined as any natural or legal person who, in selling or supplying goods or services, is contracting for purposes relating to his business. 'Business' is defined to include trades and professions and the activities of any government department or local or public authority.

The definitions of seller and supplier are important in that they restrict the 1994 Regulations to contracts relating to the supply of goods or services. The Directive is somewhat ambiguous on this point but, so far, at least as the English text is concerned, this seems to be a very reasonable interpretation and, in the absence of a judgment from the European Court of Justice which requires the UK government to change the Regulations, this is certainly the way in which the Regulations will operate.

This would mean that contracts relating to the transfer of interests in land would not be caught, although clearly a building contract (being a contract for the supply of work and materials) would be. The status of some leases and licences is also open to question. For instance, a licence of warehouse space or serviced office accommodation, could very well be a contract for the supply of services and, while a lease which confers a leasehold estate should not be caught of itself, the provisions in it which relate to the supply of services by the landlord (eg insurance, security staff, heating, etc) could well be severed and held to be covered as a separate contract for the supply of services.

It should also be noted that most financial services' contracts will be caught. This would not catch the issue of securities under a prospectus, since a security is of itself not 'goods', and the prospectus under which it is issued for subscription is probably not a contract for the supply of services. However, it would include insurance, broking (provision of the service of the sale and purchase of securities) and the provision of banking and building society services such as mortgages, deposits, loans, cash and credit cards and the sale of foreign exchange and travellers' cheques. Most of these areas are largely unaffected by the provisions of the Unfair Contract Terms Act 1977, either because they are excluded under Sched 1 or because, by and large, the provisions of the 1977 Act are not truly appropriate for the regulation of such contracts.

Regulation 3(1) provides that the 1994 Regulations apply to any term in a consumer contract which has not been individually negotiated. There is no definition of individual negotiation. Regulation 3(3) provides that if the term has been negotiated in advance and the consumer has not been able to influence the substance of the term it will not be regarded as individually negotiated. However, this is not an exhaustive definition, and no doubt the court would have to decide the question as one of fact, by applying the plain or dictionary meaning of the words to the particular circumstances of each case. In cases of dispute the burden of proof lies on the seller or supplier to show that a term was individually negotiated.

Regulation 3(2) provides that, where a term relates to the definition of the main subject matter of the contract or the adequacy of the price or remuneration as against the goods or services provided under the contract (the so-called 'core exclusion'), it will not be governed by the 1994 Regulations. Clearly, this can only apply to such terms which have not been individually negotiated since, under reg 3(1), if they have been individually negotiated they are not subject to the 1994 Regulations at all. However, reg 3(2) is subject to the proviso that, if the core term is not drafted in 'plain, intelligible language', it will be subject to the 1994 Regulations in any event. Again, this proviso has no relevance to any such core term which has been individually negotiated, since it would already have been exempt from scrutiny because of the exception under reg 3(1).

The exclusion of core terms has generated some debate in relation to insurance contracts. From the preamble to the Directive, and commentary from the DTI, it appears that the terms which define and circumscribe the insured risk and the insurer's liability, and those which define the premium to be paid are to be regarded as core terms in such contracts.

Additionally, some particular classes of contracts are excluded under Sched 1, relating to employment, succession rights, rights under family law, and the incorporation and organisation of companies or partnerships.

Also excluded under Sched 1 is any term which has been incorporated to comply with or reflects UK statutory or regulatory provisions or the provisions or principles of international conventions to which all the member states, or the EU, are parties. The first limb of this provision would prevent, for instance, scrutiny under the 1994 Regulations of warranties to be implied under the Sale of Goods Act 1979, or of the special regimes regulating terms and conditions for the supply of consumer credit under the Consumer Credit Act 1974. The second limb covers such international conventions as those which limit liability in respect of the international carriage of passengers or goods. Here, if the convention in question is one to which only some of the member states (including the UK) are parties, the second limb would not apply. However, any enabling legislation implementing the convention within the UK would be sufficient to bring the terms of the convention within the first limb of the exception.

Regulation 4(1) defines 'unfair term' as one which 'contrary to the requirements of good faith . . . causes significant imbalance to the parties' rights and obligations arising under the contract, to the detriment of the consumer'. Regulation 4(2) and (3) and Sched 2 provide some guidelines as to what should be taken into account in deciding the fairness of a term, but otherwise one is left to the short and general definition in reg 4(1).

Regulation 4(4) and Sched 3 provide 'an indicative and non-exhaustive list of the terms which may be regarded as unfair'. This list is set out in full in the Appendix to this chapter on p 223.

Where such a term is included in a contract, the 1994 Regulations make no mention of the effect of the list on the burden of proof. However, if such a term is included in a contract and the consumer complains of it, he will inevitably point to the list as one justification for the complaint. Once this happens, the burden of proof to show that, in the particular circumstances, it was not unfair, will be shifted for all practical purposes on to the other contracting party.

Thus, it is better to avoid or draft around the clauses on the list unless commercially it is essential that one of those clauses be included. In this case, it would be useful, where possible, to include in the clause, or somewhere else in the contract, at least some words which refer to the reason why its inclusion is required and why that inclusion is fair under the circumstances. This will not be conclusive in any legal proceedings but it may assist.

Regulation 5 provides that an unfair term in a contract concluded with a consumer is not to be binding on the consumer, but that the contract shall continue to bind the parties if it is capable of continuing in existence without the unfair term.

Regulation 6 imposes on any seller or supplier the obligation to ensure that any term in a written contract with a consumer shall be in 'plain intelligible language', and that if there is doubt about the meaning of a written term the interpretation most favourable to the consumer shall prevail. It should be noted that this provision does not apply only to the core terms, as discussed above, under reg 3(2), but to any written term of the contract at all except (see reg 3(1)) a term which has been individually negotiated, where the consumer has only himself to blame for any ambiguities. 'Plain intelligible language' is nowhere defined.

Regulation 7 provides that the 1994 Regulations shall apply despite the artificial imposition, through an express proper law clause, of a system of law outside those of the member states of the European Union, where the contract has a 'close connection with the territory of the member states'.

Finally, reg 8 confers certain powers on the Director General of Fair Trading to act in cases where (following a complaint) he finds that an unfair contract term is generally being used or generally recommended for use by any person (eg a trade association). The Director General can prevent continued use of such terms by injunction. These powers are intended to address fair trading issues generally, and do not provide a remedy for any individual consumer who complains of an unfair term in a contract he has entered into. In this case, the consumer concerned must apply individually for redress to the court, relying on reg 5.

Here it should be mentioned that the Directive and the 1994 Regulations work on the principle that the individual consumer does not have a remedy in terms of damages, merely because a term is unfair. Nor is a supplier who includes an unfair term subject to any criminal or civil penalty for so doing. The only effect of the Directive and the 1994 Regulations is to enable the consumer to enforce his contract with the offending clause deleted, if the contract is capable of subsisting without it.

The remedies are then left to the court, with no guidance from the 1994 Regulations. In most cases, the offending clause will have excluded or limited the supplier's liability, so that the consumer's remedy is to obtain damages or increased damages. However, if the contract can no longer subsist without the clause, then the court presumably has to deal with the issue as one where the contract was voidable for illegality, and apply some form of restitution.

There are some general problems under the 1994 Regulations, and indeed the Directive, which are worth of mention, and these will now be discussed separately.

Definition of 'unfair term' under the 1994 Regulations

Firstly, how will the definition of 'unfair term' be interpreted, and what sort of 'unfairness test' will be applied by the courts?

Although the matter is not free from doubt it seems unlikely that the standards to be applied will differ markedly from those for the reasonableness test under the Unfair Contract Terms Act 1977, which clearly has some similarities to the unfairness test. (The reasonableness test, it should be remembered, is in the 1977 Act, s 11, expressed in terms of what is 'fair and reasonable'.) So far as the reasonableness test is concerned, although it was expected that case law would give rise to sufficient precedents to flesh out the relatively few guidelines available under the 1977 Act, in fact cases have not been very helpful since they mostly seem to turn on their particular facts. The dictum in the *Mogul SS* case (1889) 23 QBD 598, CA equating reasonableness with 'the good sense of the tribunal', still seems to come closest to the mark.

It has, however, become apparent that the court is more likely to find the exclusion clause unreasonable where the plaintiff is a consumer, since a consumer is presumed to be less able to take care of his interests, suffer from greater inequality of bargaining power, and be less able to bear the economic loss that he would suffer if the defendant were allowed to rely on the exclusion clause. He is also less likely to be able to take out insurance against such risks if they are imposed on him. (Contrast *Photo Production Ltd v Securicor Transport Ltd* [1980] AC 827 and *R & B Customs Brokers Ltd v UDT Finance Ltd* [1988] 1 All ER 847, and see also *Harris v Wyre Forest District Council* [1989] 2 All ER 514.)

The unfairness test and the reasonableness test are also similar in that reg 4 of the 1994 Regulations requires that the unfairness test be applied on the basis of the relevant circumstances prevailing at the date the contract was concluded. This is broadly the same as the way in which the reasonableness test is to be applied under the 1977 Act, s 11. Additionally, there is considerable similarity between the guidelines for the two tests as set out in the 1977 Act, s 11(4) and Sched 2 and the 1994 Regulations, reg 4(2) and Sched 2. Both, for example, require a consideration of the strength of the bargaining position of the parties, and whether the consumer received an inducement to agree to the term in question. Thus, there are clearly similarities between the tests. Further, when the courts apply the reasonableness test to consumers, as discussed above, it can be seen that the reason a consumer is more likely to succeed in showing a clause is unreasonable is because the court leans in his favour as a result of his inequality of bargaining power. This approach comes very close to the concept of 'significant imbalance in the parties' rights and obligation' used to define the unfairness test under reg 4(1).

Given the above, it must be asked whether there is any essential difference between the two tests. At the end of the day, the court will decide whether, in its view, on all the facts of the case, a particular term is fair or not. This sounds very like applying the good sense of the tribunal, as referred to in the *Mogul SS* case in relation to reasonableness.

If the tests are to be different, then one has to envisage (in cases where the 1994 Regulations and the 1977 Act both apply) clauses which can (in the same circumstances) be either fair or reasonable but not both. Given the inclusion of the word 'fair' in the 1977 Act, s 11 this seems difficult. However, it is true that s 11 and reg 4 are not identical in their wording or their relevant guidelines for application and, until there are some decisions on the issue, the matter cannot be free from doubt.

Definition of 'plain intelligible language'

In a number of other jurisdictions attempts have been made either to provide a definition of 'plain intelligible language', or to set up a system of vetting standard form contracts by a regulatory authority. For instance, under the Plain Language Act 1980 of the state of New Jersey in the United States, a consumer contract must be written 'in a simple, clear, understandable and easily readable way', and a vetting authority was set up. Businesses can voluntarily submit standard agreements for review and approval to the Attorney-General's office. Approval constitutes a complete defence to an action under the statute. According to the Attorney-General's office, the review is carried out on the basis of guidelines under the Act, 'as an English teacher would, with red-pencilled comments and specific suggestions for simpler wording or sentence shortening'.

Set out below is a specimen clause before review, and as amended after review.

Before

In the event that the said edifice, of which the demised premises form a part, be so damaged by fire that the Landlord shall decide to rebuild or tear down, this lease shall be null and void and of no effect, and all agreements shall cease, terminate and be at an end, despite and notwithstanding the circumstance that the herein demised premises may not have been affected by reason of aforesaid conflagration.

After

If the building in which this apartment is located is so damaged by fire that the Landlord decides to rebuild or tear it down, this lease shall terminate even if the apartment has not been affected.

(This specimen clause is reproduced with the kind permission of Jeanne Pasmantier and CLARITY.)

Going by this example, it does not appear that the contract has to be drafted so as to be comprehensible to the lowest common denominator. Rather, it appears to be of a level that would be understandable by the reasonable man in the street.

Again, the new Civil Code of Quebec states that the clause should not be 'illegible or incomprehensible to a reasonable person'.

Taking all of the above into account although, again, it is difficult to be conclusive in the absence of precedent, the best view would be that the sort of test to be applied is whether the language would be intelligible to the ordinary reasonable man in the street with an average education—another version of the 'man on the Clapham omnibus'.

Further, although there is no vetting procedure under the 1994 Regulations, there are institutions in the United Kingdom, for instance CLARITY, which promote plain language contracts. A seal of approval from such an institution should be of some assistance to anyone asserting that his contract is in plain intelligible language.

There are two further problems which require some discussion.

Firstly, what if English is not the consumer's mother tongue? Does the other party have to make some special allowance for him, even to the extent of translating the contract? Although the 1994 Regulations are silent on this point until, and unless, a judicial decision provides to the contrary, the better view would seem to be that a consumer contracts in a language other than his own at his own risk; at least provided that the clause in question would have been in plain intelligible language so far as a native speaker of the relevant language was concerned.

The issues arising from failure to understand the language in which the contract is written go rather (like illiteracy) to the question of *consensus ad idem*. If the consumer does not understand the language at all, the failure to achieve a meeting of minds may mean that there is no contract, or that the clause in question never formed part of the contract. However, if the consumer is sufficiently fluent in the language for the other party reasonably to suppose that he understands the contract, even if he in fact does not, he may well be bound by the clause in any event, even if it is then subject to scrutiny under the 1994 Regulations so far as intelligibility to a native English speaker or fairness is concerned.

Secondly, there is a problem relating to the question of what weight, if any, should be given to the fact that, even though a clause may not be in plain intelligible language, the consumer may have understood what the clause means, either because it relates to some speciality in which he happens to be trained and knowledgeable, or because he has had it explained to him by a lawyer or other expert or, indeed, by the supplier.

Two possible situations can arise. Firstly, let us suppose that the reason for the consumer's apparent understanding is because he has come to this conclusion on his own reasoning powers or because an adviser of his (such as his solicitor) has explained it to him. In this case, his state of understanding (which may or may not be correct) is largely irrelevant. The court will simply construe the clause itself, and use reg 6 to resolve any ambiguity in favour of the consumer.

Secondly, the consumer may have asked the supplier to explain the meaning of the clause to him. In this case, either the explanation is a correct construction of the clause or it is not.

If it is a correct construction of the clause then, by definition, there can have been no ambiguity in the drafting and the court, to the extent it is asked to construe the clause, will agree with this construction. Here, reg 6 will have no application.

If the construction is not correct, one of two things can happen. The court may ignore what has passed between the parties, and construe the clause correctly, using reg 6 to resolve any ambiguity in favour of the consumer. However, it is much more likely that the court will take the view that the explanation (even though it is based on an incorrect construction of the clause) has superseded the written clause, so that the parties have now made a bargain based on the explanation given by the supplier. Here the written clause is not part of the contract between the parties at all and the court, rather than applying reg 6, will be concerned with deciding the effect of the true agreement between the parties based upon the supplier's explanation.

Finally, in dealing with this issue it should be remembered that reg 6 is only a tool that the court uses (if necessary) to construe the clause. Once it has construed the clause and resolved the ambiguity (if any), it still has to decide whether or not the clause (as construed) is unfair. It is here that the question of the understanding of the consumer is much more likely to be relevant.

There is some evidence that lack of plain intelligible language (even if it does not create any ambiguity) might of itself tip the balance to make a clause unfair. For instance, there is precedent for the fact that a clause which is in small print, and contains unnecessarily convoluted drafting will fail the reasonableness test under the Unfair Contract Terms Act 1977, s 11 (see *Stag Line Ltd* v *Tyne Ship Repair Group Ltd* [1984] 2 Lloyd's Rep 211).

However, if the supplier can show that despite convoluted drafting the clause was drawn to the attention of the consumer, and correctly explained to him before he entered into the contract, then this would certainly assist in tipping the balance back towards fairness, although it would not be conclusive.

In conclusion, it is clearly of great importance to use plain intelligible language when drafting consumer contracts so as to avoid the consideration of core terms for fairness, the unfavourable interpretation of any clause and, perhaps, a general finding of unfairness, whether or not the clause is a core term, merely because of the lack of plain intelligible language.

Differences in scope between the 1977 Act and the 1994 Regulations

There are a number of key differences in the cover for consumer transactions provided by the 1977 Act and the 1994 Regulations, which it is important to understand.

Under the 1994 Regulations a consumer is defined as a natural person acting for purposes outside his trade or business (reg 2). Under the 1977 Act, reference is to a contracting party or person who 'deals as a consumer' (ie who enters into a contract not in the course of his business) (s 12). This latter definition is wide enough to allow legal persons to be classed as consumers, not just natural persons (see *R & B Customs Brokers Ltd* v *UDT Finance Ltd* [1988] 1 All ER 847).

However, although the 1977 Act is wider in its definition of 'consumer' it is narrower in its definitions relating to goods. Sections 5, 6 and 7 of the Act only apply to consumer contracts if they are for the supply or sale of goods where the goods are 'of a type ordinarily supplied for private use or consumption' (s 12) and, in the case of s 5 (prevention of exclusion of liability for defective goods by means of manufacturers' guarantees given to consumers) the prohibition of exclusion only applies where such goods are being used otherwise than exclusively for the purposes of a business, 'goods in consumer use' (s 5(2)). The 1994 Regulations, however, apply to all types of goods and contain no such restrictions at all.

So far as concerns the differing types of contracts covered by the 1977 Act and the 1994 Regulations, this has already been discussed above, and attention has been drawn to the specific exemptions under both the Act and the Regulations. Generally, the 1994 Regulations have a much wider cover, in that they apply to all consumer contracts for the supply of goods and services, and their basis (the prohibition of unfair terms) allows them to govern all the terms of such contracts, except (if they are in plain, intelligible language) the 'core terms'.

This, in particular, makes the 1994 Regulations much more apt to deal with contracts for the supply of services, particularly financial services. The 1977 Act, quite apart from its specific exclusion of insurance contracts, can only deal with contracts for the supply of services in terms of exclusion of liability either for death, injury or damage caused by negligent performance (s 2) or for failure to perform (s 3). Even in relation to contracts for the supply of goods the 1977 Act is still limited to the regulation of exclusion clauses of one type or another, although the coverage is certainly wider and covers the most important provisions of any contract for the sale or supply of goods.

Drafting exclusion clauses under the 1977 Act and the 1994 Regulations

Now that the basic principles and theory have been explained it is possible to deal with the drafting of precedents for exclusion clauses. Because of the different regimes for business to business and consumer contracts, this chapter first deals with exclusion clauses under commercial contracts. The final section in this chapter, together with the Appendix at p 223, then covers the question of the extent to which it is possible to draft exclusion clauses in consumer contracts under the new regime of the 1994 Regulations. So far as the Unfair Contract Terms Act 1977 is concerned, the following commercial precedents in general comply with the regulatory regime under the Act for business to business transactions although, as will be noted below, some are of a more general nature and could be used where the Act has no application, for instance in a contract properly subject to a different proper law than one of the systems of law in force in the United Kingdom. However, even in this case, the precedent should not be used before the relevant governing system of law has been researched to see if it too contains any regulatory provisions which would affect the drafting of the relevant clause.

Exclusion of implied warranties

The correct way to proceed is to make clear that all warranties other than those specifically set out in the contract are expressly excluded. This can be done in several stages.

First use the warranty for conformance to specification set out below which acts as an exclusion by circumscribing the description of the goods to be supplied under the contract by reference to one defined document and excluding all others. It is important to ensure that prior representations and documentation such as sales literature do not unintentionally form part of the description.

These clauses have to be treated with a certain amount of caution where the Unfair Contract Terms Act 1977 applies. Under s 8 any clause excluding or restricting liability for pre-contract representations can only be effective if it satisfies the Act's requirement of reasonableness. The clause is likely to be acceptable in commercial situations where the parties are properly advised as to its effect (but see the discussion in relation to Clause 7.3, and in relation to 'whole agreement' clauses in Chapter 10).

7.1
The System shall conform to the System Specification. No other specification, descriptive material, written or oral representation, correspondence or statement, promotional or sales literature shall form part of or be incorporated by reference into these Terms and Conditions or the Agreement to which they relate except insofar as the same form part of a Schedule hereto bearing the signature of the Seller and the Customer.

The following clause should be added to the end of the warranty section relating to defects in the goods. This clause then excludes all other warranties covering this area which might otherwise be implied. Note that if regulatory legislation applies to the contract the clause will only be effective if all of the warranties which the legislation requires in relation to defects in goods have been given expressly. With a contract caught by the Unfair Contract Terms Act 1977, s 6 the warranties would not have to include one relating to title as provided by the Sale of Goods Act 1979, s 12 since the wording of the clause does not exclude warranties relating to title.

7.2
Except for the express warranties set out above, the Seller grants no other warranties relating to defects in the design workmanship or materials of the goods, and all other conditions, warranties, stipulations or other statements whatsoever, whether express or implied, by statute at common law or otherwise howsoever, relating to such defects in the goods, are hereby excluded; in particular (but without limitation of the foregoing) the Seller grants no warranties (other than as provided in the warranties set out above) regarding the fitness for purpose, performance, use, quality or merchantability of the goods, whether express or implied, by statute at common law or otherwise howsoever.

Finally insert the following clause to act as a blanket exclusion of all implied and pre-existing warranties. Its efficacy under any jurisdiction depends upon whether all of the warranties which cannot be excluded in respect of the relevant class of contract have been expressly included in the contract. (In cases where the Unfair Contract Terms Act 1977, s 6 applies this would also include a warranty of title.) If this is the case the clause can stand, otherwise it will be struck down under various principles of law, depending upon the jurisdiction, as an unreasonable or illegal exclusion of liability. Under sale of goods contracts it is unwise to use this clause by itself; include it as a separate stand-alone clause having already attached Clause 7.2 to the warranty clauses relating to defects in the goods.

The first paragraph needs consideration in the light of the Unfair Contract Terms Act 1977, s 8. Where the Act applies one assumes this clause would be considered reasonable in most commercial transactions.

There have been some recent cases on this point which should be considered. In *W Photoprint Ltd* v *Forward Trust Group Ltd* (1993) 12 TrL 146, QBD, such a clause was held to be reasonable where 'the parties were of equal bargaining power and could look after themselves' and 'the availability of insurance was not a crucial factor'.

However, such clauses have been struck down as being unreasonable in *St Marylebone Property Co Ltd v Payne* [1994] 45 EG 156, Mayors and City of London Court, and in *Lease Management Services Limited v Purnell Secretarial Services Limited* [1994] CCLR 127; (1994) 13 Tr L 337, where the Court of Appeal said that in their view it could not be reasonable to exclude liability for a breach of warranty which had been expressly given if it was one which was fundamental to the contract, and that exclusion clauses of this nature could only be enforceable 'where it was explained that although the seller had expressly given an oral assurance about the goods this was of no legal effect and wholly negatived by' the exclusion clause in question.

Although each of these cases turned on their own particular facts, it seems likely that in standard term contracts such exclusion clauses may well be good to deal with the common problem of preventing brochures and sales literature being incorporated into the contract, but that they will not (without very clear wording) be sufficient to exclude any express pre-contract representations made to the customer by, for instance, the seller's sales staff. Clause 7.3 attempts to provide such wording, but in any case where such express representations have been made, it would still seem prudent specifically to draw the attention of the other party to the clause, point out its effect, and retain a written record of the discussion for purposes of evidence in future. Based on the above cases, however, it does seem that such clauses are much more likely to be enforceable in one-off negotiated contracts, where the parties have been independently advised (but see the discussion in Chapter 10, in relation to 'whole agreement' clauses).

7.3

The [above-mentioned] warranties [set out in Clauses ....] are given and accepted in substitution for any representation or warranty which may have been made by the Supplier (or the sales staff or agents of the Supplier) prior to the signing of this Agreement and in consideration of the Supplier signing this Agreement the Purchaser agrees, (i) not at any future time to rely on any such prior representation or warranty, and (ii) that any such prior representation or warranty is hereby rendered null and void and of no force of effect.

All other representations or warranties (whether written or oral, express or implied by statute, common law or otherwise) other than those expressly set out in this Agreement are hereby excluded.

Warranties for the quality of goods supplied by third parties

A further problem arises where the seller assembles equipment into a system or incorporates sub-assemblies into a larger machine. Some of these items may be obtained by the seller from third parties. In these instances the seller remains liable (in the absence of any contractual term to the contrary) to the buyer under the contract in respect of all such items, particularly in the area of warranties, even though he may not be responsible in any way for defects in such items. Many sellers in this position cannot avoid taking what is called 'system responsibility' and are usually obliged to warrant the whole system or machine. If a third party item subsequently turns out to be defective, the seller then deals with it as against the buyer under the warranty in the contract of sale with the buyer and then invokes any remedies available to him under the supply contract with the third party who produced the item initially. All of the warranties under the relevant heading in Chapter 6 proceed on the basis of 'system responsibility'.

In contracts where the seller is unwilling to take system responsibility, the problem of warranty liability in respect of defects in incorporated items supplied by third parties can be solved by expressly excluding any warranty for such items on the part of the seller, and offering to pass on to the buyer any warranty that the seller has obtained from such third parties. The clause below achieves this purpose.

Like all exclusion clauses it will be subject to the appropriate regulations under legislation such as the Unfair Contract Terms Act 1977. Under ss 6(2), (3) and 7(2), (3) of this Act, since this clause is an exclusion of warranties relating to the quality of some of the goods supplied under a contract, the clause is not possible in consumer contracts and is subject to the test of reasonableness in commercial transactions.

The phrases in square brackets in the clause below respectively make the seller's obligations to pass on the warranties less absolute, and compensate him for any costs incurred in so doing.

7.4

Save as provided in this Clause the Supplier undertakes no liability and gives no warranty in relation to defects in the Third Party Equipment and in particular, but without prejudice to the generality of the foregoing, it shall have no such liability regarding the fitness for purpose, quality or merchantability of the Third Party Equipment, whether express or implied, statutory or otherwise.

The Supplier shall [use its best endeavours to] extend to the Customer, if requested, the benefit of any guarantee, condition or warranty concerning the Third Party Equipment given to the Supplier [provided that any expense reasonably incurred by the Supplier in extending such benefit shall be reimbursed to it by the Customer unless otherwise agreed in writing].

Guarantees and indemnities acting as exclusion clauses

If the express wording of the remedy under a guarantee or an indemnity is narrower than would be available under the general law for the matters dealt with in the express provision, then the express provision can itself act as an exclusion clause if there is either a phrase inserted, or a separate clause attached, stating that the express remedy is the sole remedy available in respect of those matters.

Where the Unfair Contract Terms Act 1977 applies, since all such clauses provide restricted remedies for breach of contract or limit liability for negligence under the general law, they will be subject to ss 2 and 3 of the Act. Even if the 1977 Act's provisions as to which warranties must be included have been complied with these clauses still come into conflict with ss 2 and 3, since in effect they are limiting the remedies available for breach of the relevant warranty (ie for breach of contract) to those expressly set out in the relevant guarantee or indemnity. In all cases where the 1977 Act applies, unless the limited remedies granted by such express provisions are considered reasonable, they will be void. Additionally, s 2(1) will, as discussed below, absolutely prohibit the exclusion of liability for death or personal injury caused to one party to the contract by the negligence of the other party.

Where dealing with the quality of or defects in goods supplied under contract, it is generally considered that warranties of the 'repair, replace, or money back' variety give a reasonable remedy provided that the time limit for claims is a fair one in relation to the type of goods concerned, and that there are not so many restrictions on the buyer's right to claim that the warranty is rendered practically worthless. The express guarantees in this area set out in Chapter 6 were drafted with the aim of satisfying these requirements, although since each case is decided on its particular circumstances, there can be no certainty that the combination of these clauses with a blanket exclusion clause would always be regarded as reasonable.

Two simple clauses to be added on to the relevant guarantee, which achieve the effect of turning the guarantee into an exclusion clause, are set out below.

The two clauses not only restrict the rights of the buyer in relation to correcting defects in the goods, but also exclude implied warranties as to their performance or their use, and exclude liability in relation to any loss, damage, death or injury caused by a defect in or by the use or performance of the goods. This is achieved quite subtly by the use of the words 'or caused by' in Clause **7.5** and the use of the words 'sole liability' in Clause **7.6**.

As previously discussed, these clauses will only be able to stand where there is relevant legislation governing exclusion clauses if there are express indemnities covering these points elsewhere in the contract which are not regarded under the law of the relevant jurisdiction as excluding liability in these areas to an unreasonable extent.

However, the ban on the exclusion of liability relating to death or personal injury, imposed by s 2(1) of the 1977 Act, does cause some particular problems in business to business contracts. The problem here is to decide whether a particular exemption clause relating to liability for death or personal injury is to be dealt with under s 2(1) or s 2(2).

Where the exemption clause seeks to exclude such liability suffered by a party to the contract (the 'innocent party'), because of the negligence of the other party (the 'party in default'), in a business situation this can only apply to a sole trader or a partnership, since a legal entity clearly cannot suffer personal injury or death. Here s 2(1) clearly applies, and the exemption clause will be regarded as void for the benefit of the innocent party should he suffer such personal injury or death (see also *Phillips Products Ltd* v *Hyland* [1978] 2 All ER 620).

The other category of liability for personal injury or death which the party in default can seek to exclude or pass on to the innocent party is that relating to claims made by third parties, who have suffered death or personal injury by reason of the negligence of the party in default.

This type of exemption clause obviously can apply whether the innocent party is a natural or a legal person. Such exemption clauses, shifting liability (from the party in default to the innocent party) for third party claims of this nature, relate in fact (as between the parties to the contract, and whether or not either or both are natural persons) to economic loss, so that s 2(2) will apply rather than s 2(1).

Here the basic question is who (as between the parties to the contract) will indemnify the third party. Such clauses have no effect on the primary liability to the third party for the death or personal injury he has suffered. This liability is owed to the third party in tort (or if the party is a consumer perhaps on the basis of strict liability) by the party in default, and the terms of the contract between the party in default and the innocent party can have no such liability (see *Thompson v T Lohan (Plant Hire) Ltd (J W Hurdiss Ltd third party)* [1987] 2 All ER 631).

Thus in drafting such clauses it is possible to narrow down the unlimited liability for death or personal injury to such liability where the other party can and does suffer it (s 2(1)) and exclude or limit all such liability to the other party in respect of third party claims, provided it is reasonable to do so in the circumstances of the particular contract (s 2(2)).

However, since the party excluding liability still has to contend directly with the third party claims through actions in tort or under the strict liability provisions of consumer protection legislation, he will have to carry the insurance to cover such claims in many cases anyway. Thus, many organisations prefer to cover the totality of such risks under their insurance and deal with them directly, rather than complicate the issue by excluding liability to the other party to the contract, or seeking a counter-indemnity to make the other party responsible for such claims instead.

Thus, in the following two precedents and, indeed, where applicable in the rest of the precedents in this chapter, the phrases covering the exception of liability for death or personal injury, from the operation of the exclusion clauses, have been drafted with the option of either excepting all such liability from the clauses, or only that liability which is owed in respect of death of or injury to the other party to the contract.

7.5

The Seller's liability under the foregoing provisions shall be to the exclusion of any other liability to the Buyer [(other than for death or personal injury caused [to the Buyer] by the Seller's negligence as defined in Section 1 of the Unfair Contract Terms Act 1977)] whether contractual, tortious or otherwise for defects in the goods, for any death or personal injury caused by the goods, or for any loss or damage to or caused by the goods.

7.6

The Seller's obligations to remedy defects in the goods under the warranties set out above shall be its sole liability [(other than for death or personal injury caused [to the Buyer] by the Seller's negligence as defined in Section 1 of the Unfair Contract Terms Act 1977)] to the Buyer for defects in the goods after delivery and in particular but without prejudice to the generality of the foregoing it shall have no such liability (other than as provided in the warranties set out above) regarding the fitness for purpose, quality or merchantability of the goods, whether express or implied, statutory or otherwise.

The following two clauses are longer forms with express and detailed exclusions of liability for damage caused by defects in or by the use of the goods. The phrase in square brackets should be included in each of the clauses if the Unfair Contract Terms Act 1977 applies.

7.7

The provisions set out in this Clause establish the Buyer's exclusive remedies for all defects in the System and [(with the exception of death or personal injury caused [to the Buyer] by the Seller's negligence as defined in Section 1 of the Unfair Contract Terms Act 1977)], for all death, personal injury, loss, damage, costs and expenses arising out of or caused by such defects, and are in lieu of all obligations or liabilities on the part of the Seller to the Buyer [(with the exception of death or personal injury caused [to the Buyer] by the Seller's negligence as defined in Section 1 of the Unfair Contract Terms Act 1977)], for all death, personal injury, loss, damage, costs and expenses arising out of or in connection with the use of the System, or the performance of the System, whether such obligations or liabilities would otherwise arise in contract, tort, or under statute, including negligence, even if the Seller has been advised of the possibility of such damages.

7.8

Save as provided in this Condition the Seller shall not be under any liability to the Buyer whether in contract tort or otherwise in respect of defects in the System or [(with the exception of death or personal injury caused [to the Buyer] by the Seller's negligence as defined in Section 1 of the Unfair Contract Terms Act 1977)], for any death, personal injury, damage or loss resulting from such defects or from any work done in connection therewith.

Nothing contained in this Clause or elsewhere in this Agreement shall be deemed to constitute or imply any warranty by the Seller that the System will at all times operate satisfactorily without malfunction.

The following clause is applicable in a contract for the supply of services. In nearly all jurisdictions (see the Supply of Goods and Services Act 1982, s 13) the only warranty relating to defects in services is covered by the requirement to carry out the service with reasonable care and skill. Irrespective of any other limitations on liability which may be included, it is useful to clarify this by an express clause as below. Since the failure to use reasonable care and skill amounts to negligence (see the Unfair Contract Terms Act 1977, s 1(1)(*a*) and (*b*)) the problems discussed above on excluding liability for negligence (the Unfair Contract Terms Act 1977, s 2) would apply to any clause which sought to exclude such a liability in a contract for the supply of services.

7.9
The Supplier has no obligation, duty or liability to the Customer in contract, tort, for breach of statutory duty or otherwise beyond that of a duty to exercise reasonable skill and care.

As stated above indemnities can also be used as exclusion clauses, in the same way as restricted guarantees.

The following clause is the usual way in which indemnities are used as limitations. The types of loss for which indemnity is given are restricted (note the word 'direct' in the opening line) and a limit (often arrived at by reference to the available insurance cover of the party giving the indemnity) to the total amount of the indemnity is imposed by the clause. The inclusion of the words 'wilful or negligent' will further decrease the liability of the supplier. Since there is no limit on the amount of compensation for death or personal injury caused to the customer and provided the amount inserted is reasonable in the circumstances the clause will comply with the Unfair Contract Terms Act 1977, s 2. Here the question of reasonableness may well be largely influenced by the level of insurance cover the supplier could practicably obtain. In any proceedings where evidence as to the reasonableness of such a clause is required under the Act, evidence as to the issue of practicable insurance cover will probably have to be led.

The effective use of the indemnity as an exclusion clause is achieved by the use of the words 'but not otherwise' together with the proviso. The indemnity has no application to, and therefore does not limit or exclude liability for, death or personal injury caused to the customer (if a natural person).

7.10
The Supplier will indemnify the Customer against direct damage to property or death or injury to third parties to the extent caused by the [wilful or negligent] acts or omissions of the Supplier, its subcontractors servants or agents under this Agreement, but not otherwise,

by making good such damage to property or compensating such death or injury, provided that the Supplier's total liability under this Clause shall not exceed £.........in the aggregate.

The following clause is in effect an exclusion of liability on the part of the supplier (except for death or personal injury if the phrase in square brackets is included), coupled with an obligation on the part of the customer to ensure the supplier has no liability by agreeing to indemnify the supplier against third party claims. Because of its exclusion of all liability other than for death or personal injury this clause may well be void if the Unfair Contract Terms Act 1977, ss 2(2) or 3 applies to the contract.

7.11

The [Supplier does not exclude liability for death or personal injury [caused to the Customer and] resulting from the negligence of the Supplier but subject thereto the] Supplier shall not incur any liability of any kind or nature whether in contract or tort or otherwise howsoever for any death personal injury damage loss liability or expenses suffered or incurred by the Customer (as to which the Customer expressly waives any right of recovery from the Supplier) or by any other person arising directly indirectly or in any manner howsoever out of the goods and services provided hereunder by the Supplier to the Customer or any other persons and the Customer hereby agrees to indemnify and keep the Supplier indemnified during the continuance of this Agreement and thereafter against all such liability arising as aforesaid.

The clause below is a further 'exclusion' type of indemnity clause which effectively shifts the liability from the seller to the customer. It is fuller and more wide-ranging than the previous clause. Such 'reverse' indemnities are expressly treated as exclusion clauses under the Unfair Contract Terms Act 1977, s 4 in consumer transactions and are in this case unenforceable unless they satisfy the requirement of reasonableness. They are also caught by ss 2 and 3 of the 1977 Act.

7.12

[Except in respect of any death or personal injury suffered by the Customer as a result of the Seller's negligence as defined in Section 1 of the Unfair Contract Terms Act 1977,] the Customer agrees to indemnify and hold harmless the Seller, its agents, employees, successors and assigns from and against any and all liabilities, losses, damages, claims, suits and expenses, including legal expenses, of whatsoever nature and kind imposed upon, incurred by or asserted against the Seller, its agents employees, successors and assigns relating to or arising out of the possession use selection delivery purchase or operation of the products or any failure on the part of the Customer to perform or comply with the terms of this Agreement.

Force majeure

Certain types of exclusion of liability for breach of contract are customary and even implied by law in some jurisdictions. The most usual relates to delay or failure to perform due to the happening of events outside the control of the party in default. This concept is often called *force majeure*. The term derives from the Napoleonic Civil Code and is not fully recognised in common law jurisdictions so avoid its use in drafting except as a defined term.

Since the relief allowed by law varies in each jurisdiction, it is wise to set out fully the events which excuse delay or failure in performance and the consequent relief which is to be given. English law generally only excuses breach of contract if the contract is literally impossible to perform (whether for practical reasons or because of supervening illegality) and the only remedies available are termination of the contract with limited remedies for compensation for work done or money paid in advance.

The following clauses deal with these concepts in more detail. They are regarded as reasonable under the Unfair Contract Terms Act 1977, s 3 even though they do exclude liability for what could otherwise be a breach of contract.

The key concept in such clauses is the use of the phrase 'beyond reasonable control'. The first clause is a short form based solely on this concept.

7.13

The Supplier shall not be liable for any delay or for the consequences of any delay in performing any of its obligations under this Agreement if such delay is due to any cause whatsoever beyond its reasonable control, and the Supplier shall be entitled to a reasonable extension of the time for performing such obligations.

The clause below provides mutuality and also states expressly the consequences of the occurrence of the event, namely an extension of time with a long-stop allowing termination for convenience.

7.14

Neither party shall be liable for delay in performing or failure to perform obligations if the delay or failure results from events or circumstances outside its reasonable control. Such delay or failure shall not constitute a breach of this Agreement and the time for performance shall be extended by a period equivalent to that during which performance is so prevented provided that if such delay or failure persists for more than .... months nothing in this Clause shall be taken to limit or prevent the exercise by either party of its rights of termination for convenience under Clause ....

There is often argument as to what events are within or beyond reasonable control. This is particularly so in the area of industrial action (which might have been avoided by giving in to the demands of the workers who were involved in the dispute) and of the default of sub-contractors or suppliers (who might have succeeded with more diligent supervision by the contractor). One approach is to list all of the events which will excuse liability. However, this can produce an extremely long list and the chance of missing the vital item that actually occurs. A sweep-up provision of all events beyond reasonable control is therefore usually added. The addition of this phrase must be done carefully without using the phrase 'or any other event beyond the [contractor's] reasonable control', or (by the rule of construction sometimes known as *eiusdem generis*) the argument is raised again as to whether all of the listed events are only covered if they too were beyond the reasonable control of the party concerned so that the whole purpose of the list is lost. The two clauses below adopt the listing approach with a sweep-up so phrased to avoid the *eiusdem generis* problem. In each case if the first phrase in square brackets is used the clause acts as a definition, rather than an operative clause.

7.15
[For the purposes of this Contract '*force majeure*' shall mean] [The Supplier shall not be liable for delay in performing or for failure to perform its obligations if the delay or failure results from any of] the following: (i) Acts of God, (ii) outbreak of hostilities, riot, civil disturbance, acts of terrorism, (iii) the act of any government or authority (including refusal or revocation of any licence or consent), (iv) fire, explosion, flood, fog or bad weather, (v) power failure, failure of telecommunications lines, failure or breakdown of plant, machinery or vehicles, (vi) default of suppliers or sub-contractors, (vii) theft, malicious damage, strike, lock-out or industrial action of any kind, and (viii) any cause or circumstance whatsoever beyond the Supplier's reasonable control.

7.16
[For the purposes of this Contract '*force majeure*' shall mean any circumstance beyond the reasonable control of the party affected thereby] [Neither the Contractor nor any of its employees agents or sub-contractors shall be considered in breach of this Contract or under any liability whatsoever to the Customer for non-performance, part

performance, defective performance or delay in the performance of any services supplied or to be supplied or work carried out or to be carried out by the Contractor its employees agents or sub-contractors hereunder, which is directly or indirectly caused by or is a result of any circumstance beyond its reasonable control]. Without prejudice to the generality of the foregoing, the following shall be regarded as such circumstances:

(i) Acts of God, explosion, flood, lightning, tempest, fire or accident;

(ii) war, hostilities (whether war be declared or not), invasion, act of foreign enemies;

(iii) rebellion, revolution, insurrection, military or usurped power or civil war;

(iv) riot, civil commotion or disorder;

(v) acts, restrictions, regulations, by-laws, refusals to grant any licences or permissions, prohibitions or measures of any kind on the part of any governmental authority;

(vi) import or export regulations or embargoes;

(vii) strikes, lock-outs or other industrial actions or trade disputes of whatever nature (whether involving employees of the Contractor or a third party);

(viii) defaults of suppliers or sub-contractors [for any reason whatsoever] [where such delay is beyond the reasonable control of the sub-contractor or supplier concerned];

(ix) incompleteness or inaccuracy of any technical information which it is the responsibility of the Purchaser to provide;

(x) any failure, default, delay in performance, or any act or omission of any nature whatsoever on the part of the Purchaser, or its employees, agents, suppliers or sub-contractors.

Once the fact of *force majeure* has been established and an extension of time granted further consequences have to be settled. Can the party claiming relief sit and wait for the problem to disappear? The two clauses below take opposite points of view. Clause **7.17** excuses performance and expressly relieves the contractor of the obligation to incur any extra expense by trying to work around the difficulty. (Such an obligation, unless excluded under the contract, is implied in English law if the event occurring merely makes it harder as opposed to impossible to perform the contract.) Clause **7.18** imposes a work-around obligation and restricts relief if the party concerned has contributed to the delay before the event occurred.

7.17

If the method or mode of performance contemplated or anticipated by the Contractor is affected as aforesaid the Contractor shall be under no obligation to perform by any other method or mode but may rely on the provisions of this Clause to exempt it from liability for non-performance, part performance, defective performance or delay.

If as a direct or indirect result of any of the aforesaid events performance is made more difficult or more expensive for the Contractor, the Contractor may either decline to perform or perform in part or delay performance and may rely on the provisions of this Clause to exempt it from liability therefore. Alternatively the Contractor may, at its option, notwithstanding such difficulty or expense, perform its obligations in accordance with the Contract provided that the Customer agrees to compensate the Contractor in full for all incremental or additional costs expenses and liabilities incurred by the Contractor as a result of such performance.

7.18
Notwithstanding the relief granted to the Contractor by this Clause the Contractor shall nevertheless use its best endeavours in any situation where it has invoked this Clause to perform its relevant obligations as soon as possible.

The Contractor shall not be entitled to relief under this Clause in any circumstances where it has caused or substantially contributed to any delay or failure in the performance of its obligations by any default on its part including (but without limitation) any failure to place orders or issue instructions when it ought reasonably to have done so.

Clauses **7.13** and **7.14** provide short form clauses both as to the events of *force majeure* and the relief by way of extension of time. Many contracts will require more detailed provisions. In this event Clauses **7.15** or **7.16** should be used as definition clauses together with one of the clauses below which define in detail the possible consequences of *force majeure* and the procedure to be followed in claiming relief.

The first clause is a short form for extension of time followed by termination for convenience together with some compensation. As an alternative, for the purposes of compensation for termination for *force majeure* clauses such as **3.28** or **3.29** could be used with some adaptation. Compensation on termination for *force majeure* is customarily less generous than compensation on termination for convenience; for instance, compensation for loss of profits on the unperformed part of the contract is almost never given.

7.19
In the event of *force majeure* causing a delay in the time for completion of the Contract or performance of a portion of the Contract the period of time for completion or performance, as the case may be, will be extended by a period equal to the delay provided that in the event the delay continues for a period in excess of [one hundred and twenty] consecutive days either party shall have the right to terminate the Contract.

In the event of such termination the Contractor shall be entitled to be paid for all work performed prior to the date of termination and for any unavoidable commitments entered into by the Contractor prior to the date of such termination.

The following clause can commence with the phrase in square brackets but if it does the remedies under the clause will be conditional upon the contractor having given the requisite notice. Contractors will obviously prefer that the proviso is omitted.

7.20

[Provided that the Contractor shall promptly notify the Purchaser in writing of the reasons for the delay (and the likely duration of the delay),] the performance of the Contractor's obligations shall be suspended during the period that *force majeure* persists, the Contractor shall be granted a fair and reasonable extension of time for performance sufficient to enable it to perform the obligations, performance of which has been suspended as aforesaid, and the following provisions shall have effect:

(a) any costs arising from such delay shall be borne by the party incurring the same;

(b) either party may, if such delay continues for more than [........] weeks, terminate this Agreement forthwith on giving notice in writing to the other in which event neither party shall be liable to the other by reason of such termination save that the Customer shall pay the Contractor a reasonable sum in respect of any work carried out by it prior to such termination and for that purpose the Contractor may deduct such sum from any amounts previously paid by the Customer under this Agreement (the balance (if any) of which shall be refunded to the Customer whether paid by way of deposit or otherwise).

The following clause provides for a detailed procedure and relief is conditional upon the procedure being followed. The phrase in square brackets towards the end of the first paragraph touches the same issues as those discussed under Clause **7.18**.

7.21

The party claiming that *force majeure* has occurred shall send to the other party notification (by registered letter within thirty days of the first occurrence of the *force majeure*) of full particulars thereof including its date of first occurrence and the cause or event giving rise to it. A statement by a Chamber of Commerce confirming the accuracy of the particulars contained in such notification shall be conclusive evidence of such particulars. If such notification is duly received the actual non-performance or delay in performance of the Contract resulting from *force majeure* shall not be deemed to be a breach of the Contract and the party claiming *force majeure* shall subject to the provisions hereinafter set out be excused the performance of its obligations under the Contract for so long as such performance is thereby prevented, delayed or hindered. [Both parties shall make every reasonable effort to minimise the effect of *force majeure* upon the performance of the Contract.] The party claiming *force majeure* shall notify the other immediately of the cessation of the *force majeure*.

Within a period of one calendar month from date of despatch of the notification referred to in the preceding sub-paragraph the parties to the Contract shall meet to agree upon the action to be taken to avoid further delay in the performance of the Contract. If no agreement is reached within a further period of two months or if either party shall be excused from performance of any of its obligations for a continuous period of six months from the date of the receipt of the said notification then either party may by notice in writing conveyed by registered letter terminate the Contract.

Liquidated and ascertained damages

Another way in which liability for delay is often excluded or limited is by reference to a liquidated damages clause. Although (at least under English law) such clauses are only enforceable if they are a genuine pre-estimate of the damage to be suffered per relevant period of delay, there is no doubt that in many trades (for instance the building industry) such clauses have come to be regarded as having some of the characteristics both of penalties and limitations on liability. The following clause is a standard type in common use. The first phrase in square brackets requiring the claimant to show he has suffered loss is often omitted. In many jurisdictions where penalties are enforceable, the clause becomes much simpler as it can be expressed simply as an obligation to pay conditional upon failure to meet delivery dates.

The last phrase in square brackets is also sometimes omitted. If the clause is enforceable at all in a jurisdiction which does not allow penalties there should be no other likely damages recoverable, but all those acting for the party paying the damages should include the phrase. Where penalties are enforceable the phrase is necessary or the party paying the penalty will also run the risk of facing an action at law for damages for delay on top of the penalty.

7.22

Subject to Clause [........] (*force majeure*) [and provided that the Purchaser can show that he has suffered loss] if delivery is delayed then the Contractor shall pay to the Purchaser a sum calculated at the rate of [0.25 per cent] of the Contract Price [of the goods in delay] for each [day] [week] between the delivery date in the Contract for the relevant goods and the actual date of their delivery up to a maximum of [five per cent] of the Contract Price [of the goods in delay]. Such sum shall be paid as liquidated and ascertained damages by the Contractor to the Purchaser [in full and final settlement and satisfaction of the Contractor's entire liability for any loss, damages, costs or expenses suffered or incurred by the Purchaser arising from such delay].

The converse of such a clause is of course one which redrafts the obligations for time of performance so that no obligation to perform by a fixed date is given. This provision, as discussed previously, does not fall foul of the Unfair Contract Terms Act 1977, s 3.

7.23
While the Supplier will endeavour to meet estimated dates for delivery of equipment and performance of services, the Seller undertakes no obligation to deliver or perform by such dates, and the Supplier shall not be liable for any damage resulting from any failure to deliver or perform by such dates howsoever caused.

Loss of profit and consequential loss

A matter that is almost always excluded from contractual liability is that relating to consequential or indirect damages. This is generally understood to relate to loss of profit or contracts, although it should be noted that some types of loss of profit or contracts are, legally speaking, strictly direct rather than indirect (see *Victoria Laundry (Windsor) Ltd* v *Newman Industries Ltd* [1949] 2 KB 528). The argument for exclusion is that the magnitude of the risk cannot be taken on consistently by a supplier on the basis of the normal profit margins charged by him to his customers. The problem is particularly acute where the seller is supplying capital goods which are intended to be used to earn revenue. The margin on the price of the goods will bear no relation to the possible loss of revenue if the goods are defective or their delivery is significantly delayed. Another example is the component manufacturer who supplies one component, often of very small value, to a manufacturer who will use it in the assembly of a larger and more complex item. Delay in the supply of the component may cause that manufacturer increased production costs or put him in breach of large supply contracts with damages out of all proportion to the price of the component to be supplied.

In most situations such clauses are regarded as desirable and are considered reasonable under the Unfair Contract Terms Act 1977, s 3. The following is a standard clause of the type often used.

7.24

In any event, and notwithstanding anything contained in this Contract, in no circumstances shall the Supplier be liable, in contract, tort (including negligence or breach of statutory duty) or otherwise howsoever, and whatever the cause thereof, (i) for any increased costs or expenses, (ii) for any loss of profit, business, contracts, revenues, or anticipated savings, or (iii) for any special, indirect or consequential damage of any nature whatsoever.

General exclusion clauses

Still using the principle of severability it is possible to include final sweep-up clauses which limit liability by reference to an overall amount. Such clauses will be subject, where the Unfair Contract Terms Act 1977 applies, firstly to accepting unlimited liability for death or personal injury caused to the other party to the contract by negligence (s 2(1)), and secondly for the reasonableness of the amount which is chosen as the limit of liability (ss 2(2) and 3 and perhaps s 8).

The amount depends upon the circumstances of each contract, but likely indicators are the contract value and the level of available insurance cover. A limitation of an amount significantly below the contract value is unlikely to be regarded as reasonable.

The following clause is a simple limitation of liability. The reference to death or personal injury is necessary where the Unfair Contract Terms Act 1977, s 2 applies. The last phrases in square brackets show the possible alternatives for overall limitation. The first and third phrases are more likely to be acceptable under the Unfair Contract Terms Act 1977, s 3.

7.25

In any event, and notwithstanding anything contained in this Contract, the Supplier's liability in contract, tort (including negligence or breach of statutory duty) or otherwise arising by reason of or in connection with this Contract [(except in relation to death or personal injury caused [to the Customer] by the negligence of the Supplier or its employees while acting in the course of their employment)] shall be limited to [the Contract Price] [£................] [the Contract Price or £............... whichever is the greater] [the Contract Price or £...............whichever is the lesser].

The clause below is a longer form which can be adapted with more flexibility to cover varying limits of liability for contractual obligations. It also shows the way to deal with the aggregate limits of liability relating to different incidents, which is used in insurance policies and is therefore useful to mirror the relevant insurance cover. The phrase in square brackets is needed if the Unfair Contract Terms Act 1977, s 2 applies, and the level of the limits would have to be considered carefully for the purpose of s 3 of the Act.

7.26
If pursuant to the provisions set out herein, any liability on the part of the Company shall arise (whether under the express or implied terms of this Contract, or at common law, or in any other way) to the Customer for any loss or damage of whatever nature arising out of or connected with the provision of, or purported provision of, or failure in provision of, the services covered by this Contract, such liability shall [except in relation to death or personal injury caused [to the Customer] by the negligence of the Company as defined in Section 1 of the Unfair Contract Terms Act 1977] be limited to the payment by the Company by way of damages of a sum:
(i) not exceeding £........ in respect of any one claim arising from any duty assumed by the Company which involves the operation, testing, examination, or inspection of the operational condition of any machine, plant or equipment in or about the Customer's premises, or which involves the provision of any service not solely related to the prevention or detection of fire or theft;
(ii) not exceeding £........ for the consequences of any incident involving fire theft; and
(iii) not exceeding £........ for any cause of liability (other than as set out in (i) and (ii) above) on the part of the Company under the terms hereof;
and further provided that the total liability of the Company shall not in any circumstances exceed [the sum of £........ in respect of all and any incidents arising during any consecutive period of twelve months] [the sum of £................ in respect of any one incident or series of related incidents, and the sum of £................ for any series of incidents related or unrelated in any period of twelve months].

The following clause is a further method of limitation. It states that the customer's default cannot give rise to liability. This is nearly always so in most jurisdictions but there are cases in the United States where customers have successfully claimed against a manufacturer for losses caused by their own negligence on the ground that the manufacturer should have issued a warning not to act carelessly!

7.27
The Supplier shall be under no liability whatsoever for any loss, damage, injury or expense caused by the Customer's misuse of the Equipment.

The following clause gives an example of the drafting used not to exclude liability but to ensure that no liability is being undertaken in the first part. The clause states that the customer is getting what he pays for and that the price does not justify the undertaking of more liability than is expressed in the clause. Liability for death or personal injury is accepted. The clause is generally drafted with reference to the Unfair Contract Terms Act 1977, ss 2 and 3.

7.28
It is understood that the Supplier is not an insurer, that insurance (if any) shall be obtained by the Customer, and that the amounts payable to the Supplier under the Contract are based upon the value of the [services] [equipment] to be provided hereunder and the scope of the Supplier's liability as set forth herein. The Supplier makes no guarantee or warranty that the said [services] [equipment] will avert or prevent occurrences or the consequences thereof which the [services] [equipment] are designed to detect. The Supplier shall not accept responsibility for any injurious act or default on the part of any employee or agent of the Supplier, unless the particular act or default in question could have been foreseen and avoided by the exercise of due diligence on the part of the Supplier as his employer. The Supplier shall not otherwise be liable, whether in contract tort or otherwise howsoever, for any loss, damage, death or injury arising directly or indirectly from any breakdown or failure in, or from the provision of, the [equipment] [services], all with the sole exception of any death or personal injury caused [to the Customer] by the negligence (as defined for the purposes of the Unfair Contract Terms Act 1977) of the Supplier, its servants or agents acting in the course of their employment.

Clauses interpreting and supplementing exclusion clauses

There are clauses relating to the interpretation of exclusion clauses which can be usefully included in some contracts, although in many cases their effect is achieved as part of the overall miscellaneous clauses dealt with in Chapter 11.

The first clause reinforces those clauses restricting liability by relation to stated amounts.

7.29
In the case of any breach of a term of this Contract or of any default or negligent act or omission by the Contractor (in relation to which the Contractor's liability for damages is expressed in any provision of the Contract to be limited to a stated maximum amount) no additional or separate amount by way of damages shall be claimable whether under the Contract, or in tort, or otherwise howsoever.

The second clause imposes a limitation period for actions shorter than those usually implied by law.

It should be noted that this clause, if it cuts down liability for breach of contract to a period below that prescribed by the relevant statute of limitations, should be regarded as an exclusion clause subject, in appropriate cases, to the Unfair Contract Terms Act 1977, ss 2, 3 and 8. Particular care should therefore be taken (where the Act applies) that it does not unwittingly limit the period of time in which an action can be brought in respect of death or personal injury suffered by one party to the contract as a result of the other's negligence.

7.30

No action may be brought under this Agreement more than [two] years after its termination or, in the event of default by one of the parties, more than [two] years after such default has come to the notice of the other party. [This Clause shall not apply to any action under this Agreement in respect of death or personal injury suffered by one party hereto as a result of the negligence (as defined in Section 1 of the Unfair Contract Terms Act 1977) of the other party hereto.]

The final clause provides a useful indemnity against third party claims brought against one party as a result of acts which are the responsibility of the other party.

7.31

The Customer shall indemnify the Contractor against all actions proceedings claims or demands in any way connected with this Contract brought or threatened against the Contractor by a third party except to the extent that the Contractor is liable to the Customer under this Contract.

One set of clauses which must survive the termination of the contract are the exclusions of liability: they need to be invoked in relation to claims under rights of the parties accrued at the date of termination, which normally are also subject to provisions permitting them to survive the contract's termination. The following clause provides for this and applies the principle of severability directly to the various parts of the exclusion clause.

7.32

Each provision of this Clause is to be construed as a separate limitation (applying and surviving even if for any reason one or other of the said provisions is held inapplicable or unreasonable in any circumstances) and shall remain in force notwithstanding termination of this Contract.

Omnibus exclusion clause

A clause which is useful in sufficiently important contracts is the omnibus exclusion clause, which wholly states all of the remedies for various matters under the contract, including the warranties, guarantees and indemnities and excludes all others. An example is set out below and serves as a checklist of the complex matters discussed in this chapter.

It should be said that where the Unfair Contract Terms Act 1977 applies this clause could encounter some difficulties under ss 2 and 3. It is, however, entirely suitable for a freely negotiated contract between two legal entities (so that questions of death or personal injury suffered by the parties do not arise) of equal bargaining power.

7.33

1   The Supplier and the Customer each agree that either could be harmed by improper actions taken by the other under this Agreement. Therefore, in recognition of the nature of this Agreement and as an express part of the consideration given and received hereunder, each has agreed to define and/or limit its liability to the other hereunder. This Section will define and limit the liability of the Supplier and the Customer to each other.

2   The Supplier's entire liability and the Customer's exclusive remedies against the Supplier for any damages caused by any defect or failure in the Products, or arising from the improper performance or non-performance of any work, regardless of the form of action, whether in contract, tort including negligence, strict liability or otherwise, shall be:

(a)   for failure of the Products successfully to complete the Acceptance Tests as set forth in Section ...., the remedies set forth in that Section;

(b)   for failure to supply parts, assistance, training and/or documentation as specified in Section .... , the remedies set forth in that Section;

(c)   for failure of the Products to comply with Supplier's warranties set forth in Section .... during the warranty period, the remedies set forth in that Section;

(d)   for failure of Maintenance Services set forth in Section ...., the remedies set forth in that Section;

(e)   for failure of the Products to meet the warranted availability standards during the term of Maintenance Service Order as set forth in Section ...., the remedies set forth in that Section;

(f)   for infringement of intellectual property rights as set forth in Section ...., the remedies set forth in that Section;

(g)   for damages to tangible property or for bodily injury or death to a person negligently caused by the Supplier as set forth in Section ...., the remedies set forth in that Section;

(h) for damages to the Customer's Information as defined in Section ...., the Customer's right to seek injunctive relief and for proven damages which may be provided by governing law;

(i) for failure of the Products to meet codes, laws or regulations as set forth in Section ...., the remedies set forth in that Section; and

(j) for all claims other than set forth above, the Supplier's liability to the Customer shall be limited to direct damages which are proven, in an amount not to exceed the amount received by the Supplier under the relevant Order, [or £........ whichever is less] or [£........ whichever is greater].

3   The Customer's entire liability and the Supplier's exclusive remedies against the Customer for any damages arising from the Customer's improper performance or non-performance of its obligations under the Agreement, regardless of the form of action, whether in contract, tort including negligence, strict liability or otherwise, shall be:

(a) for failure to comply with the Software licence provisions set forth in Section ...., the Supplier's right to seek injunctive relief and for proven damages which may be provided by governing law;

(b) for rescheduling of Orders as set forth in Section ...., the remedies set forth in that Section;

(c) for cancellation of Orders as set forth in Section ...., the remedies set forth in that Section;

(d) for the Supplier's invoice claims, the stated amount of those invoices, plus any applicable interest for late payment, as set forth in Section ....;

(e) for damages to the Supplier's Information, as defined in Section .... , the Supplier's right to seek injunctive relief and for proven damages which may be provided by governing law;

(f) for damages to real or tangible personal property or for bodily injury or death to a person negligently caused by the Customer, the Supplier's right to proven damages to property or person; and

(g) for all claims other than set forth above, the Customer's liability to the Supplier shall be limited to direct damages which are proven, in an amount not to exceed the amount received by the Supplier under the relevant Order, [or £........ whichever is less] [or £........ whichever is greater].

4   [Except as provided in Section 2(f) (regarding intellectual property rights infringement), Section 2(h) (regarding the Customer's Information), Section 3(a) (regarding Software) and Section 3(e) (regarding the Supplier's information) above,] neither party shall seek from the other, or be liable to the other for:

(a) loss of profits, contracts, revenue or business; or

(b) indirect, consequential, incidental, special, exemplary and/or punitive damages arising out of or relating to this Agreement.

5 The aforesaid limitations have been determined by the parties to be reasonable limitations, due to the potential for controversy, the difficulty of economic analysis of relevant loss, damages or liability, and the fact that, at the time of entering into the Contract, it is not possible to foresee and provide in the Contract (in particular by way of adjustments to the Contract Price) for all contingencies which may give rise to loss, damage or liability.

Example of a set of exclusion clauses

Set out below is a complete set of exclusion clauses using suitably adapted short form clauses from these precedents. This set of clauses could be used in a contract for the sale of goods on the basis that the contract is one between two business parties and is a one-off specially negotiated contract. The contract is subject only to the mandatory requirements of the Unfair Contract Terms Act 1977, ss 2(1) and 6(1), assuming that the reasonableness requirements will have been met in relation to ss 2(2), 6(3) and 8 of the Act.

The clauses are rather weighty and could be commercially unacceptable in some cases, but the set gives a good example of the full range of clauses and the way they fit together.

7.34
The Seller warrants that he holds full clear and unencumbered title in and to all of the Products and that upon delivery of the Products to the Buyer hereunder such title will vest in the Buyer.

7.35
The Seller warrants that the Products will conform to the applicable Product and purchase specifications listed in Schedule [........] and will be free of defects in material and workmanship for a period of one year from date of installation at the Buyer's premises.

During the said period, the Seller shall use its best efforts to repair or replace, at the Seller's option, and at the Seller's sole expense, any Product which is found not to so conform or in which such a defect manifests itself.

If the Seller is unable to repair or replace the relevant Product in accordance with the requirements of the relevant specifications, the Seller shall, upon the Buyer's request, accept the return of such Product, and refund in full any amounts paid by the Buyer therefor.

A replacement of a Product or replacement parts supplied for a Product or repairs made to a Product during the original warranty period for such Product shall be warranted for an additional period of three months after the Buyer's receipt of such replacement Product or replacement part or repaired Product, as the case may be, or until the expiry of the original warranty period, whichever is the longer period.

This warranty does not cover defects in or damage to the Products which are due to improper installation or maintenance, misuse, neglect or any cause other than ordinary commercial or industrial application. Except for the express warranties set out in this Clause, the Seller grants no other warranties relating to defects in the design workmanship or materials of the Products, and all other representations or warranties, whether written or oral, express or implied, by statute, common law or otherwise howsoever, relating to such defects in the Products, are hereby excluded; in particular (but without limitation of the foregoing) the Seller grants no warranties (other than as provided in the warranties set out above) regarding the fitness for purpose, performance, use, quality or merchantability of the Products, whether express or implied, by statute, common law or otherwise howsoever.

7.36

The warranties set out in Clauses 7.34 and 7.35 are given and accepted in substitution for any representation or warranty which may have been made by the Seller (or the sales staff or agents of the Seller) prior to the signing of this Agreement, and in consideration of the Seller signing this Agreement the Buyer agrees, (i) not at any future time to rely on any such prior representation or warranty, and (ii) that any such prior representation or warranty is hereby rendered null and void and of no force or effect.

All other representations or warranties (whether written or oral, express or implied by statute, common law or otherwise howsoever) other than these set out in this Agreement are hereby excluded.

7.37

The Seller will indemnify the Buyer against direct damage to tangible property or death or injury to third parties to the extent caused by the wilful or negligent acts or omissions of the Seller, its sub-contractors servants or agents under this Agreement, but not otherwise, by making good such damage to property or compensating such death or injury, provided that the Seller's total liability under this Clause shall not exceed the Contract Price.

7.38

[With the sole exception (where the Buyer is a natural person) of liability for death or personal injury suffered by the Buyer and caused by the wilful act or negligence of the Seller as defined in Section 1 of the Unfair Contract Terms Act 1977] the Seller's liability under Clauses 7.36 and 7.37 shall be to the exclusion of any other liability to the Buyer whether contractual, tortious or otherwise for defects in the Products, for any death or personal injury caused by the Products, or for any loss or damage to or caused by the Products.

7.39

The Seller shall not be liable for any delay or for the consequences of any delay in performing any of its obligations under this Agreement if such delay is due to any cause whatsoever beyond its reasonable control, and the Seller shall be entitled to a reasonable extension of the time for performing such obligations.

7.40

Subject to Clause 7.39 and provided that the Purchaser can show that he has suffered loss if delivery is delayed, then the Seller shall pay to the Buyer a sum calculated at the rate of 0.25 per cent of the Contract Price of the Products in delay for each week between the delivery date in this Agreement for the relevant Products and the actual date of their delivery up to a maximum of five per cent of the Contract Price of the Products in delay. Such sum shall be paid as liquidated and ascertained damages by the Seller to the Buyer in full and final settlement and satisfaction of the Contractor's entire liability for any loss, damages, costs or expenses suffered or incurred by the Purchaser arising from such delay.

7.41

In any event, and notwithstanding anything contained in this Agreement, in no circumstances shall the Seller be liable, in contract, tort (including negligence or breach of statutory duty) or otherwise howsoever, and whatever the cause thereof, (i) for any increased costs or expenses, (ii) for any loss of profit, business, contracts, revenues, or anticipated savings, or (iii) for any special indirect or consequential damage of any nature whatsoever.

7.42

In any event, and notwithstanding anything contained in this Agreement, the Seller's liability in contract, tort (including negligence or breach of statutory duty) or otherwise howsoever, and whatever the cause thereof, arising by reason of or in connection with this contract (except in relation to death or personal injury caused [to the Buyer] by the wilful act or negligence of the Supplier or its employees while acting in the course of their employment) shall be limited to the Contract Price.

7.43

The Buyer shall indemnify the Seller against all actions proceedings claims or demands in any way connected with this Agreement brought or threatened against the Seller by a third party except to the extent that the Seller is liable to the Buyer under this Agreement.

7.44

Each of the foregoing Clauses 7.34 to 7.43 is to be construed as a separate limitation (applying and surviving even if for any reason one or other of the said clauses is held inapplicable or unreasonable in any circumstances) and shall remain in force notwithstanding termination of this contract.

Drafting exclusion clauses for consumer contracts

When drafting exclusion clauses for consumers, the combined effect of the 1994 Regulations and the 1977 Act make it almost impossible to approach the exclusion of liability in the way that the draftsman does in a commercial contract.

The most important aspect of this approach is that the draftsman should not draft the contract on the basis of promising a number of positive obligations, and then include clauses which exclude or restrict liability for failure to comply with them. Instead, he should set out clearly in plain English what the supplier undertakes to do under the contract and what he does not undertake to do.

The next issue which should be borne in mind is that it is not worth attempting to exclude liability for defective products, whether by means of a clause which limits liability to some monetary amount or by means of clauses excluding the warranties which would otherwise be implied under the legislation relating to the sale or supply of goods. The better approach is to leave the contract silent on this issue, and to rely on the relevant legal principles of causation and remoteness of damage, together with product or public liability insurance to cover the risk.

The combination of the 1994 Regulations, the Unfair Contract Terms Act 1977, ss 2–7, the EC General Product Safety Directive and the Consumer Protection Act 1987 makes such exclusions almost impossible to achieve except, perhaps, in cases of pure economic loss.

Apart from the general guidelines above, the draftsman should clearly draft with one eye on the indicative and non-exhaustive list of terms which, as discussed earlier in this chapter, according to the 1994 Regulations, may be regarded as unfair. This is set out in the Appendix on p 223. It will be seen that many of the terms are more to do with preventing the supplier exercising arbitrary powers (such as forfeiture of deposit, altering the price or the terms of a contract or terminating it with immediate effect without good cause) to the detriment of the consumer, but some of the paragraphs do cover what are normally thought of as clauses excluding liability, and such clauses are clearly potentially unfair.

As discussed in Chapter 6, the practice of using consumer 'guarantees' to restrict the seller's liability has been abolished and now such terms merely give the consumer an express remedy in addition to his statutory rights. The wording for such guarantees is set out in Chapter 6.

So far as true exclusion clauses go, the most fruitful area seems to be in the field of limitation of liability for events which are beyond the reasonable control of the supplier (*force majeure*), for some forms of economic loss, particularly of a consequential nature, and, perhaps, where the contract is a supply of specially manufactured goods or bespoke services to a particular order, where there are particular issues which have been individually discussed and negotiated with the consumer.

Set out below are a number of clauses excluding or limiting liability under various aspects of consumer contracts. It should, however, be stressed that these clauses are meant very much as indications of the approach to be used in drafting, and that a very careful examination of the particular contract should always be conducted to see which, if any, are appropriate.

In addition, it should be borne in mind that the vast majority of consumer transactions are for cash over the counter, so that, in practice, the option of some written document that contains exclusions of liability is not by any means always available. However, it is in just such oral situations that (subject to evidential problems) individually negotiated terms and conditions may well appear most frequently, and these are specifically exempt from the operation of the 1994 Regulations and also more likely to be reasonable under the 1977 Act.

The first two precedents deal with liability for late delivery.

7.45
The goods will be delivered to your address as soon as they are available. Our estimated delivery time is currently [six] weeks.

7.46
We will make every effort to complete the work on time, but you will appreciate that we cannot be held responsible for delays due to weather or other circumstances beyond our control. In this case we will complete the work as soon as reasonably possible.

The next clauses deal with the extent to which it is possible to exclude liability for defects in the products or services offered. Again it will be seen that the approach is not to exclude liability for a defective product or service, but to describe the product or service in such a way that no liability is undertaken to deliver a product or service which does not have the particular defect or shortcoming.

7.47

We do not undertake structural or other types of building surveys, and therefore, if the work cannot be completed, or any damage is caused through structural or other defects in your property, we cannot be responsible for this.

7.48

The glass supplied by us is of standard commercial quality, and optical phenomena or minor cosmetic blemishes may occasionally occur in such glass due to the manufacturing process.

7.49

Our products do not in all circumstances reduce or eliminate condensation, as this depends on prevailing conditions in and around the building where the product is installed, and these conditions are beyond our control.

7.50

If you provide us with incorrect measurements or any other incorrect information, and we rely on this in preparing our quotation, we reserve the right to increase our price to cover the cost of making good any errors or doing any additional work required because of them.

7.51

The Products require special maintenance and we will provide you with the necessary instructions for this on completion of their installation. We can take no responsibility for any damage to the Products which is caused because you have failed to maintain them according to those instructions, and your Guarantee does not cover such damage.

The next clauses show various ways of dealing with consequential loss. Again they rely on describing the product in such a way that it is made clear that the product cannot operate free of faults all the time in every environment, so that total reliance on the product in particular situations, without a backup, cannot be recommended. This does not mean that a defective product does not have to be replaced, but it may limit the liability for the consequential loss suffered. Such clauses as this may also appear in user manuals or as part of operating instructions, and the question may arise as to whether they are then properly incorporated in the contract. However, even if they are not, they act as warnings as to the action to be taken by the consumer to avoid or mitigate his loss. To this extent, they should be helpful in reducing or eliminating liability to the consumer for the loss in question. It should also be said that some suppliers find them hard to use because of the negative implications in marketing the product. In some cases, therefore, suppliers dispense with such clauses, and rely on the ordinary concepts of remoteness of damage and causation to protect them.

7.52

You should regularly check that your cellular telephone is in proper working order and that the battery is properly charged. This is particularly important if you are taking your cellular telephone with you on any extended trip. However, we cannot guarantee that your cellular telephone will be able to make and receive calls at all times, and in all conditions and in all locations. Therefore you should never rely solely upon your cellular telephone for essential communications.

7.53

However carefully your camera is manufactured and tested, it may still have some defect or from time to time require repair or maintenance. Thus before using your camera for the first time, and whenever you intend to take photographs of any important event or for any special purpose, please check in advance that it is properly maintained and in full working order and consult us if necessary. If the camera fails to take photographs because of some defect and it is covered under our warranty (which is in addition to your statutory rights) we will of course repair or replace it. However, we can take no responsibility (other than, in the case of a defect covered by our warranty, to replace the spoiled film) for any disappointment, loss or expense you may suffer because the camera has failed to take the photographs you wanted.

Chapter 8

Retention of Title and Vesting

Simple retention of title clauses

The possibility of retention of title clauses in contracts for the sale
of goods arises, under English law, from the Sale of Goods Act
1979, ss 16, 17 and 19 which together permit the seller to delay
the passing of title under the contract, even though delivery has
taken place, until a specific condition (in this case payment for
the goods) has been fulfilled.

The clause is frequently used under systems of law in Europe
(particularly in Germany) and it was as a result of a case involving
a sale of goods with Dutch sellers that the clauses first came into
prominence in the United Kingdom (*Aluminium Industrie Vassen
BV v Romalpa Aluminium Limited* [1976] 1 WLR 676).

Given the rather specialised nature of the law relating to these
clauses it is unwise to draft clauses for universal application. Such
clauses should be tailored to the requirements of the governing
law of the contract in which they appear. The discussion in this
section is therefore in relation to the situation under English law
and principles.

These clauses are only of use in situations of insolvency, when
the seller can recover the goods (since they belong to him in priority
to other creditors of the buyer) rather than prove in the insolvency
for the price together with other ordinary creditors.

These clauses are often used too enthusiastically and drafted too
widely for their effective operation under English law as the post-
Romalpa cases have shown. One trap which must be avoided at
all costs is to fail to reserve the whole title in the goods and only
to reserve a beneficial or equitable interest while passing the legal
title to the buyer. This method creates an equitable charge which
is void unless registered under the Companies Act 1985, s 395 (see

158

Re Bond Worth Ltd [1980] Ch 228 and *Stroud Architectural Systems Ltd* v *John Laing Construction plc* [1994] 2 BCLC 276).

Such clauses are most useful where dealing with goods which are easily identifiable as the property of the seller, such as unique capital goods and equipment, very often with identifying serial numbers. In these circumstances a simple retention of title clause is sufficient, as set out below.

8.1
Title to the goods shall remain with the Seller and shall not pass to the Buyer until payment in full for the same has been received by the Seller.

There are certain useful ancillary provisions which should be added, such as those permitting the seller access to the buyer's premises to recover the goods. One should also specify that risk passes to the buyer upon delivery even though title does not, and impose upon the buyer the obligation as from delivery to insure the goods against loss or damage. These matters are dealt with in the clause set out below.

It should be noted that where a receiver contests a retention of title clause, but is prepared to give an undertaking to return the goods or their proceeds to the seller if his case is proved on the merits, the court is unlikely to grant an injunction under paragraph (iii) of the clause below (*Lipe Ltd* v *Leyland DAF Ltd* [1994] 1 BCLC 84, CA). However, there is nothing to prevent the seller attempting to enforce his rights by refusing to deal with the receiver, by way of supply of further goods, unless the receiver chooses to return the goods immediately or pay their price (*Leyland DAF Ltd* v *Automotive Products plc* [1994] 1 BCLC 245, CA).

8.2
Title to Equipment shall not pass to the Customer but shall be retained by the Seller until the Contract Price has been paid to the Seller in full by the Customer.
Until such time as title in the Equipment has passed to the Customer:
(i) the Seller shall have absolute authority to retake, sell or otherwise deal with or dispose of all any or part of the Equipment in which title remains vested in the Seller;
(ii) for the purpose specified in (i) above, the Seller or any of its agents or authorised representatives shall be entitled at any time and without notice to enter upon any premises in which the Equipment or any part thereof is installed, stored or kept, or is reasonably believed so to be;
(iii) the Seller shall be entitled to seek a Court injunction to prevent

the Customer from selling, transferring or otherwise disposing of the Equipment.
Notwithstanding the foregoing, risk in the Equipment shall pass on delivery of the same to the Customer and, until such time as title in the Equipment has passed to the Customer, the Customer shall insure such Equipment to its replacement value [naming the Seller as the loss payee] [noting the Seller's interest on the relevant insurance policy] and the Customer shall forthwith, upon request, provide the Seller with a Certificate or other evidence of such Insurance.

Extended retention of title clauses

Problems arise when the goods which are sold to the buyer are in the nature of commodity or consumer goods and are purchased by him for the purpose of resale. Very often he will not be able to pay the seller for the goods until he has resold them and collected the price from his end-customers. In these circumstances the original seller has little choice but to permit the buyer to sell the goods on.

The express power of resale, as agent for the original seller, coupled with either the Sale of Goods Act 1979, s 25(1) or the Factors Act 1889, s 2(1), or an equivalent provision under other systems of law, enables the buyer to transfer good title to his end-customers. It should, however, be noted that s 2(1) applies if there is an arrangement with an express power of sale, rendering the buyer, in fact, the mercantile agent of the original seller. Section 25(1) can only apply to a situation where the seller has voluntarily delivered possession of the goods to the buyer, leaving apart the question of consent to resale, but the buyer then resells and delivers possession of them to an end-customer who is a bona fide purchaser for value, acting without notice of the true owner's title in the goods.

For instance, in *Forsythe International (UK) Ltd* v *Silver Shipping Co Ltd and Petroglobe International Ltd (The 'Saetta')* [1994] 1 All ER 851, QBD, the owners of a ship retook possession of it from the charterers when they failed to pay for the charter and, in so doing, took possession of bunkers full of fuel which had been sold by the plaintiffs to the charterers under a retention of title clause, and for which the charterers had, again, failed to pay. The owners had no knowledge of the retention of title clause, but it was held that they could not claim a good title as against the plaintiffs by the operation of s 25(1) even though they had acted in good faith and the plaintiffs had clearly delivered the possession of the bunkers to the charterers. The flaw in the owners' argument was that the charterers could not be said to have delivered the possession of the bunkers to the owners. The transfer of possession was achieved not by any act or acquiescence of the charterers, but involuntarily on their part, when the owners exercised their right to terminate the charter for non-payment.

In the circumstances where the resale has vested a valid title in the end-customer, then the original seller loses any right to the goods themselves, and can only look to his security by trying to obtain rights over the proceeds of sale in the hands of the buyer.

Apart from the practical difficulties of tracing such proceeds into a mixed bank account in a situation of insolvency, there are legal problems in many jurisdictions as to whether such clauses can attach any rights at all to the proceeds of sale. It seems clear from *Romalpa* and *E Pfeiffer Weinkellerei Weinkauf GmbH* v *Arbuthnot Factors Ltd* [1988] 1 WLR 150 that under English law such a right does not arise under a retention of title clause just because title is retained. However, an express imposition of such a right amounts in effect to a charge over book debts, which in English law is void unless registered as a charge under the Companies Act 1985, s 395. The right must arise under the operation of general law resulting from the express provisions of the clause, rather than be created and imposed by an express provision in the nature of a charge in the clause itself.

This is achieved, as in *Romalpa*, by providing that the buyer holds the proceeds in a fiduciary capacity or as trustee for the seller, with an obligation not to mix the monies with his own but to pay them into a separate bank account. It is considered that under these circumstances, a trust of the proceeds arises by operation of law as a result of the fiduciary relationship imposed by the clause, so that the seller will be able to recover the proceeds which are easily identifiable as being held upon trust for him in the separate bank account.

If there is a wrongful mixing with his own monies, in contravention of such a clause and in breach of his trust (provided that they have not been paid into a bank account that has gone into overdraft so that they disappear totally), there is some authority that enforceable rights to trace into a mixed fund would arise by operation of law under the general equitable principles in *Re Hallet's Estate* (1880) 13 ChD 696.

There is a contrary argument that the creation of the fiduciary relationship between buyer and seller cannot create a trust over the whole of the proceeds of resale because these proceeds include the buyer's margin on resale. Since the parties do not intend that this margin should belong to the seller, the original fiduciary relationship cannot therefore, by operation of law, give rise to a trust over the buyer's margin. If any trust does arise it must have been created by the express words of the clause, applying the trust to the whole proceeds of sale, so that in effect the parties have created an equitable charge over the margin as additional security for the sale price owed to the seller. This charge is void unless registered and could perhaps render invalid the trust over the whole of the proceeds of resale. (See *Re Bond Worth Ltd* [1980] Ch 228, 248, 259 and *Borden (UK) Ltd* v *Scottish Timber Products Ltd* [1981] Ch 25, 45.) For this reason, some clauses provide that the buyer will hold on trust only that part of the proceeds of each resale which is equal to the original price to be paid to the seller in respect of the goods resold.

The same problem applies when the buyer is required to hold on trust not just the proceeds of resale, but also his claims against sub-sellers to be paid the proceeds of resale. Depending upon the construction of the particular provision used, this may amount to a charge, usually a floating charge, created by the buyer over his book debts as an additional security for the seller. Such a charge will again be void unless registered (see *E Pfeiffer Weinkellerei Weinkauf GmbH* v *Arbuthnot Factors Ltd*). However, this may not always be the case, if the wording of the clause amounts to an absolute assignment (see *Romalpa* and *Hughes* v *Pump House Hotel Co* [1902] 2 KB 190). Although such a clause can be added, it is very unlikely to be acceptable to buyers, particularly where they factor their debts.

The case which has most usefully explored the issues raised in this kind of extended retention of title clause, covering proceeds of sale, is *Welsh Development Agency* v *Export Finance Co Ltd* [1992] BCLC 148, CA.

Parrot Corp Limited was an exporter of computer disks. It had a standing arrangement with the finance company that whenever a buyer ordered a shipment from Parrot, Parrot would sell that shipment to the finance company and then dispose of that shipment to the buyer as the finance company's agent, on the terms that title would pass directly to the buyer when the goods were paid for in full. The proceeds of sale were in each case paid into a bank account in Parrot's name but under the sole control of the finance company. The finance company was entitled to debit certain items to that account, and pass the balance over to Parrot. This resulted in the finance company having at all times a fund of about ten per cent of the balance in the account which it could use to set off against all of the liabilities which Parrot from time to time owed to it. The Welsh Development Agency had registered a floating charge over Parrot's undertaking and, upon its insolvency, sought to contend that the arrangement between Parrot and the finance company amounted to a security which should have been registered under the Companies Acts as a floating charge.

The Court of Appeal held that there was no one clear touchstone by which it was possible to say that a transaction was a sale of goods rather than a charge or mortgage on the goods, and the court had to examine the agreement as a whole to determine the nature of the legal relationship created by the parties. Taking the agreement as a whole it clearly was a sale of goods by Parrot to the finance company, and the finance company was entitled to control and benefit in the proceeds of sale in accordance with its agreement, without the need for registration of any charge.

The problems created by the Companies Act 1985, s 395 apply of course only to companies, and since the reputed ownership provisions of the Bankruptcy Act 1914 were repealed by the Insolvency Act 1985 and not replaced in the Insolvency Act 1986, there is more scope for retention of title clauses which create security interests in the case of individuals. However, there are still considerable problems with the Bills of Sale Acts 1872 and 1878 which create an effect rather like the Companies Act 1985, s 395 —simple retention of title clauses do not have to be registered as bills of sale, but extended ones creating security interests probably do. General assignments of book debts (eg an assignment by the buyer of his book debts relating to resale of the goods) are required by the Insolvency Act 1986, s 344 to be registered under the Bills of Sale Act 1878. In practice, it is safest to assume that the same rules as to registration of security interests created by the retention of title clause apply to both companies and individuals.

A final problem encountered is the easy identification of the seller's goods. If they are not unique and easily identified (for instance by serial numbers which can be linked to unpaid invoices), the seller may not be able to enter the buyer's premises and identify the goods which are his property and which he is entitled to take away. If he cannot do this the buyer is not, as a rule, obliged to let him take an equivalent number or amount of goods of the same description from a mixed stock. This problem arises with commodities such as grain, or building materials such as glass, brick, wood or nails, or components with no serial numbers or maker's marks on them.

The problem exists even where goods have been obtained only from one seller and the seller can prove this. Obviously, unless the buyer has not paid the seller at all, the buyer's stock will contain some goods which belong to him because he has paid for them and title has passed, and some which belong to the seller because he has not paid for them, and title has yet to pass. Unless each consignment of goods can be separately identified as paid or not paid for, the problem of identifying which goods from the stock actually belong to the seller will still exist.

This can best be solved by the seller imposing an obligation upon the buyer to keep the seller's goods separate and identifiable as the seller's property, until they have been paid for and title has passed. If this obligation is not fulfilled by the buyer (which is likely to be the case), and he mixes the seller's goods with his own, then a wrongful intermixture will have taken place which results in the seller and the buyer being tenants in common of the mixed store of goods. The seller can then take from the mixed store sufficient goods to satisfy his claim for the goods which belonged to him and were wrongfully so mixed (see *Indian Oil Corporation* v *Greenstone Shipping SA* [1987] 3 WLR 869). In appropriate circumstances, such wrongful intermixture might also produce an equitable remedy under the principles in *Re Hallet's Estate* (1880) 13 ChD 696.

The following clause deals with all of these points but as can be seen there are considerable practical and legal difficulties in the way of enforcement of extended retention of title clauses. They should not be regarded as absolute and ideal means of imposing security, but may be used as insurance for those cases where all other means of security and recovery have failed.

8.3

The property in each consignment of the Products shall remain in the Seller until such time as the whole of the price therefor shall have been paid by the Buyer to the Seller in accordance with Clause .... hereof whereupon the property in the relevant consignment shall pass to the Buyer. Insofar as consignments may be delivered to the Buyer prior to the time when payment therefor is received by the Seller the Buyer shall hold the same in the capacity of a fiduciary for and on behalf of the Seller until the time when payment is received by the Seller in accordance with Clause .... hereof and in such capacity and until such time shall remain liable to account to the Seller for the same or if the same shall be sold by the Buyer, in accordance with the next paragraph of this Clause [for the proceeds of sale thereof] [for that part of the proceeds of sale thereof (the 'Seller's part of the proceeds') which is equivalent to the price at which the same were invoiced by the Seller to the Buyer].

The Buyer shall have the right to sell any consignment or part thereof before payment for the same shall have been received by the Seller provided that the Buyer shall pay the [proceeds] [Seller's part of the proceeds] of such a sale into a separate bank account clearly denoted as an account containing monies deposited for the benefit of the Seller by the Buyer acting in a fiduciary capacity.

Risk in each consignment of the Products shall notwithstanding the first paragraph of this Clause pass to the Buyer upon delivery by the Seller to the Buyer.

In the case of consignments of the Products sold while the property is still vested in the Seller the Seller hereby gives the Buyer the right to pass the property therein to the buyers in the normal course of its business.

The Seller shall be entitled at any time while payment is outstanding in respect of a consignment of the Products to re-take possession of such consignment from the Buyer and the Buyer undertakes to deliver the same to the Seller or its duly authorised agent upon request, and the Seller or its duly authorised agent shall have the right during normal business hours to enter upon the land or buildings of the Buyer to take possession of the said consignment.

The Buyer shall store or otherwise denote consignments of the Products in respect of which property remains with the Seller in such a way that the same can be recognised as the property of the Seller.

Seller's right to sue for price

An unpaid seller who has delivered goods under a retention of title clause cannot sue for the price, since under the Sale of Goods Act 1979, s 49(1) the seller can only sue for the price when title has passed to the buyer unless (see s 49(2)) the price has to be paid on a 'day certain'. This problem can be avoided by express provisions as to payment, providing for a 'day certain', as set out below.

8.4

The Buyer shall pay for each consignment of the Products supplied to it hereunder [by draft payable sixty days after the date of shipment from the United Kingdom Port of Exit], [thirty days after the date of delivery to the buyer's premises] [at the end of the month following the month in which the relevant invoice is issued] or by such other method of payment as shall from time to time be agreed between the time of [shipment] [delivery] [issue] as aforesaid and the time that payment becomes due as aforesaid.

Payment shall fall due as aforesaid in respect of each consignment of the Products despite the fact that title therein has not passed to the Buyer and the Seller shall accordingly be entitled to sue for the price once the same is due notwithstanding the fact that the property in the said consignment has not so passed.

Where the Seller recovers possession of a consignment of the Products title in which has not yet passed to the Buyer such recovery of possession shall be without prejudice to the rights of the Seller to sue for the purchase price under this Clause.

Retention of title clauses with wider scope

Many retention of title clauses have attempted to go further than the ones above but under English law have nearly all failed upon the principle that the clause created a security interest, which was then void for want of registration.

This is obvious where goods are purchased, with the knowledge and therefore the express or implied permission of the seller, to be used in a manufacturing process which alters or destroys their substance. The original goods cease to exist as soon as the buyer starts working on them in the manufacturing process, the seller therefore can no longer claim any title to them, and any provision that he may have inserted in the clause to claim title to the end product, until he has been paid for the raw material, will be regarded as a security interest created by the clause and therefore void if not registered. This was the situation with resin sold to be used to make chipboard (see *Borden (UK) Ltd* v *Scottish Timber Products Ltd* [1981] Ch 25), leather to be made into handbags (see *Re Peachdart* [1984] Ch 131), yarn to be spun into fabric (see *Clough Mill Ltd* v *Martin* [1985] 1 WLR 111), cardboard to be made into cartons (see *Modelboard Ltd* v *Outer Box Ltd* [1993] BCLC 623) and fabric to be made into dresses (*Ian Chisholm Textiles Ltd* v *Griffiths* [1994] 2 BCLC 291).

The only exception to the above rule appears to be in the area of large components or sub-assemblies which, while they have been assembled into part of a larger machine, have not been altered or worked upon so that they can be detached and restored to their separate existence in their original state. This was held to be the case with diesel engines in *Hendy Lennox (Industrial Engines) Ltd* v *Grahame Puttick Limited* [1984] 1 WLR 485. Looking at *Re*

Peachdart and *Clough Mill* it appears the criteria for the seller retaining ownership are not only that the sub-assembly must be easily separable but that the seller must have carried out very little (preferably no) work to change or adapt the sub-assembly himself, as the very act of carrying out such work may create a proprietary interest in the sub-assembly for the buyer and extinguish the title retained by the seller.

The remaining type of extended clause is one which is often called an 'all-monies' or 'all-accounts' clause, which provides that title in any one consignment of goods shall not pass until all sums owing by the buyer to the seller for that or any other consignments of goods shall have been paid. The clauses can go as far as to impose that all sums owing by the buyer to the seller under any contract and in any capacity must be paid. Based on *Romalpa, Borden, Clough Mill* and *John Snow and Co Ltd v DGB Woodcraft Co Ltd* [1985] BCLC 54, there seems no reason why such a clause is not a permissible condition for the passing of title under the Sale of Goods Act 1979, s 19(1). However, this type of clause creates two problems.

Firstly, title may never pass in any of the goods until the business relationship is at an end, further orders are not placed and all orders have been paid for.

Secondly, if at any time the buyer's account has a zero balance or goes into credit, title to all of the goods delivered up to that time will vest in him to the extent that he has not already sold them and all of the proceeds of sale at that date in the separate bank account, if any, will also so vest, while from then on new goods delivered and new proceeds of sale collected will continue to be subject to the clause. The seller will then have to contend with a mixed stock of goods, some of which will belong to him and some of which will belong to the buyer, and the obligations of separation and identification which this will entail. Also the separate bank account, if the buyer does not remove the monies which belong to him, will become a mixed fund with the consequent necessity to attempt to invoke the principles of equitable tracing under the doctrines in *Re Hallet's Estate* (1880) 13 ChD 696.

Clauses imposing the duty to keep the seller's and the buyer's goods separate and to pay the seller's proceeds of sale into a separately identifiable bank account, may save the seller by creating a wrongful mixing of goods and funds as described above. Nevertheless, in the circumstances of an all-accounts or all-monies clause, these concepts appear artificial, since both parties know that such separation will hardly be practical in the event of the zero balance or credit balance occurring—the buyer and seller will probably not even know the exact date upon which such a balance occurs. For this reason there must be some doubt about the enforceability of such clauses. Indeed, in Scotland 'all-accounts' clauses have been struck down as attempts to obtain security without possession, falling outside the Sale of Goods Act 1979 by virtue of s 62(4) which provides that the Act (and hence the rules on conditional passing of title) does not apply to 'a transaction in the form of a contract of sale which is intended to operate by way of mortgage, pledge, charge or other security'.

In a recent English case, an 'all-accounts' clause was held to amount to the provision of a security for all debts from time to time outstanding between the buyer and the seller, notwithstanding that the clause attempted to characterise the relationship between the buyer and seller as a bailment which imposed fiduciary duties upon the buyer by operation of law. The clause was thus held to be a floating charge and, in the particular circumstances, void as against the receiver for want of registration (see *Compaq Computer Ltd* v *Abercorn Group Ltd* [1993] BCLC 602). The retention of title clause in *Stroud Architectural Services Ltd* v *John Laing Construction Ltd* [1994] 2 BCLC 276, discussed above, was also an all-monies clause, but this aspect of the clause was never really discussed since the clause failed at the first hurdle on the principle set out in *Re Bond Worth Ltd* [1980] Ch 228, since it failed to reserve the legal title to the goods, and only retained the equitable and beneficial interest in the goods instead. In the light of these cases, unless a contrary decision is given in a subsequent case in the Court of Appeal, it appears highly unlikely that all-monies clauses will be enforceable against a company unless registered under s 395.

The case of *Welsh Development Agency* v *Export Finance Co*, discussed above, can also be seen superficially as upholding the validity of an unregistered all-monies clause, but this is not in fact correct. So far as the all-monies aspect of the agreement between Parrot and the finance company was concerned, this was only created in relationship to the funds built up in the account out of the individual transactions in relation to each consignment of goods that Parrot sold to the finance company. Thus, the beneficial interest in a certain part of the funds became vested in the finance company, by operation of law, on the occasion of each transaction when Parrot sold the goods as its agent, acting in a fiduciary capacity, and the proceeds were paid into the separate bank account. Once the beneficial interest had so vested in the finance company, it could choose to use those funds as it saw fit to satisfy any liabilities owed to it by Parrot, not just those in respect of the goods whose sale had generated those particular goods.

Set out below is a fairly conservative type of all-monies clause, which is probably enforceable, subject to the question of the need to register it.

The additional provisions show alternative ways of dealing with the questions of resale, keeping goods separate and payment into a separate bank account, which can also be used or adapted for the simple clauses set out above. In the light of the discussions above on the rights to the whole proceeds of resale, as opposed to just that part of the resale proceeds which is equal to the price to be paid by the buyer to the seller, the last three lines of the second paragraph may go further than is justified if used in a clause which is not to be registered as a security. However, in the case of this clause which on present law will not be enforceable unless registered, there seems no harm in seeking to bind the whole of the resale proceeds rather than just a part of them.

It must be said that the use of such a clause appears generally to be of doubtful commercial practicality. Firstly, only a supplier who is in a very strong bargaining position with the buyer will ever be able to impose such a clause. Secondly, the requirement to register the clause as a floating charge is likely to be impossible to fulfil without the consent of the bankers who provide the buyer's working capital. Such credit arrangements are usually secured by a first floating charge, so that the registration of the clause would only create a second floating charge. In the event of the buyer's insolvency, there is unlikely to be anything left after the bank has put in its receiver and paid off the buyer's debts to the bank. In any case, whether or not the bankers have required a first floating charge by way of security, their lending agreement will certainly contain a negative pledge covenant, preventing the buyer from granting any security at all to a third party without the bank's consent and, in most cases, such consent is unlikely to be forthcoming.

8.5
Notwithstanding the passing of risk in the goods in accordance with Condition ...., legal title to the goods shall remain with the Seller until such time as the Seller has received payment of the purchase price of the goods and of the purchase price of any other goods or services

previously or subsequently supplied by the Seller to the Purchaser whereupon such title shall pass to the Purchaser.

Insofar as the goods may be delivered to the Purchaser prior to the time when title thereto passes to the Purchaser as aforesaid the Purchaser shall until such time hold the goods as the fiduciary agent of the Seller and shall accordingly remain liable to account to the Seller for the goods or, if the same shall be sold by the Purchaser (which the Purchaser shall be entitled to do as the fiduciary agent of the Seller but, as between the Purchaser and the Purchaser's customer, only as principal and without creating any relationship, disclosed or undisclosed, between the Seller and such customer), for all of the proceeds, tangible and intangible (and including without limitation insurance proceeds and proceeds of proceeds), thereof.

The Purchaser shall, as trustee for the Seller, pay such proceeds into a bank account separate from all other bank accounts and other monies and assets of the Purchaser and of third parties. The Purchaser shall store the goods separate from any other goods of the Purchaser and of third parties and shall identify the goods as the property of the Seller. The Purchaser shall not remove any identifying marks placed on the goods by the Seller.

Notwithstanding the retention by the Seller of legal title to the goods, the risk in the goods shall pass to the Purchaser as provided in Clause ...., and the Purchaser shall arrange for the Seller's interest in the same to be noted on all relevant insurance policies.

The Purchaser may exercise its right to sell the goods as the fiduciary agent of the Seller in the usual course of the Purchaser's business but such right:

(i) may be revoked at any time by the Seller giving notice to that effect if the Purchaser is in default for longer than seven days in the payment of any sum whatsoever due to the Seller (whether in respect of the goods or of any other goods or services supplied at any time by the Seller to the Purchaser or for any reason whatsoever) or if the Seller has bona fide doubts as to the solvency of the Purchaser; and

(ii) shall automatically cease if a receiver, manager or administrator is appointed over the assets undertaking or property of the Purchaser, or a winding up or administration order against the Purchaser is made or petitioned, or any petition or order in bankruptcy against the Purchaser is presented or made, or the Purchaser goes into voluntary liquidation (otherwise than for the purposes of reconstruction or amalgamation while solvent) or calls a meeting of or makes arrangements or compositions with creditors.

Upon determination of the Purchaser's rights of sale under paragraph (i) or (ii) above, the Purchaser shall place the goods at the disposal of the Seller (who shall be entitled to enter any premises of the Purchaser for the purpose of removing the goods and to remove the goods from the said premises) and/or as the case may be pay to the Seller the proceeds then held by the Purchaser as trustee for the Seller in accordance with this Clause.

Insolvency

There are problems with bad debt relief for VAT in insolvency situations where the goods are subject to a retention of title clause (see the Value Added Tax Act 1983, s 22(2)) although Customs and Excise have agreed that relief will be granted where title has passed to the insolvent debtor by the time relief is claimed. Also, a seller cannot enforce a retention of title clause where a petition for an administration order has been presented (and not dismissed) or during the period that such an order is in force. The goods cannot be repossessed except with the consent of the administrator or by a court order. The administrator may, subject to obtaining the consent of the court, override the rights of the seller, sell the goods and apply the net proceeds of sale towards the sums payable under the agreement (see the Insolvency Act 1986, ss 10, 11, 14 and 15).

Vesting

The converse of a retention of title clause is a vesting clause which vests title in the buyer before delivery and or payment. Such clauses are possible because of the flexibility given by the Sale of Goods Act 1979, ss 16, 17 and 19 and are mostly used in construction contracts or manufacturing projects relating to capital goods. Their object is to protect the customer against the insolvency or default of the contractor, so as to enable the customer to complete the contract using the contractor's work in progress whether situated on site or in the contractor's factory.

The following clause deals with the main points necessary to achieve this.

8.6

As and whenever goods, materials and other items have been billed to the Customer, or have been allocated to or incorporated in any Equipment assembled pursuant to the Contract, or have been delivered to the Customer (whichever shall first occur) the same shall belong to, and all legal and beneficial title therein and thereto shall vest in, the Customer.

While any goods, materials or other items are vested in the Customer in any of the circumstances detailed above, the Contractor shall hold the same, or ensure that the same are held by the person in whose possession they are, for the sole purpose of completing the Equipment and delivering it when completed to the Customer, and the same shall not be within the ownership, control or disposition of the Contractor.

The Contractor shall ensure that so far as is reasonably practicable all such goods, materials or other items vested in the Customer as aforesaid are identified as being the property of the Customer whether by marking, segregation or in some other reasonable and practical manner, or recorded as such in the Contractor's books of account.

Problems arise with these clauses, when the customer attempts to enforce them. Firstly, if the goods are still with the contractor and he has not been paid he can resist delivery despite the passing of title to the customer by raising either an unpaid seller's lien under the Sale of Goods Act 1979, s 41, or an unpaid workman's lien under common law in the case of a contract for work and materials. These liens may be excluded by the express provisions of the contract and should be excluded if the customer wants full protection, particularly where he wants to take possession of the work in progress to complete the contract himself but is refusing to pay the contractor because of a contractual dispute.

Secondly, the question arises of whether the customer actually does want to take possession of all of the work in progress vested in him in the event that he has terminated the contract. If he does he will be accepting liability to pay for this work in progress to the extent that he has not already done so by way of advance payments. Most vesting clauses give the customer the right to pick and choose, at least for work in progress, so that he can reject what he does not require and take possession of what he does want, subject only to full payment for the latter.

The clause below, which should in most cases be added to the vesting clause set out above, covers both of these matters.

8.7
Neither the Contractor, nor a sub-contractor, nor any other person shall have a lien on any equipment, goods, materials or other items which have vested in the Customer under this Clause for any sum due to the Contractor, sub-contractor or other person, and the Contractor shall take all such steps as may be reasonably necessary to ensure that the title of the Customer, and the exclusion of any such lien, are brought to the notice of all sub-contractors and other persons dealing with any such equipment, goods, materials or other items.
In the event of the determination of the Contract by the Customer whether for breach or for convenience or otherwise howsoever any equipment which has not been finally accepted by the Customer, and any goods, materials or things which have not been incorporated in equipment which has been finally so accepted, shall re-vest in the Contractor on the expiration of thirty days from the date on which such determination takes effect unless and to the extent that the

Customer shall have given the Contractor before the expiration of such period notice that the Customer elects to retain the property in any of the same.

The Contractor shall hand over to the Customer any equipment, goods, materials or other items the property in which the Customer has elected to retain under the previous paragraph of this Clause, and if he shall fail to do so the Customer may enter any premises of the Contractor and remove such equipment, goods, materials or other items and recover the cost of so doing from the Contractor.

The Customer shall (to the extent he has not already done so) pay a fair and reasonable price for any equipment, goods, materials or other items the property in which the Customer has elected to retain as aforesaid and which are handed over to him by the Contractor or otherwise come into his possession.

Chapter 9

Service of Notices

Proper provision for the service of notices is a necessary part of the formalities of almost any agreement. Any notice clause has to provide for the places at which notice is to be served, the method of service and when the notice shall be deemed to have been delivered. Notice clauses have become considerably more complicated because of the variety of means of communication that are available to the parties. Although from a substantive legal point of view there is no need for notices under most commercial agreements to be made in writing, nearly all notice clauses do not permit oral notices to be given, for reasons relating to evidence of transmission and receipt and the need for certainty.

The question always arises as to whether any form of notice other than that in the notice clause will be a proper notice under the agreement. To some extent this depends upon the exact wording of the clause. If it prescribes certain forms of notice as the exclusive methods of service it is likely that any other form will not be a proper notice, but there are cases which suggest that a notice which is served with some procedural defect may suffice if there is clear evidence that it was received by the party to be served, and he understood its contents.

Means of communication

The first clause is a standard short form which permits the use of telex or facsimile facilities, but has a certain vagueness about the means of communication that may be used, provided they are in writing. This allows some flexibility in that its provisions are not necessarily exclusive.

174

9.1

All notices and other communications hereunder shall be in writing and shall be deemed to have been duly given: when delivered, if delivered by messenger during normal business hours of the recipient; when sent, if transmitted by telex or facsimile transmission (receipt confirmed) during normal business hours of the recipient, or on the third business day following mailing, if mailed by certified or registered mail, postage prepaid, in each case addressed as follows:

Address: ....
....
....

For the attention of: [Company Secretary]
Address: ....
....
....

For the attention of: [Company Secretary]

The following clause is a long form which excludes facsimile and electronic mail as means of communication. It is also an exclusive clause in that it prescribes as mandatory certain forms of communication and specifically excludes others.

9.2

Any notice and any permission consent licence approval or other authorisation to be served upon or given or communicated to one party hereto by the other (in this clause called a 'communication') shall be in the form of a document in writing including without limitation a telex or cable but not a facsimile or an electronic mail message.

All communication shall be made to the Contractor at the following address or to the following telex number:

Address: ....
....
....

Telex No: ....
For the attention of: [the Company Secretary]
and to the Customer at the following address or to the following telex number:

Address: ....
....
....

Telex No: ....
For the attention of: [the Company Secretary]
All communications shall be delivered by hand during normal business hours or sent by cable or telex or sent by registered post (where possible by airmail).

A communication shall have effect for the purposes of this Agreement and shall be deemed to have been received by the party to whom it was addressed:

if delivered by hand upon receipt by the relevant person for whose attention it should be addressed as provided above, or upon receipt by any other person then upon the premises at the relevant address who reasonably appears to be authorised to receive post or other messages on behalf of the relevant party; and

if sent by telex upon the transmission of the communication to the relevant telex number and the receipt by the transmitting telex machine of an answer-back code showing that the telex message has been received properly by the telex machine to which it was transmitted; and

if sent by cable [seventy-two hours] after the text of the cable has been given to the relevant telegraph company or other authority for transmission unless before the expiry of that period an advice of inability to deliver is received by the party making the communication; and

if sent by registered post [seven days] after the date upon the registration receipt provided by the relevant postal authority.

Each party shall be obliged to send a communication to the other in accordance with this Clause notifying any changes in the relevant details set out in the second paragraph of this Clause, which details shall then be deemed to have been amended accordingly.

Alternative provisions

The next clause is a shorter form but contains alternative provisions for service in the event of a strike or suspension of any particular means of communication. Again, it is not an exclusive type of clause.

9.3

Any and all notices or other information to be given by one of the parties to the other shall be deemed sufficiently given when forwarded by prepaid, registered or certified first class air mail or by facsimile, telex or hand delivery to the other party at the following address:

If to the Contractor:

Address: ....

....

....

....

Attention: [Company Secretary]

If to the Customer:

Address: ....

....

....

....

Attention: [Company Secretary]

and such notices shall be deemed to have been received five business days after mailing if forwarded by mail, and the following business day if forwarded by cable, telegram, telex, facsimile transmission or by hand. The aforementioned address of either party may be changed at any time by giving prior notice to the other party in accordance with the foregoing. In the event of a generally-prevailing labour dispute or other situation which will delay or impede the giving of notice by any such means, in either the country of origin or of destination, the notice shall be given by [such specified method as] [that method, whether or not previously specified in this Clause, which] will be most reliable and expeditious and least affected by such dispute or situation.

The following clause is drafted so as to provide that notice is not served (in certain cases) until actual delivery of the message takes place. This is useful for the person receiving the notice but less beneficial to the person who is serving it.

9.4
The respective addresses for service of notices under this Agreement shall be as set out below provided that any party may by written notice to the other substitute another address in England which shall then become the notice address:

....
....
....

Notices and other communications under this Agreement shall be made by first class prepaid mail, either recorded delivery or registered (and by air mail where the address of the recipient is outside the United Kingdom), addressed to the recipient at its notice address and will be deemed to have been communicated upon the date of actual delivery.

The clause below takes advantage of modern methods of communication including electronic mail and provides that transmission rather than receipt is all that is necessary to ensure proper service of a notice.

9.5
Any notice, invoice or other document which may be given by either party under this Agreement shall be deemed to have been duly given if left at or sent by post (whether by letter or, where the parties agree, by magnetic tape or any other form), telex or facsimile transmission (confirmed by letter sent by post) or [where the parties expressly agree] by electronic mail to each party's registered office or any other address notified to each other in writing in accordance with this Clause as an address to which notices, invoices and other documents may be sent.

Any such communication shall be deemed to have been made to the other party (if by post) four days from the date of posting (and in proving such service or delivery, it shall be sufficient to prove that such communication was properly addressed, stamped and put in the post), and if by telex or facsimile transmission at the time of the transmission provided that the same shall not have been received in a garbled form. Any communication by electronic mail shall be deemed to have been made on the day on which the communication is first received in the other party's electronic mailbox.

Agents for service of process

Where a party to an agreement is outside the jurisdiction, it is often useful to appoint, by way of a specific provision of the agreement, an agent within the jurisdiction who can be validly served in that party's place. This avoids the need (in the event of a dispute) for the other party to go through the time-consuming procedure necessary to obtain service outside the jurisdiction. Clause **9.6** is an example of such a provision.

9.6 *Address*
The Vendor hereby irrevocably appoints the [Vendor's Solicitors] [ABC Limited] as its agent for the service of process in England in connection with this Agreement, service upon whom shall be deemed completed whether or not forwarded to or received by the Vendor. Nothing contained in this Agreement shall affect the right to serve process in any other manner permitted by law, nor affect the right to bring proceedings in any other jurisdiction whether in connection with this Agreement or for the purpose of the enforcement or execution of any judgment or other award obtained against the Vendor in the courts of England, or as a result of arbitration proceedings conducted in England. [All documents sent to [the Vendor's Solicitors] [ABC Limited] in connection with their role as agent for service under this Clause must be addressed 'for the attention of ..../Service of Proceedings'.]

Chapter 10

Whole Agreement and Variation Clauses

Whole agreement clauses

In the interests of certainty, parties to a commercial agreement generally wish to record all of their obligations in relation to a transaction in one document, or one set of documents, and to exclude from any legal force or effect any other documentation that may have passed between them, such as preliminary correspondence, quotations, sales literature, etc. They will also, because of evidentiary difficulties, normally wish to exclude all oral representations and discussions.

As discussed in Chapter 7 such clauses could be affected by the Unfair Contract Terms Act 1977, s 8 which prevents exclusion of liability for pre-contract misrepresentations unless the exclusion satisfies the Act's test of reasonableness. The 1977 Act is unlikely to be a problem in negotiated one-off contracts but may be more problematic in standard form or consumer transactions.

This issue has already been discussed in Chapter 7 in regard to clauses which exclude pre-contract representation in relation to contracts for the sale of goods. (See *W Photoprint Ltd v Forward Trust Group Ltd* (1993) 12 Tr L 146, QBD, *St Marylebone Property Co Ltd v Payne* [1994] 45 EG 156, Mayors and City of London Court, and *Lease Management Services Limited v Purnell Secretarial Services Limited* [1994] CCLR 127; (1994), 13 Tr L 337.)

There are also two unreported decisions on the question of the more general type of whole agreement clause for which precedents are set out below. These are *Alman and Benson v Associated Newspapers Limited* (1980) *unreported*, 20 June, Browne-Wilkinson J and *Witter Limited v TBP Industries Limited* Ch 1990-W-5354 15 July 1994, Jacob J.

The first case held that a whole agreement clause which only stated that the agreement 'sets forth the entire agreement and understanding of the parties' is not sufficient to exclude a claim for rescission or damages based upon a pre-contractual representation. However, there was no reason why appropriate wording should not be added which would have this effect. To this extent the case is no more than an example of the way in which exclusion clauses are construed by the court strictly in accordance with their terms. It will be seen that the precedents set out below conform to this suggestion of the court by expressly excluding such pre-contractual representations. This approach would also be in line with *W Photoprint Ltd v Forward Trust Group Ltd.*

The second case was actually concerned with a different situation. Although there was a whole agreement clause, nothing turned on its construction, so far as the exclusion of pre-contract representations went.

The clause read 'This Agreement sets forth the entire agreement and understanding between the parties . . . In particular, but without prejudice to the generality of the foregoing, the Purchaser acknowledges that it had not been induced to enter into this Agreement by any representation or warranty other than the statements contained or referred to in [the Warranty Schedule]'. The defendant further represented that the express warranties in the schedule were true, and was then found to be in breach of one of them.

Jacob J found that in such a case, by the application of the Misrepresentation Act 1967, s 1, the whole agreement clause could not preclude the plaintiff from seeking rescission or claiming damages on a tortious basis, in respect of the breach of the express warranty in the schedule, in addition to his right to claim damages for breach of contract. This could only have been achieved if the clause had contained an express provision excluding the right to rescission in the event of such a breach. Again, this seems nothing more than an example of the strict construction of an exclusion clause.

However, the judge went on further to consider the effect of the clause more generally. He considered that (contrary to the remarks of Browne-Wilkinson J) merely stating that a party has not relied on pre-contract negotiations is not sufficient to exclude liability, but that the clause would have to go further and expressly exclude any remedy in respect of any untrue statement upon which he had relied in entering the contract, other than breach of contract.

Again, this seems merely another example of strict construction of an exclusion clause.

However, he also remarked that in his view the clause failed to satisfy the reasonableness test under the Unfair Contract Terms Act 1977, s 8 because it was so wide that it excluded fraudulent misrepresentation which was clearly unreasonable.

If the learned judge was saying that, as a rule of law, it is always unreasonable to exclude liability for a fraudulent misrepresentation, neither the Unfair Contract Terms Act 1977 nor the Misrepresentation Act 1967 contains a provision to this effect, and this would not seem a correct way to apply the reasonableness test under the Unfair Contract Terms Act 1977, which requires the court to look at the specific circumstances of each case. If he was saying that in this particular case exclusion of such liability was unreasonable then there seems to have been no real evidence led on which he could have based his finding. Indeed the defendant himself never complained that liability for fraudulent misrepresentation had been excluded, nor even as to the reasonableness of the clause as a whole, so it is hard to see how any such evidence could have been led, or how counsel for either side could have made considered submissions on the issue.

Certainly this issue has never been raised in the first three cases discussed above, and any idea that there is a general principle of law, that exclusion of this liability is always unreasonable, would appear to run contrary to *W Photoprint Ltd* v *Forward Trust Group Ltd*, which did find the standard type of whole agreement clause reasonable. In that case the reasonableness test was considered from the aspect of whether it was reasonable to have such a clause in the contract at all, given that the parties were of equal bargaining power and independently advised, not whether it was reasonable or not on the basis of the particular categories of liability which it excluded.

The lessons from all these cases seem to be as follows. As usual, always draft the exclusion clause clearly. Thus, where a party is to be under no liability for pre-contract representations, specifically exclude liability for this issue. Then, so far as applicable warranties are concerned, if there is to be no right of rescission in the event of a breach of one of them, then this too should be stated in the contract.

Finally, should the standard clause exclude liability for fraudulent misrepresentation as a matter of course or not? Given the above analysis, which would conclude that there is no general principle of law requiring this, the case comes down to one of the reasonableness of the clause in the particular circumstances of each case. Here, given that the insertion of the clause in the contract at all would be reasonable (eg because it was a one-off negotiated contract between parties of equal bargaining power, independently advised), it seems hard to see why it is not just as reasonable to exclude pre-contract misrepresentations which are fraudulent as well as those which are merely negligent, or even innocent.

The following precedents have thus proceeded on the basis that no specific exception in relation to fraudulent misrepresentation is to be made, but that a specific exclusion of the right to rescind has been included in square brackets in appropriate places.

The first clause deals with the exclusion of prior representations, whether orally or in writing.

10.1

This Agreement supersedes and invalidates all other commitments, representations and warranties relating to the subject matter hereof which may have been made by the parties either orally or in writing prior to the date hereof, and which shall become null and void from the date this Agreement is signed. Each party warrants to the other that it has not relied on any such commitment, representation or warranty in entering into this Agreement.

The following clause cancels any prior agreements relating to the matters covered by the current agreement. Note the importance of referring to the survival provisions of the previous agreement or the cancellation may be incomplete.

10.2

This Agreement hereby cancels all prior agreements between the parties (if any) relating to [the products] [the subject matter hereof] and also cancels and nullifies all rights (if any) of either party arising against the other by virtue of all or any of the said prior agreements, or any of the provisions thereof, notwithstanding the existence of any provision in any such prior agreement that any such rights or provisions shall survive its termination.

The following clause is a long form of whole agreement clause. It attempts to deal with the various issues raised by the cases discussed above. In particular, paragraph 4 deals with the issue of exclusion of the right to rescind for breach of the contract.

10.3

1   This Agreement (including the documents and instruments referred to herein) supersedes all prior representations, arrangements,

understandings and agreements between the parties (whether written or oral) relating to the subject matter hereof and sets forth the entire complete and exclusive agreement and understanding between the parties hereto relating to the subject matter hereof.

2 Each party warrants to the other that it has not relied on any representation, arrangement, understanding or agreement (whether written or oral) not expressly set out or referred to in this Agreement.

3 Without prejudice to the generality of the foregoing, save as expressly provided in this Agreement, (a) the Vendor gives no promise, warranty, undertaking or representation to the Purchaser, (b) the Vendor shall be under no liability in respect of the transactions contemplated by, and the subject matter of, this Agreement, and (c) all other warranties express or implied by law legislation or otherwise howsoever are hereby expressly excluded.

4 Each party further agrees and undertakes to the other that no breach of this agreement shall entitle it to rescind this Agreement, and that its remedies for any breach of this Agreement shall be solely for breach of contract, which remedies shall be subject to and in accordance with the provisions of this Agreement.

Variations

Variation of a contract after its signature has two aspects, a procedural and a substantive one. As regards procedure it is important that any such changes are made in a disciplined way, that proper consideration as to whether they should be made is given by duly authorised persons and that a proper record of all variations is kept. Variations should not be made informally, or as it were by accident.

It is not certain that a procedural clause can render invalid any variation which is not made in compliance with it, since in theory the parties could when making such a variation agree implicitly or even expressly to vary or ignore the variation procedure clause itself. Nevertheless, such a clause should always be inserted for its evidentiary value. Its presence makes it difficult for one party to claim that an informal variation (particularly an oral one) is valid, since he knows the proper procedure for instituting variations and therefore cannot easily rely on any doctrine of ostensible authority (on the part of the person representing the other party) in order to bind the other party to honour the informal variation.

The clause below provides for a formal amendment procedure, and a very restricted one. It is most suited for agreements which are not likely to require variation.

10.4

This Agreement may be amended or modified in whole or in part at any time by an agreement in writing executed in the same manner and by the same persons as this Agreement.

The following clause, although beginning with a wide prohibition on variations and changes of all kinds, provides for a rather more flexible procedure for variation.

10.5

This Agreement may not be released, discharged, supplemented, interpreted, amended, varied or modified in any manner except by an instrument in writing signed by a duly authorised officer or representative of each of the parties hereto.

The following clause provides a still more flexible procedure, but remains subject to proper safeguards against inadvertent changes, and also provides against any unintended general waiver of rights by means of a contract variation.

10.6

The parties may expressly agree in writing any variation in the provisions hereof, provided that unless expressly so agreed no such agreement shall constitute or be construed as a general waiver of any of the provisions hereof by any of the parties and the rights and obligations of the parties hereunder shall remain in full force and effect notwithstanding any variation agreed between the parties on any particular occasion.

The substantive questions in relation to variations concern changes in the performance required of one of the parties to the contract. The question to be decided with such variations is whether and to what extent one party can have a unilateral right to vary either his or the other party's performance obligations under the original contract.

The clause below relates to the supply of goods and is quite a common instance of the supplier's right to change the specification of goods supplied. The words in square brackets are added to ensure that the changes to the supplied products are not such as to concern the customer.

10.7

The Supplier reserves the right to improve or modify any of the products without prior notice [provided that such improvement or modification shall not affect the form, fit, function or maintenance of the relevant product].

Another approach to variations is to permit the supplier to make them but, in the case of material modifications, to give the customer the chance of refusing to accept them by cancelling the order, unless the order can be filled from unmodified product. When dealing with mass-produced goods for many different customers, this type of clause is a fair one for the manufacturer to impose, in order to enable him to implement general modifications to his product range without being hindered by a long order book for unmodified products.

10.8
The Supplier reserves the right to improve or modify any of the products without prior notice provided that details of any modification affecting form, fit, function or maintenance shall be notified to the Buyer in which event the Buyer may vary or cancel any order for the relevant product placed prior to the receipt of such notification except to the extent that such orders can be met by the supply of stocks of the relevant product which do not incorporate the improvement or modification notified hereunder.
Variation or cancellation hereunder shall be effected by the Buyer notifying the Supplier thereof within fourteen days of receipt by the Buyer of the relevant notification of the relevant improvement or modification. The Buyer's rights of variation or cancellation under this Clause shall be its sole remedy in the event of any improvement or modification being made to a product, and in particular, but without limitation, no compensation or damages for breach of contract shall be payable to the Buyer by reason of such improvement or modification.

The following clause looks at the buyer who wishes to have a certain amount of freedom to change the specifications of what he is buying. This clause is appropriate in the area of the supply of special products to a particular customer, often developed to the customer's own specification. The clause not only has to deal with the change in specifications, but with any consequential changes to the contract price or time scales. Even if the seller is bound to implement the buyer's variations (as he is in this clause) he must be allowed sufficient extra time to implement the changes and be compensated for the extra cost in doing so.
The second and third paragraphs of the clause return to the procedural area, but are particularly important where there is development under the contract and interchange of information, opinions and advice between technical staff of both parties. It is easy for technical staff to change specifications informally by agreement among themselves, or for one party to claim that it was implementing such a change upon the advice, or at least with the knowledge, of the other party's technical staff. These paragraphs

permit the interchange of technical information, but do not allow the technical staff to create informal contract variations.

10.9

The Buyer reserves the right at any time to make changes in any specification, drawing or other data incorporated in this Agreement. If any such change causes any increase or decrease in the cost of or the time required for performance of this Agreement an equitable adjustment shall be made in the relevant price and/or to the relevant time scales. Any claim by the Seller for increase of cost and/or time scale under this Clause shall be deemed void unless asserted within fifteen days from receipt by the Seller of the Buyer's change notification. However failure to agree on any claim for equitable adjustment shall not excuse the Seller from proceeding immediately in the performance of this Agreement as so changed, pending resolution of the relevant claim under the dispute resolution procedure set out in Clause.....

Whether made pursuant to this Clause or by mutual agreement, changes shall not be binding upon the Buyer except when confirmed in writing by an authorised member of the Buyer's purchasing department. The provision of information advice approvals or instructions by the Buyer's technical personnel or by any other person shall be deemed expressions of personal opinion only and shall not affect the Buyer's and the Seller's rights and obligations hereunder unless the same is issued in a written document, signed by an authorised member of the Buyer's purchasing department, expressly stating that it constitutes a change to this Agreement.

The Buyer's personnel may from time to time render assistance or give technical advice to or effect an exchange of information with the Seller's personnel concerning the products to be furnished under this Agreement. However such exchanges shall not grant the Seller authority to change the relevant products or any provisions of this Agreement, nor shall such changes be binding upon the Buyer unless issued as a change to this Agreement in accordance with the previous paragraph.

The following clause sets out a different variation procedure. Its important difference is that the supplier has far more control over whether or not a variation will be implemented, and has greater protection as to the right to demand what he regards as sufficient increases in contract price and time scale to enable him to implement the variation without suffering loss. Unless the relevant changes to the contract price and time scales have been agreed, the supplier has no obligation to implement any agreed variation.

10.10

The Client may at any time during the Agreement require the Supplier to revise the dates specified in the Schedule including the Completion Date and/or to undertake any reasonable alteration or addition to or omission from the System or any part thereof (in this Clause called a 'Variation'). In the event of a Variation being required, the Client shall formally request the Supplier to provide a proposal in writing setting out the effect such Variation will have on the System and what adjustment if any, will be required to the Total Contract Price and to the dates specified in the Schedule.

The Supplier shall satisfy the Client as to the reasonableness of changes to the dates specified in the Schedule and of the extra costs resulting from Variations under this Clause. The Supplier shall furnish such details within fourteen days of receipt of the Client's request or within such period as may be mutually agreed.

The Supplier shall not and shall have no obligation to vary the System in accordance with the relevant Variation unless and until the relevant proposal or any mutually agreed amended proposal has been accepted by the Client in writing.

No Variation under the above shall invalidate this Agreement but if such Variation involves an increase or decrease in the cost to the Supplier for carrying out the Variation and/or a change to any of the dates specified in the Schedule as aforesaid an appropriate adjustment to the Total Contract Price and/or to the dates set out in the Schedule (being the adjustment set out in the relevant proposal or amended proposal accepted by the Client in writing pursuant to the above) shall be deemed to have been made with effect from the date of the relevant acceptance by the Client as aforesaid.

Chapter 11

Miscellaneous Clauses

There are a number of miscellaneous clauses towards the end of the agreement which are often called 'boilerplate', even though the term actually goes much wider than this. These clauses do not have a great deal in common, but tend to relate to the inter-relationship between the general law and the specific terms of the contract, and to modify the operation of certain general rules of law upon the contract.

Agency partnership or joint venture excluded

In the absence of express provisions to the contrary many types of commercial agreements can set up unwanted relationships of agency or partnership between the parties. The general effect of the existence of such relationships would be that one party could bind the other towards third parties in a way not contemplated by the express provisions of the agreement, or one party could similarly become liable towards third parties in respect of the acts and omissions of the other party. Various unintended provisions as to the division of profits or losses or indemnification for expenses could also arise.

The following two clauses are simple exclusions of such relationships. The third clause excludes all such relationships and expressly prohibits one party from binding the other with obligations to third parties.

11.1
Nothing contained in this Agreement shall be so construed as to constitute either party to be the agent of the other.

11.2
This Agreement shall not operate so as to create a partnership or joint venture of any kind between the parties hereto.

11.3
Nothing in this Agreement shall be construed as establishing or implying any partnership or joint venture between the parties hereto, and nothing in this Agreement shall be deemed to constitute either of the parties hereto as the agent of the other party or authorise either party, (i) to incur any expenses on behalf of the other party, (ii) to enter into any engagement or make any representation or warranty on behalf of the other party, (iii) to pledge the credit of, or otherwise bind or oblige the other party, or (iv) to commit the other party in any way whatsoever, without in each case obtaining the other party's prior written consent.

Assignment and sub-contracting

In most jurisdictions commercial contracts are not easily assignable so as to enable one party by assignment to release himself from all obligations under the agreement and pass them on to the assignee. The case law is complicated and not always certain. In addition, sub-contracting is often permitted under general law since the original party to the contract remains liable for the performance of his sub-contractor. These matters are therefore better regulated expressly under the contract.

In most cases where the identity of the party performing the obligations is important assignment and sub-contracting are forbidden, as seen in the two clauses below.

11.4
This Agreement shall not be assigned or transferred (nor the performance of any obligations hereunder sub-contracted) by either party except with the written consent of the other.

11.5
Neither the rights nor the obligations of any party under this Agreement may be assigned, transferred, sub-contracted or otherwise disposed of, in whole or in part, without the prior written consent of the other parties.

The following provision can be inserted with either of the foregoing clauses for the avoidance of doubt.

11.6
No attempted assignment shall relieve the assignor of any of its obligations hereunder without the written consent of the other party or parties hereto.

Finally it is often useful to state specifically the usual rule of law relating to privity of contract, which holds that the contract generates rights and obligations only between the parties to the contract and that third parties cannot directly enforce those rights or obligations for their own benefit.

11.7
No provision of this Agreement is intended for the benefit of any third party.

Costs, stamp duty and VAT

On general legal principles the costs in performing an agreement in the absence of specific provision to the contrary lie where they fall. The general law also provides as to which party to a transaction is liable to bear sales or transfer taxes or stamp duties related to the transaction. In most commercial agreements these matters are better clarified, although the commercial customs usually follow the general rules of law.

11.8
Each party shall be responsible for all of its own costs incurred in the performance of its obligations hereunder.

11.9
Except as specifically agreed to the contrary, any costs in relation to this Agreement and the subject matter hereof which are incurred by any one of the parties hereto shall be borne by the party incurring the same.

It will be noted in the following clause that the purchaser is required to bear stamp duty and transfer taxes. This is usually the position under most systems of taxation and the commercial customs follow this rule.

11.10
The Vendor shall bear all legal, accountancy and other costs and expenses incurred by it in connection with this Agreement and the sale of the Business. The Purchaser shall bear all such costs and expenses incurred by it. The Purchaser shall bear all stamp duties and sales and transfer taxes [including without limitation value added tax] arising as a result or in consequence of this Agreement.

Counterparts

It is often important either for evidentiary or stamp duty purposes to produce the original of an agreement rather than a copy. In many cases each party therefore requires an original of the agreement that has been executed. The problem is solved by a counterpart clause which in effect creates more than one original document so that each of the parties may possess one.

The first clause does this in a straightforward manner but does not require each party to sign all of the counterparts. It is useful when there are only two parties who each sign one copy of the agreement and bring it into effect by exchanging their copies.

11.11
This Agreement may be entered into in any number of counterparts and by the parties to it on separate counterparts, each of which when so executed and delivered shall be an original.

The following clause states that each counterpart must be signed by all of the parties and that the agreement cannot become effective until at least one such counterpart has been so signed and delivered to each of the parties to the agreement. Where dealing with an agreement that has more than two parties this clause is the one to use. The number in square brackets is equal to the number of parties.

11.12
This Agreement shall be executed in at least [three] counterparts, each of which shall be deemed to constitute an original, and shall become effective when at least [three] counterparts have been signed by all of the parties hereto and such a counterpart (so signed) has been delivered to each of the parties hereto.

Export control regulations

Although they are becoming of slightly less importance in east–west relationships today, controls on the export of high technology products and information to potentially unfriendly nations are features of both the North American and Western European systems of export control. The two main regimes are the United States Export Administration Regulations and the new European Union regime (set up under a new Council Regulation) which has superseded the old Western European COCOM rules (Council Regulation (EC) 3381/94).

The purpose of these regimes is to control the spread of nuclear, chemical and biological weapons and missile technology, and of material, plant and equipment which can be used in their development and manufacture, but has peaceful uses as well ('dual use goods').

The EC Regulation has two main aims. The first is to harmonise the list of dual use goods subject to export controls by member states and to ensure that the Union is surrounded by a strong 'external fence'. The second is to free up the movement of these dual use goods between member states.

The Regulation is directly applicable in the United Kingdom, but there are some optional controls in the EC Regulation, including maintaining additional national controls for some dual use goods not covered by the Regulation. The UK government has decided to implement these optional controls by the introduction of the new UK Regulations (the Dual Use and Related Goods (Export Control) Regulations 1995 (SI No 271).

The date for implementation of both the Regulation and the statutory instrument was originally 1 March 1995 but, at the time of writing, the date of implementation has been slightly postponed, and a new date has not yet been fixed.

Although the Regulation only applies to dual use and atomic and nuclear goods, this is not the end of the matter. Most member states have local regulations controlling the export of military goods and weapons as well. In the United Kingdom this is dealt with under the current Export of Goods (Control) Order 1994 (SI No 1191), which will no longer apply to dual use or atomic and nuclear goods, but will remain in force for exports of military goods.

The new system relies to a great extent on self-certification, and on checking by the exporter as to the use to which dual use goods are to be put by the end user.

Violation of both the United States and European Union regimes is a criminal offence, and can result in severe penalties upon exporters who are found guilty of such contraventions. The regulations of both regimes are complicated and indeed the whole subject is extremely complex, and should not be approached without consulting someone with detailed knowledge of the subject. In the first instance, in the United Kingdom, for newcomers to the field, it is possible to direct general enquiries to the Department of Trade and Industry.

It is usual for suppliers of dual use goods not only to comply with such regulations themselves before making the initial supply under the contract, but also to impose further obligations on their customers as to the use or onward disposal of the products or technology to prevent the customer in his turn violating the regulations. Where the customer is later found guilty of such violation the original supplier has some defence in that he brought the obligations to the attention of the customer and presumably did not aid or assist in the customer's violation.

The first two clauses provide in general terms for observation of relevant systems of rules by the customer.

11.13
The Customer shall not use any knowhow, product or software furnished to it under this Agreement in a manner that would cause the Supplier to violate the regulations of the Export Administration of the United States of America, or the export control regulations of the United Kingdom.

11.14
The Licensee undertakes that, if the same shall be necessary, it shall obtain (to the exclusion of the Licensor) any governmental or other approvals required for manufacture or supply of the Products, including without limitation consents under the procedure relating to the United States Export Control Regulations.

Since the United States Export Control Regulations in particular are concerned with the ultimate destination of goods exported from the US, where these regulations apply, a clause controlling re-export by the customer is usually included.

11.15
Regardless of any disclosure made by the Purchaser to the Seller of an ultimate destination and end use of the Products, the Purchaser agrees (a) not to export either directly or indirectly any product or system incorporating such product, without first obtaining a licence to export or re-export from the United States Government as required and (b) to comply with United States Government Export Control Regulations as applicable.

The following clause deals with consents in a more general manner and relates to knowhow rather than purely to the supply of products.

11.16
The parties recognise that the transfer of Confidential Information, to [the United Kingdom] or to [......................] may be subject to the specific approval of the governments of the respective countries of export, or various agencies thereof, and that such governments or bodies may require further approval before the communication or transfer of any Confidential Information or the sale of products or services exploiting Confidential Information is made to or for a country other than the United Kingdom or [......................]. Each party undertakes to do all that is reasonably possible to obtain any Government approvals required from its Government(s) in order to permit the activities contemplated by this Agreement.

The next clause deals in more detail with United States Export Administration Regulations.

11.17

If the Customer is located outside the United States, then the Customer warrants that it will comply in all respects with the export and re-export restrictions set forth in the export licence for the Products shipped to the Customer. If the Customer is located in the United States, then the Customer warrants that it will comply in all respects with the export and re-export restrictions specified by the United States Government with regard to the Products and the Software.

The final clause in this section deals with export and re-export in a general way and contains the important provision relating to prohibited end use. Since the seller is required to enquire about end use, particularly where he is selling to someone he knows is a reseller, this clause does not absolve him of the obligation to make proper enquiries, but it does go some way towards helping him to show he has properly considered the issue.

11.18

If the Reseller wishes to export any Products supplied under this Agreement it is the Reseller's responsibility to obtain all such consents and licences as may from time to time be required under United Kingdom and/or United States laws and Export Control regulations, or under laws of any other country regulating such export. No Products supplied under this Agreement may be exported or resold for export if the Reseller has any grounds for suspecting that such Products are intended to be used for any purpose related to nuclear, chemical or biological weapons, or missile technology.

Further assurance

The completion of a transaction may not take place when the main agreement relating to it is signed. Various other documents may be necessary such as formal assignments of contracts with third parties, conveyances for the vesting of real property or intellectual property rights, the registration of charges or the joining together of both parties to make applications to regulatory authorities for permission to do various acts contemplated under the agreement.

Although a general obligation to do these things is probably implied into the contract by most systems of law, it is convenient to state the obligation in the contract. The following two clauses give respectively a short and a long version of such obligations, with the second clause concentrating on the obtaining of necessary regulatory permissions.

11.19

Each party shall from time to time upon the request of the other party execute any additional documents and do any other acts or things which may reasonably be required to effectuate the purposes of this Agreement.

11.20
Subject to the terms and conditions hereof, each party agrees to [use all reasonable endeavours to] do, or cause to be done, all things necessary, proper, or advisable under applicable laws and regulations to consummate the transactions contemplated by this Agreement as expeditiously as practicable including, without limitation, the performance of such further acts or the execution and delivery of any additional instruments or documents [as any party may reasonably request] [as may be necessary] to obtain any [governmental] [or stock exchange] permits, approvals, licences or waivers required for effecting the purposes of this Agreement and the transactions contemplated hereby.

The following clause concentrates, in the context of a sale agreement, upon the question of perfecting the vesting of assets and the continuing provision of necessary information by one side to the other. The phrases in square brackets draw attention to who is to bear the expense of further assurance. In most cases, it is customary for the party who receives the benefit of the further assurance to bear the expenses of the party who gives it.

11.21
The Vendor shall [in each case at the Purchaser's expense] from time to time execute such further assurances and do such things and afford to the Purchaser such assistance as the Purchaser may reasonably require for the purpose of vesting in the Purchaser or its nominee the full benefit of the assets, rights and benefits to be transferred to the Purchaser under this Agreement (including, so far as consistent with the terms of this Agreement, the benefit of any rights accruing against third parties, whether such rights have or have not accrued or become enforceable at the date of signature hereof).
The Vendor shall [in each case at the Purchaser's expense] from time to time supply to the Purchaser such information and assistance as the Purchaser may reasonably require for the purpose of implementing the provisions of this Agreement.

The following clause is useful where one party requires a document executed by the other party to the agreement to perfect rights he has under the agreement. One of the most likely areas is where there is an obligation to assign to one party intellectual property rights generated by the other party. The other party may refuse to sign the documentation and then the party requiring execution can sign on his behalf using the authority created by the power of attorney.

In some countries the use of powers of attorney is regulated by provisions relating to formalities of execution. These can include execution under seal, legalising, witness by a notary public and sometimes the preparation of a certified translation into the language of the territory where the power is to have effect. There can also be formalities connected with registration and stamping in the territory where the power is to be used. In these cases such a clause is not likely to be held to confer a valid and exercisable power of attorney. If this is the case then if it is felt essential to have such a power a separate instrument should be executed in accordance with the local law's requirements.

11.22

The Customer hereby irrevocably appoints the Contractor to be his attorney in his name and on his behalf to execute and do any instrument or thing and generally to use his name for the purpose of giving to the Contractor (or his nominee or assignee) the full benefit of the provisions of Clauses [........], and in favour of any third party a certificate in writing (accompanied by a certified copy of this Agreement) signed by any authorised signatory of the Contractor (in the presence of and witnessed by a Notary Public) that any instrument or act falls within the authority hereby conferred shall be conclusive evidence that such is the case.

Guarantees of and undertakings to procure performance

The following two clauses deal with third party guarantees of contractual obligations. They are not elaborate guarantees (which should be dealt with in separate documents, particularly where the obligations to be guaranteed are complex or onerous, and the sums of money at state are large) but are useful in more ordinary circumstances where a parent company and a subsidiary are both parties to the same transaction. It is then sensible for the parent company to be required to guarantee the performance by its subsidiaries of their obligations under the contract.

The first clause below is in the form of an undertaking to procure and is suitable when talking about a related set of documents and agreements, some of which will be executed and performed by the parent and some by its subsidiaries, while the second is in the form of a normal parent company guarantee, where the parent company would join in the agreement expressly and only for the purpose of guaranteeing performance by its subsidiary.

11.23

The Company hereby unconditionally and irrevocably undertakes to procure the execution and delivery of each of the Subsidiaries' Agreements and of each instrument and agreement referred to therein by each of the Company's Subsidiaries party thereto and undertakes to procure the prompt performance or payment when due of each and every obligation and liability which any of them may have under any such agreement or instrument.

11.24

In consideration of the Vendor entering into this Agreement the Guarantor hereby unconditionally and irrevocably guarantees to the Vendor the due and punctual performance and observance by the Purchaser of its obligations under this Agreement. If the Purchaser fails for any reason whatsoever punctually and duly to perform or observe any of the said obligations the Guarantor shall cause such performance or observance to occur, as if the Guarantor instead of the Purchaser were expressed to be the primary obligor in respect of the said obligations under this Agreement, and not merely as surety (but without affecting the Purchaser's obligations). Notwithstanding any other provision in this Agreement this guarantee shall not be affected by the granting of time or other indulgence or waiver on the part of the Vendor to the Purchaser.

Supervening illegality and severance

Unfortunately, an agreement when drafted in accordance with the wishes of the parties sometimes turns out to have provisions which are illegal or unenforceable under the general law governing the agreement. Such matters usually occur in relation to restraint of trade or restriction on competition clauses, but can also occur in the area of warranties and exclusions of liability, where the general law can prevent parties to a contract from excluding certain warranties or contracting out of certain liabilities imposed by law (see Chapter 7 relating to exclusions of liability).

The following clauses are attempts to readjust the contract terms in the light of a subsequent discovery or ruling of illegality.

The first clause simply provides that the offending provision, to the extent that it is deemed illegal, shall be severed from the agreement and ignored, without affecting the validity of the remainder of the agreement. This is a way of setting out the 'blue pencil' or 'red pencil' rules which most systems of law have. These provide that if a provision can be deleted (literally by running a pencil through it) leaving the remainder of the contract intact, then the court will do this to preserve the remainder of the contract.

11.25

If any term or provision in this Agreement shall be held to be illegal or unenforceable, in whole or in part, under any enactment or rule of law, such term or provision or part shall to that extent be deemed not to form part of this Agreement but the validity and enforceability of the remainder of this Agreement shall not be affected.

The following clause provides for the same procedure, but allows that where various jurisdictions may have to rule on a contract, what is illegal under one system of law may not be illegal under another. It therefore provides for a concept of severability in relation to particular jurisdictions.

11.26

Any provision of this Agreement which is held invalid or unenforceable in any jurisdiction shall be ineffective to the extent of such invalidity or unenforceability without invalidating or rendering unenforceable the remaining provisions hereof, and any such invalidity or unenforceability in any jurisdiction shall not invalidate or render unenforceable such provisions in any other jurisdiction.

The 'pencil' rules, whether imposed by law, or set out in an express clause, can lead to a style of drafting in the alternate (see Chapter 7) so for instance a number of exclusions of liability or covenants restricting competition are set out separately, or in extreme cases in ascending order of likelihood of enforceability (for example three separate covenants for non-competition, one for two years, one for three years and one for five years). The court can then 'pencil' out the clauses that have gone too far and leave the ones it finds acceptable. In such a case the following clause is a useful addition to help the arguments that this is what the court should do.

11.27

Each undertaking in this Agreement shall be construed as a separate undertaking and if one or more of the undertakings contained in this Agreement is found to be unenforceable or in any way an unreasonable restraint of trade the remaining undertakings shall continue to bind the parties.

There are alternative ways other than pure severance of dealing with unenforceable or illegal provisions. The following clause provides for the possibility of renegotiation of the offending term to a legally acceptable form. This is particularly used in the case of renegotiating the area or time period in covenants against competition. The clause may in some jurisdictions be invalid, as an agreement to agree (this is probably the case in most common law countries), but it gives an indication of the parties' intentions and (in some jurisdictions, particularly civil law ones) may well bind them to negotiate such a variation in good faith. It should, however, be noted that such clauses are of little use under English law.

11.28
The parties agree that should any provision of the Agreement be invalid or unenforceable then they shall forthwith enter into good faith negotiations to amend such provision in such a way that, as amended, it is valid and legal and to the maximum extent possible carries out the original intent of the parties as to the point or points in question.

The following two clauses attempt to deal with the matter not through negotiation, but by an automatic replacement, which is as close to the original as it is legally possible to attain. This is a difficult type of clause to operate as many offending provisions are struck out on the grounds that they are 'unreasonable', and in the absence of a ruling by the court or an arbitrator as to what a reasonable provision would have been, there is no real certainty as to what the replacement provision should contain. The parties will probably, in practice, have to negotiate this between themselves perhaps with an appeal to previous decided cases by way of argument. Again, the enforceability of such clauses in common law jurisdictions is doubtful.

11.29
Any clause covenant or provision hereof that is hereafter found invalid or unenforceable in whole or in part for any reason shall whenever allowed by the context be deemed replaced by such valid and enforceable clause covenant or provision whose contents are as close as permissible to those of the invalid or unenforceable clause covenant or provision.

11.30
If any undertaking contained in this Agreement is found to be void but would be valid if the period of application were reduced or if some part of the undertaking were deleted the undertaking in question shall apply with such modification as may be necessary to make it valid and effective.

Finally, what is the situation where a severability clause has operated, but this fundamentally alters the bargain contained in the agreement, or one of the parties is not happy with the agreement as it now stands without the offending provision? It is possible to provide that in such circumstances the agreement may be terminated in its entirety. However, since this really does away with the purpose of the severability clause, it is important not to allow such a clause to operate too widely. Here the difficulty is to distinguish between provisions which can be deleted without affecting the fundamental bargain of the parties, and those which cannot.

One way is to specify a particular clause, and to provide that if it is found to be unenforceable the whole agreement will automatically terminate. However, since this calls the attention of (for instance) competition law authorities to the particular clause in question, this degree of precision may not always be welcome. The clause below sets out a number of ways of approaching the problem, but none of them is free from difficulty, and all should be used with caution. Generally, it is better to avoid such clauses, unless the particular facts of a case indicate a high degree of likelihood that a particular clause could be unenforceable, and the parties are certain they do not wish to proceed if it cannot be included.

Another way of dealing with such issues (particularly where non-competition clauses are concerned) is to provide that the agreement will not come into effect until the relevant regulatory authority has cleared the clause in question and that, if the clause is not so cleared, the agreement shall thereupon terminate automatically. This provides certainty, but may not be commercially acceptable to the parties if the regulatory authority in question is not required to deal with references to tight deadlines, so that the agreement remains in limbo for an unacceptably long time.

11.31

If any term or provision of this Agreement shall be held to be illegal or unenforceable, in whole or in part, under any enactment or rule of law, such term or provision or part (the 'Illegal Term') shall to that extent be deemed not to form part of this Agreement but the validity and enforceability of the remainder of this Agreement shall not be affected PROVIDED THAT [where a party can demonstrate that it would not have entered into this Agreement without the inclusion of the Illegal Term, then that party may terminate this Agreement forthwith by notice to the other parties hereto] [where the exclusion of the Illegal Term fundamentally alters the balance of the rights and obligations of the parties, as set out in this Agreement prior to such exclusion, any party may terminate this Agreement forthwith by notice to the other parties hereto] [if this Agreement is not capable of continuing in existence without the Illegal Term, any party may terminate this Agreement forthwith by notice to the other parties hereto].

Time to be of the essence

Where a time is stated to be of the essence in the performance of an obligation, failure to perform strictly to time entitles the other party to terminate the contract immediately and without notice. Under general law in most jurisdictions time is not of the essence unless specifically made so by an express provision, or by the subsequent service of notice, in relation to any particular failure by a party to perform to time under a contract, giving reasonable notice of the requirement to perform by a given date and stating time is of the essence in complying with that date. For instance, under English law in a contract for the sale of goods, neither the time for payment nor the time for delivery are of the essence, unless expressly stated so to be in the contract or made so by service of a subsequent notice as described above.

The following clause makes time of the essence for compliance with all obligations under the contract. This may be too severe in many cases, but it is possible to limit its application to certain clauses under the contract. Nevertheless, a party who is in a strong bargaining position may well insist on the inclusion of the clause in the form set out below.

11.32
Time shall be of the essence of this Agreement, both as regards the dates and periods mentioned and as regards any dates and periods which may be substituted for them in accordance with this Agreement or by agreement in writing between the parties.

Waiver

Many systems of law state that failure to enforce rights under an agreement may in some circumstances amount to a waiver of those rights. Since parties often, either deliberately or through an oversight, fail to enforce their rights under an agreement to the full, it is advisable to provide for this situation under express clauses.

The first clause provides for the rule that any one instance of forbearance does not amount to a waiver of a party's right to demand performance on a future occasion of the same obligation. For instance, if the contract provides for payment 30 days after delivery of invoice, and on one occasion the creditor does not press for payment on time and accepts late payment, this clause will enable him to insist on payment to time on a future occasion, without having to argue that he has waived his rights by the previous forbearance.

11.33

The waiver or forbearance or failure of a party in insisting in any one or more instances upon the performance of any provisions of this Agreement shall not be construed as a waiver or relinquishment of that party's rights to future performance of such provision and the other party's obligation in respect of such future performance shall continue in full force and effect.

The following clause goes further and provides that any failure to enforce or forbearance in respect of any particular matter does not prevent the party who has given it changing his mind or insisting upon compliance in respect of that matter itself.

11.34

Any waiver (whether effected by a positive waiver or by a delay or failure in enforcement) by any party hereto of its right, in any instance, to require compliance with any of the provisions of this Agreement by the other party shall not prevent that party (subject to reasonable notice where a positive waiver has been given) subsequently requiring such compliance in respect of that instance by the other party.

The following clause combines the effect of the two previous ones. It makes the point that the waiver of one right cannot be taken as a waiver of any other relevant right on that or any other occasion. This clause cannot cover the case of a positive waiver, which would have to be dealt with separately by the previous clause, suitably adapted, if it were felt to be a live issue in the circumstances of the particular contract being drafted.

11.35

In no event shall any delay failure or omission on the part of either of the parties in enforcing exercising or pursuing any right, power, privilege, claim or remedy, which is conferred by this Agreement, or arises under this Agreement, or arises from any breach by any of the other parties to this Agreement of any of its obligations hereunder, be deemed to be or be construed as, (i) a waiver thereof, or of any other such right power privilege claim or remedy, in respect of the particular circumstances in question, or (ii) operate so as to bar the enforcement or exercise thereof, or of any other such right, power, privilege, claim or remedy, in any other instance at any time or times thereafter.

Chapter 12

Disputes and Conflict of Laws

Proper law and the jurisdiction of the courts

Neither an arbitration nor an expert clause removes the need for a proper law clause, specifying the legal system that will govern the contract and its performance and interpretation, and for a clause deciding which courts shall have jurisdiction in the case of legal disputes. In the restricted circumstances in which an appeal to the courts can lie against the award of an arbitrator or where one party contests the decision of an expert on grounds of bad faith or fraudulent behaviour of the other party, a resort to the courts may be necessary. A proper law clause may be necessary to decide whether the arbitration or the expert clause itself is valid, or the way in which it should be operated. Arbitration or expert clauses do not remove all possibility of resort to the courts, they only circumscribe it. There are many circumstances in which the parties may prefer an agreement in which there is no arbitration or expert provision at all, and in which the only regulation of disputes is either by informal agreement and negotiation or resort to the courts.

The clause below states the proper law and gives jurisdiction to one court. The use of the word 'non-exclusive' means that although proceedings can certainly be instituted in the English courts, they can also be brought in others if that court rules that under any relevant conflict of law provisions it has jurisdiction to hear the case. This degree of flexibility is useful to bring an action against a party (for instance to obtain an injunction or recover assets) in a jurisdiction other than that of the proper law. To the contrary a provision conferring exclusive jurisdiction on a particular court would normally prevent actions being brought before other courts. In some circumstances, the system of law governing any other court which (but for that exclusivity provision) could have assumed jurisdiction might have rules relating to ouster of jurisdiction or paramountcy of local law, with the result that the exclusivity provision would be ignored and the court would hear the dispute anyway.

12.1

This Agreement shall be governed by and construed in accordance with English law and each party agrees to submit to the [non-exclusive] [exclusive] jurisdiction of the English courts as regards any claim or matter arising under this Agreement.

The next clause is a more complicated one. It can be used to compromise where the parties cannot agree on a proper law and a court, but it is also useful in international situations generally. If the defendant is always on home ground then, if judgment is obtained, it will be from the court in the jurisdiction where the defendant has his assets, removing the problem of enforcing a foreign judgment. Since the defendant is on home ground, he will be confident of his rights under his own law, the proceedings will be in his native language, he can use legal representatives that he is familiar with, his witnesses will not have far to travel, and generally his costs will be less than those of the plaintiff.

This means that both parties are unlikely to raise claims as plaintiffs unless they feel a genuine grievance and think their claim is likely to result in a judgment in their favour. Since claims of this nature are the ones which the other party is most likely to want to settle, and frivolous claims are deterred, this form of clause cuts down litigation. Also neither party can be forced against his will to the expense of foreign litigation by the other party. This type of clause gives some certainty to both parties that the costs of litigation can be controlled and that the other is unlikely to institute legal proceedings against them lightly.

In the clause shown below there is reference to the courts of each party's domicile, but in practice it is better to state the name of the country and specify the court concerned in more detail perhaps by referring to the district court of the town where each party's principal offices are. It should be remembered that in countries with a federal constitution a reference to the state in which the party is resident must be made; reference to country of domicile is not enough.

12.2

Any legal proceedings instituted against the Distributor by the Principal shall be brought in the courts of the Distributor's country of domicile and any legal proceedings against the Principal by the Distributor shall be brought in the courts of the Principal's country of domicile and for the purposes of such proceedings the law governing this Agreement and such proceedings shall in each case be deemed to be the law of the country in which the relevant proceedings have been instituted in accordance with this Clause. For the purpose of proceedings brought against it by the other party under this Clause each party agrees to submit to the jurisdiction of the courts of the other party's country of domicile.

Arbitration

The usefulness of arbitration clauses depends on how easy it is to enforce rights under a law other than that of the country of the party against whom enforcement is sought. In many cases arbitration awards cannot be implemented (if the party against whom they are made refuses to comply with them) without a retrial of the case in the local courts to obtain a court order under which the award can be enforced. The advisability of inserting an arbitration clause has to be seen in this light.

However, if such a clause is used two matters should be considered: that its drafting is sufficiently wide to enable all disputes which arise to be covered whatever their nature; and that the procedure for arbitration is laid down either in the contract or by reference to a general system of arbitration procedure. Time limits are very important to ensure that the arbitrator is appointed promptly, that both sides conduct the various interlocutory stages of the case with a minimum of delay and that the decision is given by the arbitrator within a reasonable time after the case has been heard. Provision should always be made for an independent third party to appoint an arbitrator if the two parties cannot agree upon an appointee.

The first three clauses below are usual types of clauses. Clause 12.4 is of a type often favoured in commercial arbitrations of an international character. The last sentence in square brackets is sometimes used to resolve the problem where neither party can agree to the proper law which should govern the agreement.

Clause 12.6 provides for an internal escalation procedure for the resolution of disputes before submission to outside arbitration. The Rules of the London International Court of Arbitration provide for arbitration by a sole arbitrator if the parties so specify and the sentence in square brackets can be included if required. The advantages of a single arbitrator are speed and lower costs. The disadvantages are the difficulty of agreement upon an arbitrator by the parties in dispute, the uncertainty of his identity and his possible unsuitability to one side or the other. If there is no agreement then the London International Court of Arbitration can appoint him by default.

Clause 12.7 is a longer version, which deals with the procedural problems that arise over the appointment of arbitrators and the constitution and method of operation of the arbitral tribunal.

12.3

Any dispute or claim arising out of this Agreement shall be finally settled by arbitration in [Japan] pursuant to the rules of [the Japanese Commercial Arbitration Association] by which each party agrees to be bound.

12.4

Any dispute or claim arising out of this Agreement shall be referred to and resolved by the International Chamber of Commerce ('ICC') in Paris in accordance with the ICC Conciliation and Arbitration Rules. [The ICC shall decide which system of law shall be applied in relation to the dispute].

12.5

Any question or difference which may arise concerning the construction meaning or effect of this Agreement or concerning the rights and liabilities of the parties hereunder or any other matter arising out of or in connection with this Agreement shall be referred to a single arbitrator in London to be agreed between the parties. Failing such agreement within thirty days of the request by one party to the other that a matter be referred to arbitration in accordance with this Clause such reference shall be to an arbitrator appointed by the President for the time being of the London Chamber of Commerce. The decision of such arbitrator shall be final and binding upon the parties. Any reference under this Clause shall be deemed to be a reference to arbitration within the meaning of the Arbitration Acts 1950 and 1979.

12.6

The Customer and the Contractor shall use their best efforts to negotiate in good faith and settle amicably any dispute that may arise out of or relate to this Agreement or a breach thereof. If any such dispute cannot be settled amicably through ordinary negotiations by appropriate representatives of the Customer and the Contractor, the dispute shall be referred to the Chief Executive Officers of the Customer and the Contractor who shall meet in order to attempt to resolve the dispute. If any such meeting fails to result in a settlement, the matter shall be submitted to the arbitration in London of the London International Court of Arbitration under and in accordance with its rules at the date of such submission, which Rules are deemed to be incorporated by reference within this Clause. [The tribunal shall consist of a sole arbitrator.] The parties hereto acknowledge that service of any notices in the course of such arbitration at their addresses as given in this Agreement shall be sufficient and valid.

12.7
All disputes or differences which arise out of or in connection with this Agreement or its construction, operation, termination or liquidation shall if practicable be settled by means of negotiation between the parties. If the parties cannot settle any such dispute or difference within twenty-one days after first conferring, then such dispute or difference shall be settled by arbitration. The award of the arbitrators shall be final and binding upon the parties.
The venue of such arbitration shall be decided by the parties to the dispute in each case.
If the parties fail to reach agreement on the venue of such arbitration within five days then the arbitration shall take place at the Vienna Chamber of Commerce.
The arbitration shall be in accordance with the UNCITRAL Arbitration Rules in effect on the date of the referral to arbitration, except that in the event of any conflict between those Rules and the arbitration provisions of this Agreement, the provisions of this Agreement shall govern.
The Vienna Chamber of Commerce shall be the appointing authority save as provided below.
The number of arbitrators shall be three.
Each party to the arbitration proceedings shall appoint one arbitrator. If within fifteen days after receipt of the Claimant's notification of the appointment of an arbitrator the Respondent has not, by telegram or telex, notified the Claimant of the name of the arbitrator he appoints, the second arbitrator shall be appointed in accordance with the following procedures:
If the Respondent is the Purchaser, the second arbitrator shall be appointed by the [................] Chamber of Commerce and Industry;
If the Respondent is the Seller the second arbitrator shall be appointed by [the President of the Law Society of England and Wales];
If within fifteen days after receipt of the request from the Claimant, the [................] Chamber of Commerce and Industry or [the President of the Law Society of England and Wales] as the case may be has not, by telegram or telex, notified the Claimant of the name of the second arbitrator, the second arbitrator shall be appointed by the Vienna Chamber of Commerce.
The arbitrators thus appointed shall choose the third arbitrator who will act as the presiding arbitrator of the tribunal. If within thirty days after the appointment of the second arbitrator, the two arbitrators have not agreed upon the choice of the presiding arbitrator, then at the request of either party to the arbitration proceedings the presiding arbitrator shall be appointed by the Vienna Chamber of Commerce

and shall be of a nationality other than that of the Purchaser or the Seller. The arbitration, including the making of the award, shall take place in Vienna, Austria and (except in those cases where this Agreement expressly refers to the applicability of [English] law) the arbitrators shall resolve any such dispute or difference referred to them (excluding conflict of laws) in accordance with the substantive laws of Austria. All submissions and awards in relation to arbitration hereunder shall be made in [English] and all arbitration proceedings shall be conducted in [English].

The problem relating to arbitration clauses in any jurisdiction is the relationship under the local law between the process of arbitration and the court. This presents three basic questions:

(1) How far can parties to a contract set up their own private tribunal to resolve disputes under the contract, outside the jurisdiction of the court?

(2) How far can the courts intervene in the process of arbitration to regulate the conduct of the arbitration (procedural questions) and to overturn the arbitrator's award (substantive questions of law and/or fact)?

(3) Will the court assist in the enforcement of the award and if so how?

The answers to these questions depend upon the particular provisions of the local law, and the questions should be addressed to a local lawyer if one is considering detailed arbitration provisions in an agreement.

A full discussion of these questions and of all other aspects of commercial arbitration under English law can be found in one of the leading works in this field, Mustill and Boyd's *Commercial Arbitration* (Butterworths, 2nd edn, 1989). The first chapter of the book is particularly useful as it gives a succinct overview which, although somewhat simplified as the authors state, does provide a good introduction to the subject and the key issues involved.

Under English law, where a valid arbitration agreement in writing exists, unless both parties agree (tacitly or expressly) to ignore it, the courts require that the agreement be honoured, so preventing either party ignoring the agreement and proceeding through the courts instead. The remedy available is for the defendant in the relevant legal proceedings to apply to the court for the action to be stayed. The plaintiff must then either proceed under the arbitration agreement or give up his claim, as the court will no longer listen to applications once the stay has been granted.

Under the Arbitration Act 1950, s 4 the court has a power (which it can exercise at its discretion) to grant a stay in relation to domestic arbitration agreements; that is, agreements between United Kingdom nationals, persons resident in the UK, or companies controlled in the UK, where the agreement provides for arbitration in the UK, irrespective of whether the agreement is to be performed in England or is subject to English law. Under the Arbitration Act 1975, s 1 the court must grant a stay of proceedings when it is requested in any non-domestic arbitration agreement. Here it has no discretion in the matter. However, no stay is to be granted if the arbitration agreement is found by the court to be null and void or inoperative or incapable of being performed. It must be emphasised that the remedy is not something the court will grant of its own volition, but only upon the request of the defendant in the proceedings.

As a procedural point, the defendant will lose this right if he takes part in the proceedings to any further extent other than entering an appearance and asking for the stay. The filing of a defence will be taken to be an assent to the legal proceedings, which is sufficient to waive the right to ask for a stay.

As regards the procedure to be followed by the arbitrator, Mustill and Boyd consider that English law is such that in the absence of any express or implied terms to the contrary the arbitrator should adopt a procedure that is adversarial in nature (broadly along the same lines as those followed in a High Court action) and that, at least in the absence of an express provision to the contrary, the arbitrator is obliged to decide the dispute according to the proper law of the contract.

The court will allow a wide range of procedures to be followed if the contract has express provisions or if there are customs which govern arbitrations in a particular trade. However, in practice the court is moving towards a position where it would be free to intervene in any case where it is shown that the proceedings have been conducted unfairly or give the appearance of being unfair, or which does not comply with the express or implied terms of the agreement to arbitrate. These situations are grouped together under the description of 'misconduct'. Mustill and Boyd state that the word means that the reference has not been conducted in an appropriate manner. This may be due to discreditable behaviour on the part of the arbitrator, but it is more likely to be the result of an honest mistake.

The remedies granted by the court in these circumstances are either to set aside the award or to remit the award for reconsideration by the arbitrator (see the Arbitration Act 1950, ss 22 and 23). Mustill and Boyd make the point that since arbitration agreements are construed as tolerating a high degree of procedural informality and unorthodoxy, the prospect of establishing that there has been a sufficient deviation to justify an intervention by the court is comparatively small.

Appeals which may be made against awards of an arbitrator are now governed by the Arbitration Act 1979. Generally, no appeal lies against a finding by an arbitrator on a question of fact.

The 1979 Act provides for exclusion agreements which enable the parties to contract out of their right to appeal to the court on questions of law. Where the exclusion agreement is permitted under the Act, the decision of the arbitrator cannot be appealed. This is not to say that it cannot be remitted or set aside for 'misconduct' or that the court cannot refuse to lend its aid to enforce the award. Further, the court can still rule on the basic elements of the arbitration clause to see if its wording covers the reference and whether there is a valid and enforceable arbitration agreement in the first place.

Exclusion agreements apply in the case of domestic arbitration agreements only if the exclusion agreement has been entered into after the commencement of the arbitration agreement. A similar rule applies to 'special category' agreements, those relating to admiralty matters, insurance contracts and commodity contracts. Special category agreements can contain an exclusion agreement inserted in the initial contract and prior to the commencement of the arbitration proceedings, if there is an express provision in them stating that the contract is to be governed by a law other than the law of England and Wales.

Even where no exclusion agreement exists or is permitted, an appeal can only be made to the High Court with the leave of the court, and leave is similarly required to appeal from the High Court to the Court of Appeal.

The proper wording and the exact extent of an exclusion agreement under the 1979 Act is discussed in detail in Mustill and Boyd. The authors conclude that 'there is some room for uncertainty as what exactly the Act contemplates by way of exclusion agreement, and we believe that the safest course will be to use a form of words which by express reference to s 3(1) of the 1979 Act, excludes all rights of appeal'.

Based upon this opinion, the author would suggest that where the draftsman contemplates an exclusion agreement the following wording would be appropriate. It should, however, be borne in mind that doubt does exist as to the way in which this wording would be interpreted by the courts.

12.8

The parties hereby enter into an exclusion agreement pursuant to Section 3(1) of the Arbitration Act 1979 to exclude and hereby exclude all rights which each party would (in the absence of such exclusion agreement) enjoy under the said Act (including without limitation under Section 1 of the said Act) to appeal and to apply to the court:

    (a) in relation to any and all awards made under any and all references to arbitration pursuant to Clause [refer specifically to the relevant arbitration clause] of this Agreement; and

    (b) in relation to questions of law arising during the course of such references; and

    (c) otherwise in relation to such references.

As regards enforcement of awards the court will assist either by holding the party against whom the award has been made to his contractually binding promise (in the arbitration agreement) to honour the award or by the summary procedure under the Arbitration Act 1950, s 26. In addition, the Arbitration Act 1950 incorporates the procedure for the enforcement of foreign arbitration awards set out in the Geneva Convention on the Execution of Foreign Arbitration Awards of 1927, and the Arbitration Act 1975 incorporates the procedure under the New York Convention on the Recognition of Foreign Arbitral Awards of 1958.

Experts

Where the parties try to resolve a problem of fact, such as compliance with a technical specification, whether a particular standard of quality has been reached, the value of an item or the proper drawing up of a balance sheet, it is possible to use an expert and to provide that his decision is final and binding. In all circumstances, except perhaps outright fraud or manifest error on the face of the award, there will be no right of appeal to the courts and the rules as to the ouster of the jurisdiction of the court have no application. The following clause is a standard example of the type used.

12.9

If any dispute arises between the parties with respect to any matter within the expertise of a technical expert then such dispute shall at the instance of either party be referred to a person agreed between the parties, and, in default of agreement within twenty-one days of notice from either party to the other calling upon the other so to agree, to a person chosen on the application of either party by the President for the time being of the [British Computer Society]. Such person shall be appointed to act as an expert and not as an arbitrator and the decision of such person shall be final and binding. The costs of such expert shall be borne equally by the parties unless such expert shall decide one party has acted unreasonably in which case he shall have discretion as to costs.

Amiable composition

Amiable composition is an attempt to remove nearly all elements of technicality which are seen as problems in the formal settlement of disputes in simple commercial matters. Arbitration had a similar beginning, but over the years the proceedings of arbitration have become more formal. In some cases the procedure of an arbitration can be as lengthy as a trial in court and in some cases can cost more, as both parties not only have to pay for experts, witnesses, advisers and representatives, but also for the 'court' and the 'judge' as well. This is particularly true of large-scale international arbitrations.

The basis of the following amiable composition clause is rather that of 'rough justice' than fine detail. In the interests of saving costs and time, the parties present their problem to a person whom they feel is likely to have a sufficient blend of commercial and contractual knowledge and judgment, to decide what is fair and reasonable in all the circumstances. An advocate has been used in Clause **12.10** as an example, but many other professional experts would be equally appropriate depending upon the scope of the agreement and the desire of the parties.

The importance of the clause lies in the shortness and inquisitorial nature of the proceedings. Firstly, this enables the expert to reduce the delays and expenses that formal proceedings give rise to, particularly in the area of discovery of documents by one side to the other, and the giving of oral evidence, arguments and submissions. Proceedings can be speedy and simple. Secondly, the expert has no need to give reasons or to follow particular legal rules in reaching his decision.

This type of clause is probably not possible where the proper law of the contract is English. It does not fall within the various English Arbitration Acts and is not an exclusion agreement within the meaning of the Arbitration Act 1979, s 3. There are other jurisdictions, particularly civil law ones, which recognise such types of clauses which are often called 'amiable composition' clauses or 'equity clauses'. Under English law, as a general principle of public policy, agreements to oust the jurisdiction of the courts are void. Most commentators consider that such a clause amounts to an ouster clause.

Mustill and Boyd point out that in the absence of an express equity clause, an arbitrator who deliberately refused to apply the relevant system of law could be checked by the English courts (if they had jurisdiction) through the 'misconduct' route, perhaps for exceeding his mandate under the arbitration clause or for bad faith, even if there were an applicable exclusion agreement. It is one thing to have an exclusion agreement which leaves the arbitrator to apply the law as best he can, but it is quite another to let him ignore the law, which the parties expected him to apply, and substitute his own ideas of what is fair and equitable (Lord Denning's 'palm-tree justice'). It would also be open to the court when a party applied to enforce an award obtained where the arbitrator had acted by deliberately ignoring principles of law, to decline to enforce it.

These arguments do not apply where an express equity clause is inserted in the agreement, but Mustill and Boyd consider that in these circumstances, probably based upon public policy grounds, an English court would be likely to regard the clause as unenforceable, and claim jurisdiction to the agreement (ignoring the offending clause) according to principles of English law.

12.10

Any dispute of whatever nature in respect of or arising out of this Agreement or its termination shall at the instance of either of the parties be referred to an advocate who has been admitted to practice in the Courts of [...............] for at least twenty years and who is currently and has been for at least the last ten of such years actively engaged in the practice of [commercial] law, to be agreed upon by the parties or (failing agreement within thirty days after one party has first requested to the other that their dispute be dealt with in terms of this Clause) to be appointed by the President for the time being of the Bar council of [...............].

Such advocate (the 'expert') shall not be bound to follow principles of law but may decide the matter submitted to him according to what he considers fair and reasonable in all the circumstances of the case.

The parties shall use their best endeavours to procure that the expert shall hold the hearing referred to in this Clause and give his decision within thirty days of the reference to him. In giving his decision the expert shall not give reasons therefor and shall also make a ruling in his entire discretion as to which party shall bear the costs of the reference or as to whether the costs shall be borne by both parties and (if so) in what proportions.

There shall be an oral hearing (at which both parties and the expert shall be present) at which each party shall make an oral submission, present documents and have the opportunity to comment upon the submission of the other and answer any questions which the expert or (with the leave of the expert) the other party may put to him. The parties shall be [present in person] [represented by a duly authorised officer], and shall not employ legal representatives or any other third parties to put their case. No witnesses shall be called but each party shall deliver to the other party prior to the hearing copies of any documents which he proposes to rely upon in his oral submission provided that a copy of each such document is also at the same time delivered to the expert. Unless otherwise agreed by both parties and the expert the oral hearing shall take place in [......................] and shall not last longer than [two] working days. Subject to the foregoing the expert shall have the sole and entire discretion as to the procedure and the conduct of the reference to him of the matter in question, including without limitation the viewing of the subject matter of the dispute.

The expert's decision shall be final and binding on the parties and shall be carried into effect and may be made an order of any competent court at the instance of either party.

This Clause constitutes an irrevocable consent by the parties to any proceedings in terms hereof and neither of the parties shall be entitled to withdraw therefrom or claim at any proceedings before a court that it is not bound by this Clause.

This Clause shall survive the expiry or other termination for whatever reason of this Agreement.

Alternative Dispute Resolution and mediation

There is no particular need to insert a clause in commercial contracts to provide for a process of consultation or negotiation between the parties before they turn to more formal procedures for the resolution of disputes, but clauses providing for an escalation of disputes to higher levels of management are sometimes included as a way of avoiding an immediate break-down in relations between the parties. An example of such a clause is set out below.

12.11

The Customer and the Contractor shall use their best efforts to negotiate in good faith and settle amicably any dispute that may arise out of or relate to this Agreement or a breach thereof. If any such dispute cannot be settled amicably through ordinary negotiations by appropriate representatives of the Customer and the Contractor, the dispute shall be referred to the Chief Executive Officers of the Customer and the Contractor who shall meet in order to attempt to resolve the dispute. If any such meeting fails to result in a settlement, the matter at the election of either party may be submitted for resolution [by arbitration pursuant to Clause .... hereof] [to a court of competent jurisdiction].

Another possibility is to provide for a more formal process of negotiation assisted by the mediation of a third party. This process has gained in popularity in the United Kingdom over the last five years or so (having spread originally from North America) under the name of Alternative Dispute Resolution or ADR. ADR involves the use of an impartial, specially trained third party who acts as a mediator to facilitate a mutually acceptable settlement between the parties. The mediator is given no power (even under contract) to impose a solution on the parties, who are free at any time to abandon the procedure and resort to more formal means of dispute resolution.

The procedure used under ADR can vary considerably. The mediator can act as a go-between for the parties who do not, at least initially, meet face to face. He can also conduct formal joint settlement discussions. Additionally, the parties can opt for an 'executive tribunal' or 'mini-trial' where a formal presentation by each party is made to a panel made up of senior executives from each party with the mediator as the neutral chairman.

Just as discussed in relation to amiable composition, ADR has to contend with the various formal legal problems concerning the invalidity of agreements which attempt to set up any system of dispute resolution which ousts the jurisdiction of the courts. This is one of the reasons why ADR has to be a non-binding process. The other reason why ADR is non-binding is that its whole spirit is an attempt at achieving a meeting of minds between the parties with a solution that leaves both of them feeling satisfied.

Where ADR is appropriate it can result in a substantial saving of cost and time over the normal processes of arbitration or litigation, and often keep alive a commercial relationship between parties who have to do business with each other in the future.

Clause **12.12** provides an example of an informal mediation clause. Clause **12.13** is a suggested ADR clause for inclusion in an agreement before disputes have occurred to provide for their resolution in advance by ADR. The various ADR bodies also provide standard clauses which can be obtained on application.

The drafting of an ADR agreement to cover particular disputes after they have arisen is a more detailed task, which must be tailored to the particular circumstances of the dispute, and is outside the scope of this book although, again, the various ADR bodies are prepared to assist in this connection if required.

Finally, it should be remembered that all such clauses are probably not enforceable in English law, as being no more than agreements to negotiate in good faith and, for the reasons relating to the invalidity of agreements to oust the jurisdiction of the courts, are also unlikely to assist one of the parties to gain a stay of legal proceedings on the ground that the negotiation procedures envisaged by the clauses have either been ignored or not yet completed. Nevertheless, in commercial contracts such clauses do at least signify an intention of good faith on the part of the parties which may be useful, when disputes do arise, in persuading the parties to undertake the prescribed form of negotiation, even if they are not legally obliged to do so.

12.12

Before resorting to [arbitration pursuant to Clause ....] [legal proceedings] the parties shall attempt to settle by negotiations between them in good faith all disputes or differences which arise between them out of or in connection with this Agreement. The parties further agree that (provided both parties consider that such negotiations would be assisted thereby), they will appoint a mediator by mutual agreement, or (failing mutual agreement) will apply to the [President of the London Chamber of Commerce] to appoint a mediator, to assist them in such negotiations. Both parties agree to co-operate fully with such mediator, provide such assistance as is necessary to enable the mediator to discharge his duties, and to bear equally between them the fees and expenses of the mediator.

12.13

Before resorting to [arbitration pursuant to Clause ....] [legal proceedings] the parties shall attempt to settle in good faith all disputes or differences which arise between them out of or in connection with this Agreement, by negotiations between them in good faith and, in the event of failure of such negotiations, by the use of the procedure known as Alternative Dispute Resolution ('ADR').

Where failure of negotiations in respect of such dispute or difference occurs the parties shall together refer such dispute or difference to [name of ADR body] for resolution in accordance with such of the ADR Procedures offered by [name of ADR body] as [name of ADR body] considers appropriate in all of the circumstances.

The parties agree to be bound by the relevant rules of [name of ADR body] relating to the conduct of the relevant ADR Proceedings, as if the same were incorporated in this Agreement. Each party shall bear its own costs incurred in the relevant ADR Proceedings, and one half of the fees and expenses of [name of ADR body], unless a different agreement is reached as part of any settlement arrived at as a result of the relevant ADR Proceedings.

Settlement clauses

Although the drafting of a full settlement agreement is sometimes necessary, it can also be the case that a short form clause to be included in an agreement is also called for. Clause 12.14 deals with this issue in relation to terminated agreements and claims which may have arisen under them. The clause can, however, easily be adapted to a more general, and shorter, form of release as in Clause 12.15.

It should be noted that since they compromise existing claims, rather than modify prospective liability, settlement clauses are not regarded as secondary contracts excluding liability under the Unfair Contract Terms Act 1977, s 10 and therefore such clauses are not exclusion clauses subject to the scrutiny of the Act (*Tudor Grange Holdings Ltd* v *Citibank NA* [1992] Ch 53, ChD).

12.14
Upon [the Effective Date] [Completion] each of the Terminated Agreements shall be immediately cancelled and, with effect from [the Effective Date] [Completion], all rights and obligations thereunder shall terminate and be of no further force or effect (including any provision of any Terminated Agreement which by its terms is intended to survive such termination). While no party acknowledges or admits to any breach or default of any Terminated Agreement, each party hereby irrevocably releases, waives and discharges forever each of the other parties from any and all claims, debts, liabilities, demands, obligations, costs, expenses, actions and causes of action of every nature, character and description, vested and contingent, whether known or unknown, which such party may have owned or held against any of the other parties with respect to any period ending on or prior to [the Effective Date] [Completion] arising out of or in connection with the Terminated Agreements, including without limitation in connection with any breach or alleged breach of any of the Terminated Agreements.

12.15
While no party acknowledges or admits to any breach, default or liability arising out of or in connection with .... (the 'Dispute'), each party hereby irrevocably releases, waives and discharges forever each of the other parties from any and all claims, debts, liabilities, demands, obligations, costs, expenses, actions and causes of action of every nature,

character and description, vested and contingent, whether known or unknown, which such party may have owned or held against any of the other parties with respect to any period ending on or prior to [the Effective Date] [Completion] arising out of or in connection with the Dispute.

Governing language

In international agreements translations are often used and it is useful to specify the language in which the original of the agreement shall be. This is easier for interpretation of the document if ever litigation or arbitration takes place. In some countries the local law specifies the local language as the authoritative governing language for all agreements subject to that law. This is, for instance, the case in Saudi Arabia where Arabic is specified as the governing language.

12.16
This Agreement is drawn up in the English language (save that certain of the Schedules may in whole or in part be drawn up in the .... language). This Agreement may be translated into any language other than English provided however that the English text shall in any event prevail.

Payment of interest

Not all tribunals automatically award interest along with judgments for liquidated or unliquidated damages and when they do the rate is not always a commercial one which compensates the party for the time he was out of money. It is useful to include an express provision covering the payment of interest at a rate which reflects the interest at which the party concerned will have had to borrow money pending payment in order to finance his operations.

12.17
If the Vendor or the Purchaser defaults in the payment when due of any sum payable under this Agreement (whether determined by agreement or pursuant to an order of a court or otherwise) the liability of the Vendor or the Purchaser (as the case may be) shall be increased to include interest on such sum from the date when such payment is due until the date of actual payment (as well after as before judgment) at a rate per annum of [three] per cent above [the base rate from time to time of [Midland Bank plc]] [three month LIBOR]. Such interest shall accrue from day to day and shall be paid subject to any withholding tax.

Specific performance

Damages are not always an adequate remedy for breach of contract. Specific performance is an alternative. Although in most jurisdictions it is not a remedy granted as of right, but at the discretion of the court (English courts in particular treat specific performance as a discretionary remedy) the inclusion of this clause aids the arguments of the party seeking specific performance even though its presence is not conclusive.

12.18

The parties acknowledge and agree that in the event of a default by the Contractor on the one hand and the Customer on the other hand in the performance of their respective obligations under Clause .... of this Agreement, the loss or damage incurred by the non-defaulting party by reason of such default will be such that damages will not be an adequate remedy. Accordingly, the non-defaulting party shall have the right to specific performance of the defaulting party's obligations under the said Clause. Such remedy shall be in addition to, and not in lieu or limitation of, other remedies provided to the non-defaulting party hereunder or otherwise at law or in equity.

Set-off

Self-help is an important weapon in any dispute. The withholding of sums of money due by way of set-off is permissible under the general law in most jurisdictions, but is subject to various restrictions. The inclusion of an express right of set-off makes the use of the remedy easier. The clause below is a wide one, permitting set-off not just of sums owed under the contract to which the dispute relates, but also of sums owed under any other contracts with the party concerned.

12.19

Whenever under the Contract any sum of money shall be recoverable from or payable by the Contractor, the same may be deducted from any sum then due or which at any time thereafter may become due to the Contractor under this or any other contract with the Customer. Exercise by the Customer of its rights under this Clause shall be without prejudice to any other rights or remedies available to the Customer under the Contract, or otherwise howsoever, at law or in equity.

Although the inclusion of set-off clauses is common, equally common is the inclusion of clauses excluding those rights. The following is a standard clause of this type.

12.20

All amounts due under this Agreement to be paid by the Customer to the Supplier shall be paid in full (without any deduction or withholding other than—if any—that required by law in respect of withholding or deduction of tax) and the Customer shall not be entitled to assert any credit set-off or counterclaim against the Supplier in order to justify withholding payment of any such amount in whole or in part.

One word of caution. Until *Stewart Gill v Horatio Myer Co* [1992] 2 All ER 257, CA no one doubted such clauses preventing set-off were enforceable, but this is no longer entirely correct. This case held that such a clause can fall, in appropriate cases, to be considered as an exclusion clause under the Unfair Contract Terms Act 1977, s 3. Thus while such clauses are still completely enforceable in a negotiated contract between business parties, they will have to satisfy the requirement of reasonableness imposed by s 3 if they are to be enforced either in a consumer contract, or where the party seeking to enforce the clause in a business contract was dealing on his written standard terms. This, it appears, from the case, is not likely to be easy to do. In addition, such clauses may well be generally unfair in consumer contracts under the Unfair Terms in Consumer Contracts Regulations 1994 as discussed in Chapter 7 (see reg 4(4) and Sched 3, para 1(*b*) on p 223).

Cumulative remedies

There is sometimes a presumption, even in the absence of a specific exclusion or whole agreement clause, that the parties have written down the whole of the rules governing the relationship between them, and that by doing this, they have demonstrated an intention to displace any additional remedies that would otherwise be available to them under the general law (see Chapter 6). The extent to which express terms exclude implied ones is not free from doubt under the law, although it is likely that a court would hold for such exclusion in an area where the parties were commercially sophisticated, properly advised and had negotiated a specially drafted one-off contract.

Where a party intends to preserve rights under the general law in addition to the rights specifically granted under the contract, it is advisable that an express clause to this effect is inserted in the contract.

Additionally, it is wise to add that the exercise of any one remedy under the contract (for example asking for an injunction or claiming liquidated damages) does not prejudice the exercise of any other right under the contract or under the general law (for example cancellation).

12.21
The provisions of this Agreement, and the rights and remedies of the parties under this Agreement are cumulative and are without prejudice and in addition to any rights or remedies a party may have at law or in equity; no exercise by a party of any one right or remedy under this Agreement, or at law or in equity, shall (save to the extent, if any, provided expressly in this Agreement or at law or in equity) operate so as to hinder or prevent the exercise by it of any other such right or remedy.

Appendix

The Unfair Terms in Consumer Regulations 1994 (SI No 3159), Sched 3

Terms referred to in reg 4(4)

1 **Terms which have the object or effect of:**

(a) excluding or limiting the legal liability of a seller or supplier in the event of the death of a customer or personal injury to the latter resulting from an act or omission of that seller or supplier;

(b) inappropriately excluding or limiting the legal rights of the consumer vis-à-vis the seller or supplier or another party in the event of total or partial non-performance or inadequate performance by the seller or supplier of any of the contractual obligations, including the option of offsetting a debt owed to the seller or supplier against any claim which the consumer may have against him;

(c) making an agreement binding on the consumer whereas provision of services by the seller or supplier is subject to a condition whose realisation depends on his own will alone;

(d) permitting the seller or supplier to retain sums paid by the consumer where the latter decides not to conclude or perform the contract, without providing for the consumer to receive compensation of an equivalent amount from the seller or supplier where the latter is the party cancelling the contract;

(e) requiring any consumer who fails to fulfil his obligation to pay a disproportionately high sum in compensation;

(f) authorising the seller or supplier to dissolve the contract on a discretionary basis where the same facility is not granted to the consumer, or permitting the seller or supplier to retain...

Appendix

The Unfair Terms in Consumer Regulations 1994 (SI No 3159), Sched 3

Terms referred to in reg 4(4)

1 Terms which have the object or effect of:

(a) excluding or limiting the legal liability of a seller or supplier in the event of the death of a customer or personal injury to the latter resulting from an act or omission of that seller or supplier;

(b) inappropriately excluding or limiting the legal rights of the consumer *vis-à-vis* the seller or supplier or another party in the event of total or partial non-performance or inadequate performance by the seller or supplier of any of the contractual obligations, including the option of offsetting a debt owed to the seller or supplier against any claim which the consumer may have against him;

(c) making an agreement binding on the consumer whereas provision of services by the seller or supplier is subject to a condition whose realisation depends on his own will alone;

(d) permitting the seller or supplier to retain sums paid by the consumer where the latter decides not to conclude or perform the contract, without providing for the consumer to receive compensation of an equivalent amount from the seller or supplier where the latter is the party cancelling the contract;

(e) requiring any consumer who fails to fulfil his obligation to pay a disproportionately high sum in compensation;

(f) authorising the seller or supplier to dissolve the contract on a discretionary basis where the same facility is not granted to the consumer, or permitting the seller or supplier to retain the sums paid for services not yet supplied by him where it is the seller or supplier who dissolves the contract;

(g) enabling the seller or supplier to terminate a contract of indeterminate duration without reasonable notice except where there are serious grounds for doing so;

(h) automatically extending a contract of fixed duration where the consumer does not indicate otherwise, when the deadline fixed for the consumer to express this desire not to extend the contract is unreasonably early;

(i) irrevocably binding the consumer to terms with which he had no real opportunity of becoming acquainted before the conclusion of the contract;

(j) enabling the seller or supplier to alter the terms of the contract unilaterally without a valid reason which is specified in the contract;

(k) enabling the seller or supplier to alter unilaterally without a valid reason any characteristics of the product or service to be provided;

(l) providing for the price of goods to be determined at the time of delivery or allowing a seller of goods or supplier of services to increase their price without in both cases giving the consumer the corresponding right to cancel the contract if the final price is too high in relation to the price agreed when the contract was concluded;

(m) giving the seller or supplier the right to determine whether the goods or services supplied are in conformity with the contract, or giving him the exclusive right to interpret any term of the contract;

(n) limiting the seller's or supplier's obligation to respect commitments undertaken by his agents or making his commitments subject to compliance with a particular formality;

(o) obliging the consumer to fulfil all his obligations where the seller or supplier does not perform his;

(p) giving the seller or supplier the possibility of transferring his rights and obligations under the contract, where this may serve to reduce the guarantees for the consumer, without the latter's agreement;

(q) excluding or hindering the consumer's right to take legal action or exercise any other legal remedy, particularly by requiring the consumer to take disputes exclusively to arbitration not covered by legal provisions, unduly restricting the evidence available to him or imposing on him a burden of proof which, according to the applicable law, should lie with another party to the contract.

2 Scope of sub-paragraphs (g), (j) and (l)

(a) Sub-paragraph (g) is without hindrance to terms by which a supplier of financial services reserves the right to terminate unilaterally a contract of indeterminate duration without notice where there is a valid reason, provided that the supplier is required to inform the other contracting party or parties thereof immediately.

(b) Sub-paragraph (j) is without hindrance to terms under which a supplier of financial services reserves the right to alter the rate of interest payable by the consumer or due to the latter, or the amount of other charges for financial services without notice where there is a valid reason, provided that the supplier is required to inform the other contracting party or parties thereof at the earliest opportunity and that the latter are free to dissolve the contract immediately.

Sub-paragraph (j) is also without hindrance to terms under which a seller or supplier reserves the right to alter unilaterally the conditions of a contract of indeterminate duration, provided that he is required to inform the consumer with reasonable notice and that the consumer is free to dissolve the contract.

(c) Sub-paragraphs (g), (j) and (l) do not apply to:
— transactions in transferable securities, financial instruments and other products or services where the price is linked to fluctuations in a stock exchange quotation or index of a financial market rate that the seller or supplier does not control;
— contracts for the purchase or sale of foreign currency,

travellers' cheques or international money orders denominated in foreign currency;

(d) Sub-paragraph (l) is without hindrance to price-indexation clauses, where lawful, provided that the method by which prices vary is explicitly described.